Business L

Business Law in Ireland

By
Anthony Thuillier
Cathy Mac Daid

CLARUS
PRESS

Published by
Clarus Press Ltd,
Griffith Campus,
South Circular Road,
Dublin 8.

Typeset by
Deanta Global Publishing Services

Printed by
Sprint Print, Dublin

ISBN
978-1-905536-77-1

PREFACE

"I'm a *business* student, why do I have to do law?" Most people who have taught law to undergraduate business students will recognise this question. There's the feeling that law is a whole other world, and not a particularly easy one to understand. We decided to write this book for those very students, in an attempt to dispel that feeling. We also thought that members of the public who ran their own businesses, or who were simply curious about some of the basic legal principles involved, would welcome a text that offered a clear overview of these important areas. "Business law" is a collection of law topics rather than a subject in its own right. It takes in aspects of contract and tort law, of company and employment law, and it even needs to address issues that arise out of EU law. What is reckless trading? What is a fundamental term in a contract, and what can I do if one is breached? What are the rights and duties of employers and employees? When is my insurer entitled to repudiate my contract of insurance? These are the type of questions addressed in this book. This is not a book for lawyers: it is a book for non-lawyers who need to know the law as it affects business life in Ireland. If you are a company director or an entrepreneur, the book will allow you to make informed decisions; and if at some point you have to seek legal advice you'll be arriving in to your solicitor's office with some idea as to issues in your case. If you are a student of business law, you will find all of the concepts you need to know, explained clearly and with the most recent cases.

We would like to thank David McCartney of Clarus Press for all his work in bringing this book to publication, our colleagues in Independent College Dublin, DIT and DCU, and our families for their support.

Anthony Thuillier BL and Cathy Mac Daid BL
1 October 2015

CONTENTS

TABLE OF CASES

TABLE OF LEGISLATION

Statutory Instruments

EU Directives and Regulations

Treaties and Conventions

INTRODUCTION TO LAW

Introduction

Irish law comes from a number of sources—our Constitution, the laws passed in the Dáil, laws that come from Europe, the wealth of case law that is the legacy of our having been part of the British Commonwealth—but if there is one thread flowing through our law it is that people should act reasonably. Thousands of situations could be listed in every branch of the law, but they all invariably come down to that question, which is weighed up by a judge who is considering all the facts of the case.

Was a company director knowingly a party to the carrying on of reckless or fraudulent trading? Ought that person to have known, given the skill and experience that could reasonably be expected of a person in their position, that their behaviour would cause loss to creditors? Is a director exercising his powers in a manner that is oppressive to a shareholder, or is the exercise reasonable, bona fide, and in the interests of the company? Has a director shown a want of proper standards, such that should cause him to be restricted from acting as a director? Did one party exercise undue pressure on another to enter into a contract, or was the contract to be reasonably expected, in the context of the rough and tumble of commercial life? Is it reasonable for a person who contracted for a swimming pool 7 ft 6 in in depth, and got a swimming pool that was shallower, to insist on the builder paying the full cost of redoing the pool? What happens when an employee feels they are being unfairly selected for redundancy compared to other employees? What does an employer do if their employee is guilty of gross misconduct? Can the employee be summarily dismissed without any disciplinary procedures being invoked? What rights does a pregnant employee have? These are the kinds of questions that the courts are asked on a daily basis, in company, contract and employment law. If we take this idea of reasonableness as the thread that runs through our law, we next have to ask: where do our laws come from? This is what we turn our attention to now.

Common Law and Equity

The first source of rules that make up our body of law are rules that have arisen in common law and in equity. When we say that something is a common law rule, what we mean is that the rule has been developed over time—often over centuries—and is a rule that is generally acknowledged and applied in reported cases. For example, the Companies Act 2014 incorporates the three common law duties of directors ("directors must exercise their powers in good faith and in the interests of the company" is one of them). These duties are now codified: they are incorporated in statute. Before this, they were not written down in any one document.

Common law develops in the courts, and we see its development in case law: the written decisions of judges which have been recorded since before the nineteenth century. When Ireland was part of the British Commonwealth, the highest court of the jurisdiction was the House of Lords (now renamed the UK Supreme Court). All lower courts were bound to follow the decisions of the highest court. Since independence, we have had our own Supreme Court. Its decisions have been binding on all our lower courts. But we did not decide to ignore English case law. We still find it useful. While it is not binding on Irish courts, it is often "persuasive". Sometimes the English courts deal with issues which have not arisen here. When a given issue finally does arise here, we look at the decision of the English courts and often adopt their reasoning. Examples in contract or company law where Irish courts have not followed English decisions are very thin on the ground.

The next thing to understand – because it has some influence on contract law, in particular—is that there are two streams of law: common law and equity. Hundreds of years ago there was simply "the law"—an accumulation of rules—rules that at times were rigid and so at times produced harsh results. As a reaction to that, the judges developed a series of doctrines which all had at their heart the idea of fairness, or equity. These became known as equitable doctrines. You can find the full list of the maxims online, but you might take these three as the most important, and most representative:

> He who comes to equity must come with clean hands.
> He who seeks equity must do equity.
> Equity looks to the intent and not to the form.

At first the two streams were separate but in time equity came to influence and overlap with the rest of the law. Depending on the dispute, a party might seek damages—the most common relief—or might seek an equitable remedy, for example, seek to rectify a contract or to have a contract performed, or seek an injunction.

The Constitution

The next thing to consider is our Constitution. This is the fundamental law of the State, and no legislation can be passed which is at variance with it. The French have had no problem changing their Constitution again and again, but we are more cautious. Our current Constitution was passed by referendum in the summer of 1937. A lot of people opposed it. Many thought a new constitution was unnecessary. Ireland had a constitution at that time, one which was only fifteen years old. But Éamon de Valera believed that it was a "tattered and torn document which never represented the wishes of the Irish people".[1] This was an exaggeration of course, and it would be true to say that, at that period in time, Irish people were more concerned with the economic "war" that de Valera's government had continued for four years against the United Kingdom. W.T. Cosgrave, the leader of the opposition, said that the proposed constitution was "a party measure, and had been dealt with almost exclusively by one man".[2] But this was a time when a person could be branded a West Brit or a Blueshirt for supporting Fine Gael, a time when political debate could be silenced by men shouting down opponents with "Up the Republic!". Richard Mulcahy, a Fianna Fáil TD, said that Fianna Fáil was going to give "the greatest and most successful bull-fight that ever was seen in Europe, when [de Valera] would wave the red rag of a new Constitution before the nose of John Bull".[3] It is sometimes forgotten that some people supported the new Constitution because it was a way of expressing anti-British sentiment. The Constitution was put to the people and approved.

It took decades to root out the worst parts of the 1937 Constitution, and the job is still not finished. The Constitution claimed a "special position" for the Catholic Church (Articles 44.1.2 and 44.1.3 were repealed in 1972). It claimed sovereignty over the six counties of Northern Ireland (Articles 2 and 3 were repealed in 1998). But perhaps the most damaging innovation was the attitude towards women. This was an issue at the time. WT Cosgrave said that the rights of women "were not guaranteed and… might be menaced" if the Constitution was passed.[4] The day before the

---

[1] *The Irish Times*, Saturday, 26 June 1937 at p 10.
[2] *The Irish Times*, Thursday, 24 June 1937.
[3] *The Irish Times*, Saturday, 26 June 1937 at p 10, under the title "Feeding the Bull".
[4] *The Irish Times*, Thursday, 24 June 1937.

vote, the National University Women Graduates' Association, a non-party organisation, placed an advertisement in *The Irish Times*, addressed to women voters.[5] It pointed out that "under Article 40 your equality of status guaranteed in the 1916 Proclamation and the old Constitution can be taken away"; "under Article 41 the State can interfere in the private concerns of the Home"; and "under Article 45 the State can interfere in a woman's choice of occupation". No one has yet thought of repealing the article that says "the State recognises that by her life within the home, woman gives to the State a support without which the common good cannot be achieved". The legacy of this attitude to women runs through modern Irish history, from the law that stated that women must give up their jobs when they married to the victimisation of Eileen Flynn and the death of Savita Halappanavar.

The Constitution was not, of course, all bad, and where they could the courts interpreted certain of the articles to allow for a right to privacy, and right to bodily integrity and so on. In fact it was to be the judiciary of the 1960s that proved to be a liberalizing force for the State through their use of the "doctrine of unenumerated rights". The judgment of Kenny J in *Ryan* is famous for its claim that there are unenumerated rights in the Constitution:

> "I think that the personal rights which may be involved to invalidate legislation are not confined to those specified in Article 40 but include all those rights which result from the Christian and democratic nature of the State".[6]

This doctrine of unenumerated rights was then used to find the right to marital privacy, the right to marry, the right to bodily integrity and the right to earn a living among others from within the Constitution which was in fact silent on all these "rights". One academic, writing in 1980, could say that

> "[i]f the judgment of the average liberal observer were asked for, he would probably say the overall impact of the courts on

---

[5] *The Irish Times*, Wednesday, 20 June 1937 at p 3; see also *The Irish Times*, 26 June 1937 at p 15 for report on a crowded meeting of women's rights activists in the Dublin Mansion House.
[6] *Ryan v Attorney General* [1965] IR 294, 312

modern Irish life, in their handling of constitutional issues, has been beneficial, rational, progressive and fair".[7]

The same can still be fairly said today. Gerard Hogan, now a judge of the High Court, has said that of the almost ninety separate instances of declarations of unconstitutionality since 1937, "in the majority of these cases the judicial branch has forced the Oireachtas to come up with a fairer and better law than that which was invalidated".[8]

Domestic Legislation

We elect representatives–Jackie Healy Rae, Mick Wallace, Gerry Adams, Tom Barry and so on–to attend parliament, where they propose and debate laws, and finally enact them. The Dáil and the Seanad are our Houses of Parliament (though our Seanad can play only a very limited role). A Bill must pass through five stages in the Oireachtas.[9] When it does pass these stages, it becomes an Act (you can search for any Act on irishstatutebook.ie). Even then it might not necessarily be "the law": for that to happen, the Act must be "commenced" by the relevant Minister. All of the laws passed by the Oireachtas enjoy the "presumption of constitutionality". This means that an Act of the Oireachtas "will not be declared invalid where it is possible to construe it in accordance with the Constitution".[10] This presumption also applies to every law that was passed before Ireland achieved independence.

When the courts are interpreting legislation there are a number of established rules that help them. The first is to give the words their literal meaning ("the literal rule"). The second is to be used if the first doesn't work: if, by applying the literal meaning, there would be something inconsistent or absurd or something that went against the purpose of the statute, then a judge is allowed to opt for a meaning that is "consistent with the smooth working of the system which the statute

---

[7] JM Kelly, *The Irish Constitution*, Preface to the first edition, Butterworths, 1980.
[8] Dermot Keogh & AJ McCarthy, *The Making of the Irish Constitution 1937*, Mercier Press 2007, Foreword, fn 1.
[9] The Kubler-Ross model.
[10] *East Donegal Co-op v AG* [1970] IR 317.

purports to be regulating".[11] This is called "the golden rule". The third rule is "the mischief rule", where mischief is an old-fashioned way of saying "the bad thing"; in this case, the court can look at the bad thing that the statute was supposed to resolve, and give the corresponding interpretation.

EU Law

While it is true to say that the Supreme Court is "the highest court in the land", this is a quaint expression, because since 1973 Ireland has been a member of the European Union. Did Irish people know what they were getting themselves into when they voted to join the EU (it was then called the European Economic Community (EEC))? It is interesting to look back to the eve of the referendum. One Labour TD promised that "massive redundancies" would occur if Ireland entered into full membership of the EEC, as well as a *decrease* in the cost of living for farmers.[12] Leaflets were distributed that said that tea would jump from 40p per pound to £1.20 per pound, and the Taoiseach had to refute this.[13] Maeve Binchy said: "although I never voted Fianna Fáil in my life nor never intend to I don't feel ashamed of voting yes next week".[14] She was refuting, among many things, "this new-found hysteria about foreign capitalists coming in twirling moustaches and buying up land". Fianna Fáil was arguing that entry into the Community would help end partition, something Sinn Féin thought a "snide and deceitful" piece of "propaganda".[15] The general secretary of the Amalgamated Transport and General Workers' Union said that both Fine Gael and Fianna Fáil, in supporting EEC entry, were "exhorting the public to sell out our independence and sovereignty in all matters political, social and economic".[16] One pamphleteer thought that being asked to enter the EEC was strikingly similar to Ireland being asked to vote for the Act of Union; he suggested that too much time was being spent on discussing possible

---

[11] *The People (AG) v McGlynn* [1967] IR 232, approving a *dictum* of Lord Shaw.

[12] Dr John O'Connell TD, speaking in Ballyfermot, *The Irish Times*, 25 April 1972 at p 9 (it was sometimes referred to as the Common Market Referendum); see also comments of Brendan Corish, *The Irish Times*, 27 April 1972 at p 9.

[13] *The Irish Times*, 2 May 1972 at p 5.

[14] *The Irish Times*, 3 May 1972 at p 6.

[15] Frank Graham of Sinn Féin, speaking in Baldoyle, quoted in *The Irish Times*, 28 April 1972 at p 9.

[16] Matt Merriman, quoted in *The Irish Times*, 28 April 1972 at p 9.

price increase, when the real issues were defence commitments and political integration.[17] It would seem that the last two concerns have aged best. Whatever people thought back then, and whatever your view on our membership is now, the key point is this: by becoming members we agreed to be part of an evolving system. We are bound by European Treaties (which set out the Union's objectives and help organise it), by its secondary legislation (regulations, directives and so on), and by decisions of the European courts (the Court of Justice in Luxembourg and the Court of Human Rights in Strasbourg). European law trumps national law, just as European objectives trump national objectives, or even the national interest, as recent history has shown.

The Distinction between Civil and Criminal Law

Most of the time it is easy to understand that the law has one major division–the division between criminal and civil law. This has always been the case, but recently it has taken on a physical dimension in Dublin, where the Criminal Courts of Justice are housed in a modern building by the main entrance to the Phoenix Park and the civil courts have remained in the Four Courts complex. This book is concerned only with civil matters–contractual disputes, company law issues, employment law issues and so on. These disputes are entered into by private citizens, or companies, and the most common remedy is damages (the legal word for compensation). Defendants are not found "guilty" in civil disputes; they are found "liable", i.e. the fault lies with them and they must pay damages to the plaintiffs as a result.

Criminal law deals with murder, rape, assault, theft and so on. It is the Office of the Director of Public Prosecutions that issues proceedings in a criminal law case. A private citizen can never issue criminal proceedings: it is always a matter for the State.

Sometimes there can be overlap. It is rare, and it will not concern you very much in this course, but it is important to understand the distinction. Say you are involved in a fight on a night out and a person causes you injury. In this case, two possible sets of proceedings may issue: one will

---

[17] Pamphlet by Pádraig Ó Snodaigh, "historian and poet", of the Common Market Study Group, *The Irish Times*, 5 May 1972 at p 9.

be issued by the DPP, seeking to have the perpetrator fined or imprisoned for assault (for example); the other may be issued by you, an action for battery, which is a civil law action, founded on the law of tort, the result of which—if you were successful—would be an award of damages in your favour.

A key difference between criminal and civil law is the burden of proof. In civil proceedings, the plaintiff must prove his case "on the balance of probabilities". In criminal proceedings, the State must prove that the accused committed the crime in question "beyond reasonable doubt".

There is a simple way of recognising a criminal case by its title. All criminal cases begin with "DPP", for example *DPP v Hegarty*, *DPP v Wright*. The people who work in the Office of the Director of Public Prosecutions actually prosecute criminal cases. The long title of a case such as *DPP v Hegarty* is actually *"The People (at the suit of the Director of Public Prosecutions) v Hegarty"*. The DPP prosecutes on behalf of the Irish people, because we consider crime to be an attack on the fabric of society. Therefore, when you see a case name like *Moore v Westwood Club Ltd* or *O'Connell v Breanagh Catering Ltd*, you can be sure they are not criminal cases. The plaintiff in these cases is a civil person (remember that a legal "person" can be a company).

Structure of the Legal System in Ireland

There are five levels of court in Ireland. In ascending order they are: the District Court, the Circuit Court, the High Court, the Special Criminal Court, the Court of Appeal and the Supreme Court. First, the country is divided into twenty-three districts. Each district has its District Court. All criminal proceedings begin in a District Court (although some of them only appear there to be sent forward to higher courts). Road traffic offences are dealt with in the District Court. People who have not paid their television licence, or bus fare, appear there; barring and custody orders in family proceedings, orders to do with the Control of Dogs Act, licensing applications for pubs and clubs: these kinds of things take place in the District Court. It is the lowest court. Each District Court deals with offences and matters which took place within that district. Civil cases should be taken in the District Court where the amount of damages claimed does not exceed €15,000.

The next level up is the Circuit Court. The country is divided into eight circuits. Each circuit deals with matters which took place within that circuit. The Circuit Court's jurisdiction extends to claims worth €75,000. Criminal cases can be heard here—although not criminal matters of the most serious kind – and they will be heard by a judge and jury. The High Court, with its thirty-six judges—has full jurisdiction to hear all matters, civil or criminal. There is no limit on the size of a claim taken in the High Court. When the High Court hears criminal matters – mainly rape and murder cases—it is known as the Central Criminal Court. The Special Criminal Court was established under the terms of the Offences against the State Act, 1939 and deals with two categories of offence: those which are known as 'scheduled offences' (i.e. IRA and subversive crime) and those in respect of which the Director of Public Prosecutions has certified that the ordinary courts are inadequate to secure the effective administration of justice. The Special Criminal Court sits with three judges and no jury. The Court of Appeal is a new court, established in 2014 to hear many of the appeals that would have traditionally been heard by the Supreme Court. Finally, the highest court in the land, the Supreme Court, has nine judges and a Chief Justice (usually, three or five judges hear any one matter). If you have taken a matter all the way to the Supreme Court, and are dissatisfied with the outcome, you may be able to have recourse to either the Court of Justice of the European Union or if it involves a convention right to the European Court of Human Rights (as Mary Robinson, when she was a barrister, took David Norris' case to the European Court of Human Rights, for example).

In Ireland legal practitioners are divided into two kinds, solicitors and barristers. What is the difference between the two? Solicitors have a personal relationship with the client. A person can walk in off the street to a solicitor's office, explain their problem, and instruct the solicitor. From that moment on, the solicitor and client will be in contact about issues arising in the case, what needs to be done next and so on. The barrister is contacted by the solicitor and hired on behalf of the client (a layperson cannot contact a barrister directly). The barrister never has as close a relationship with the client as the solicitor does. Solicitors handle clients' money; barristers never do this. Solicitors draw up contracts, wills, conveyance documents and company constitutions (to give four examples). Barristers do not usually draw up these kinds of documents; their area of expertise is the drafting of pleadings (Statements of Claim, Defences, Motion papers). Barristers are often called upon to advise on points of law. Solicitors often handle their own cases in the District Court, but when a matter goes to a higher court they usually instruct a barrister. One of the key skills of a barrister is advocacy – presenting a case before a judge.

The Attorney General is the legal advisor to the government. The post-holder changes with each new government, because the post is usually given to a barrister with political sympathies matching one of the main governing parties (Cearbhall Ó Dálaigh in the 1940s and 1950s, Declan Costello and John Kelly in the 1970s, John Rogers, John Murray, Peter Sutherland in the 1980s and so on). The Attorney General is the chief law officer of the State.

WHAT IS TORT LAW?

Introduction to Tort Law

A woman was taking a walk one evening with two friends. They were walking on the footpath by the old Bray Road. A car passed them and the backseat passenger hurled an egg at the three strolling friends. It hit the woman in the eye and she fell to the ground, her eye bleeding. Surgery could not save it, and her eye was removed and replaced with an artificial eye. These are facts of *Doody v Clarke*.[1]

The moment you ask the question "who is to blame?" or "who should the woman sue?", you have entered the world of tort law.

The woman sued Niall Clarke, the seventeen-year-old driver, who had only recently bought the car. She did not sue the thrower of the egg. Niall's insurer had repudiated liability and he was defending the case on his own. The plaintiff argued that Niall should have (a) ordered the passengers to put the eggs away, (b) ordered that the window be put up, (c) stopped his car or (d) put the passengers out of the car. While these are practical arguments, and – with hindsight – sensible ones, do they chime with what the law requires?

Was Niall liable for the acts of his passenger? The law says that the owner of a "mechanically propelled vehicle" is vicariously liable for the actions of a driver.[2] First of all, what does "vicariously liable" mean? A good example is *Curley v Mannion*.[3] The defendant was the owner of the car. His thirteen-year-old daughter opened a passenger door without looking and hit Kathleen Curley, who was cycling by. The court ruled that "a person in charge of a motor car must take precautions for the safety of others, and this will include *the duty to take reasonable care* to prevent conduct on the part of passengers which is negligent".[4] So, when it comes to cars, the owner and driver will of course be liable in negligence for his own acts, but he will also be liable for the negligent acts of others while the car is under his "control and supervision" when he could reasonably foresee those negligent acts. The father was vicariously liable for the acts of his passengers because he had failed to take reasonable care to ensure such an

---

[1] [2013] IEHC 505.
[2] s 118 of the Road Traffic Act 1961.
[3] [1965] IR 543.
[4] Ó Dálaigh CJ at p 546.

accident would not happen. If a teacher hits a pupil, the school might be vicariously liable. If a surgeon removes the wrong kidney, the hospital might be vicariously liable. And so on. The key to vicarious liability is the level of control that a person has over the person who commits the fault.

Curley v Mannion also shows some of the key elements that create liability in tort law: behaviour or conduct is measured by what is reasonable, and if a wrong happens, we ask "was it reasonably foreseeable?" and "what was the standard of care owed by the defendant to the plaintiff?"

The judge decided in *Doody v Clarke* that the arguments of the plaintiff – that Niall should have ordered the passengers to put the eggs away and to put the window up, stopped his car or put the passengers out of the car – were "too extreme and ultimately not reasonable".[5] There was no conversation in the car about egging people who were out walking. The judge said it would not be reasonable to say that Niall knew or ought to have known that an egg was going to be thrown from his car at a woman who was out walking. Niall certainly had a duty of care to the woman, but as the facts stood, the plaintiff had not established that Niall was in breach of the duty of care he owed her. To impose liability on Niall, the judge said, would be "too high...a standard of care". The judge would have decided differently had a conversation about egging pedestrians taken place in the car. Niall might well have been held liable had his passengers thrown a couple of eggs before the tragic incident occurred. Each case turns on its own facts. In *Doody v Clarke* the actions of the passenger were not reasonably foreseeable by the driver.

Personal injury cases are one of the most well-known kinds of tort law. In *Moore v Westwood Club Ltd*[6] a woman who fell in a nightclub was awarded €56,000. In *O'Connell v Breanagh Catering Ltd*[7] a woman who was injured while dancing backwards with a colleague was not awarded damages. In *Wright v AIB Finance & Leasing*[8] the manufacturer of a combine harvester was liable for a hand injury due to defective design. In *McGorman v Lakeland Electrical Ltd*[9] a fall from a ladder at work was not

---

[5] [2013] IEHC 505 at para [31].
[6] [2014] IEHC 44 (High Court, Herbert J, 5 February 2014).
[7] [2013] IEHC 426 (High Court, Ryan J, 28 June 2013).
[8] [2013] IESC 55 (Supreme Court, Clarke J, 11 December 2013).
[9] [2013] IEHC 471 (High Court, Irvine J, 30 July 2013).

the fault of the employer. To simply state the facts of the accident and the award as we have done here is not to say very much: the only thing being said is that personal injury cases are a very well-known kind of tort. What is important is a concept that will have been present in each of the foregoing cases: the idea that the defendant owed a "duty of care" to the plaintiff not to allow him or her to come to harm.

The Duty of Care

The duty of care is a massive concept. It is used in many contexts. Whether a duty of care existed or not will always have to be considered with regard to the specific fact scenario of each case. The duty of care to another person exists where there is a legal right or interest which creates the duty of care; it exists where the harm complained of was reasonably foreseeable and where there was a relationship of proximity (a kind of closeness brought about by law) between the two parties. For example, for an action in negligence to succeed, the plaintiff must demonstrate four things: a duty of care between the parties, a breach of that duty, damage which was reasonably foreseeable, and a causal link between the breach and the damage.[10]

The Tort of Trespass

A second example of tort law is trespass. In *Kessopersadh v Keating*[11] three gardaí entered the house of the plaintiffs, a husband and wife, after their twenty-two year old son had been involved in a road accident which caused the death of a pedestrian. The gardaí searched the Kessopersadhs' house without their consent and they took an action seeking damages for trespass. The gardaí had come to the house to arrest the son for dangerous driving. The Kessopersadhs told the gardaí he was not there, which was true, but the gardaí decided to search the house to make sure. The Kessopersadhs were awarded €50,000 in compensation for trespass and entry into their home and for the distress and anxiety it caused. In *Royal Dublin Society v Yates*[12] the judge said:

---

[10] John Tully, *Tort Law in Ireland*, Clarus Press 2014, at p 15.
[11] [2013] IEHC 317 (High Court, O'Malley J, 9 July 2013).
[12] Unreported, High Court, Shanley J, 31 July 1997.

"[t]respass to land consists in any unjustifiable intrusion by one person upon land in the possession of another. The intrusion may be intentional or it may be negligent: in either case it is actionable in the absence of lawful justification".

The law of trespass can be invoked in many different situations. In *Savill v Byrne*[13] a former tenant was restrained from trespassing on property. In *Inland Fisheries Ireland v Ó Baoill*[14] the plaintiff used it to assert their right to manage and control a river. In *Swinburne v Geary*[15] it was invoked to get people out of a holiday home so that it could be sold by a receiver.

What is the Tort of "Nuisance"?

Nuisance is one of those words whose everyday meaning is different from its legal meaning. In law, the tort of nuisance consists of "any interference with a person's use and enjoyment of his land".[16] There are two different kinds: public nuisance and private nuisance. Public nuisance is a crime and is not of interest to us.[17] It is private nuisance that is concerned with a person's use of their land, the term "person" including a company, as we can see in *Campbell-Sharp Associates Ltd v MVMBI JV Ltd*,[18] an ongoing action and a good example of what may feature in a nuisance case. The plaintiffs claim that during three years of the construction of the Green Line Luas in Dublin there were persistently high levels of noise, vibrations, dirt, dust and grime, and the obstruction of access to their premises on Harcourt St. Any of these elements on its own, if persistent enough, would constitute a "nuisance" in the legal sense. In *O'Callaghan v Limerick City Council*[19] the nuisance in question was water damage. The plaintiff, whose house is ten metres from a canal wall, sought damages arising out tunnelling work that was carried out under the Limerick Drainage Scheme and that damaged his house. The judge awarded €404,800 (and ruled that

---

[13] [2012] IEHC 415 (High Court, Laffoy J, 19 October 2012).
[14] [2012] IEHC 550 (High Court, Laffoy J, 19 December 2012).
[15] [2013] IEHC 412 (High Court, Mac Eochaidh J, 19 August 2013).
[16] *Per* Shanley J, *Redfont Ltd v Custom House Dock Management Ltd* (High Court, 31 March 1998).
[17] The Supreme Court, in *Re Article 26 and the Employment Equality Bill 1996* [1997] 2 IR at 321, said it is "an act which obstructs, or causes inconvenience or damage to, the public in the exercise of rights common to all citizens". In civil actions for public nuisance, only the Attorney General can take proceedings.
[18] [2013] IEHC 470 (High Court, Hanna J, 31 July 2013).
[19] [2012] IEHC 293 (High Court, Hedigan J, 12 July 2012).

25% be paid by the first defendant and 75% by the second defendant, because of their varying liability).

The Reasonable Man and the Test for Nuisance

One of the most famous Irish nuisance cases was *Hanrahan v Merck, Sharp & Dohme (Ireland) Ltd,*[20] a legal battle between a Tipperary dairy farmer and a large American-based pharmaceutical company which had set up a factory in the valley where the plaintiff's farm was located. In that case the nuisance came from the chemicals emanating from the factory – gases, dust and liquids – which had a harmful effect on the Hanrahan family and their cattle, as well as plant life on the farm, for over five years. In the course of its judgment the Supreme Court approved a test for nuisance, which is that the plaintiff must show that the interference caused to the comfort and enjoyment of his or her property would be an interference to any reasonable person living in the same locality. It is not a defence to claim that the activities complained of were carried out in accordance with the highest standards. For decades the courts referred to "the reasonable man" – conduct, nuisance and so on were to be judged by what the reasonable man would have done, or what the reasonable man could have put up with, and so on. The court in *Hanrahan* approved a definition of the qualities of the reasonable man:

> "the reasonable man connotes a person whose notions and standards of behaviour and responsibility correspond with those generally pertaining among ordinary people in our society at the present time, who seldom allows his emotions to overbear his reason, whose habits are moderate and whose disposition is equable."[21]

The court found for the Hanrahans, stating that to succeed in a claim in nuisance it was enough for plaintiffs to establish that they had not enjoyed the comfortable and healthy use of their land to the degree that would be expected by an ordinary person whose requirements are objectively reasonable.

---

[20] [1988] ILRM 629.
[21] [1988] ILRM 629 at 634, Henchy J approving Gannon J in *Halpin v Tara Mines* (High Court, 16 February 1976).

Occupier's Liability

What is occupier's liability? Let's look at it in action in *O'Connell v Breanagh Catering Ltd*.[22] The plaintiff, Ciara O'Connell, was on a night out with work colleagues. One of them was Noel Humphries. They went to Copper Face Jack's nightclub after midnight and some of them danced. The judge noted: "It was modern dancing of the kind that takes place in night clubs and which is not easy to describe in terms that make sense". At one point, when Ciara and Noel were dancing backwards together, he fell on her, and she hit the ground heavily and injured her left arm. She stayed on the ground. Security staff came. An ambulance was called. Ciara was brought to hospital. The judge had to answer the following essential question regarding liability: what made Noel fall? Was the surface of the dance floor dangerous or was it allowed to be in a state that would lead to accidents? Could fault be laid at the door of the nightclub? The nightclub – through the private limited company called Breanagh Catering Ltd – was the occupier of the premises. Persons – human or corporate – who occupy buildings have duties to those who come into them. The level of duty owed depends on how the person coming onto the premises can be categorised. There are three categories, and they are set out in the Occupiers' Liability Act 1995, *the* essential piece of legislation for this area. The three categories of persons who come on to another person's property are visitors, recreational users and trespassers.

An occupier of premises owes a duty of care towards a visitor. This means "a duty to take such care as is reasonable in all the circumstances" to ensure that a visitor to the premises does not suffer injury or damage by reason of any danger existing there.[23] A visitor is someone who is on the premises because they have been invited by the occupier, or given the permission of the occupier, such as a customer in a shop; someone there because of a term in a contract (a cinema-goer); or an "entrant as of right" such as a garda or fire fighter.

A lesser duty of care is owed to recreational users and to trespassers, and the duty owed to each of those two is the same. A recreational user is a person who has come on to the premises with or without the occupier's

---

[22] [2013] IEHC 426 (Ryan J, 28 June 2013).
[23] Occupiers' Liability Act 1995, s 3.

permission and is there without having paid any admission fee (paying for car parking does not count). The recreational user is defined as being present on the premises "for the purpose of engaging in a recreational activity". The Act states that the duties owed by the occupier to recreational users and trespassers include the duty not to injure the person intentionally, and not to act with reckless disregard for the person.[24] Whether the occupier has acted with reckless disregard for the recreational user or trespasser will depend on the circumstances of the case, but in particular the court will take into account whether the occupier knew (or had reasonable grounds for believing) that a danger existed on the premises.

So – back to Copper Face Jack's. Those in charge of a nightclub can control the surface of the dance floor but not the way people dance. Ciara O'Connell and Noel Humphries were clearly visitors to Coppers, according to the legal definition. This meant the nightclub had a duty to take reasonable care to ensure that they did not suffer injury by reason of any danger on the premises. If the dance floor was one that got slippy when wet, that clearly would be a danger. That was the plaintiff's case. But the dance floor was substantially made of pine, which did not become slippy when wet, as the plaintiff's engineer found when he tested it. Reasonable care had been taken and the judge dismissed the case.

One tort that does not exist – but which a lot of people have wanted to exist since the property crash – is the tort of reckless lending. In *Healy v Stepstone Mortgage Funding Ltd*,[25] Hogan J found such claims "completely unsustainable in law and…doomed to fail".

Damages

The two main remedies available in tort law are damages and injunctions. "Damages" is the legal word for money or compensation. What is the

---

[24] Occupiers' Liability Act 1995, ss 4(a) and (b). This includes a duty not to intentionally damage that person's property.
[25] [2014] IEHC 134. Claims for mis-selling (and negligence) are also bound to fail: see *Parsley Properties Ltd v Bank of Scotland* [2014] IEHC 624 (McGovern J). Nor do banks have a fiduciary duty to a borrower of €36m—see *IBRC Ltd v Morrissey* [2013] IEHC 208 (Finlay Geoghegan J).

function of damages? In *Kelleher & Kelleher v Don O'Connor & Co.*[26] the judge said:

> "It is important to start with the fundamental proposition that, in almost all cases, the principal function of the award of damages is to seek to put the party concerned back into the position in which they would have been had the relevant wrongdoing not occurred.... In the case of a tort, the court has to attempt to put the plaintiff back into the position in which that plaintiff would have been had the tort not occurred at all. It is the pre-incident position that the court must look at as a starting point."

Injunctions

Injunctions are an important weapon in civil law. A person or a company can seek an injunction to make someone stop doing something, or, in some cases, one which will order them to do something. A party can seek an injunction before the full case has been heard (an "interim injunction", which will last until the outcome of the case), and may be granted an injunction that will remain in force after the case has ended (a "perpetual injunction"). If an injunction is granted and not obeyed, the person in breach of it will be in contempt of court. An injunction is not a cause of action; it is a remedy, in the same way that an award of damages is a remedy.

The test for succeeding in an injunction application was clearly put by one judge in a recent case:

> "A plaintiff seeking an injunction must show not that he or she has an arguable case but rather a strong case which means a case that is likely to succeed at a full hearing. Even if the plaintiff succeeds in doing so, he or she must still satisfy the court that the balance of convenience lies in granting the injunction".[27]

---

[26] [2010] IEHC 313 (*per* Clarke J at para [9.1]).
[27] *Per* Ryan J, *Hartnett v Advance Tyre Company* [2013] IEHC 615, at 2. This test is known as the Campus Oil test, after the case in which it was first enunciated: *Campus Oil v Minister for Industry and Energy (No. 2)* [1983] 1 IR 88. Put in point form, the test is: (i) Is there a fair bona fide question to be tried? (ii) Are damages an adequate remedy? (iii) Does the balance of convenience fall in favour of the granting of an injunction?

This reference to the balance of convenience means that if damages would be an adequate remedy (if the plaintiff wins the case in the end), then the court will not grant an injunction. The court is making a call: any wrong that may be done because no injunction is granted is outweighed by the ability to award compensation.

Injunctions can be sought in a great variety of situations. An example of a high-level injunction application is *Pringle v The Government of Ireland*.[28] The plaintiff, a TD, was afraid that a European Treaty was going to transfer Irish sovereignty away from the Irish parliament to a degree that was incompatible with the Constitution. He sought an injunction restraining the government from ratifying the Treaty pending the outcome of his challenge (Mr Pringle thought a referendum was necessary, and that the government was not going to hold one, but was going to simply ratify the Treaty in the Dáil). At a more everyday level, in *Goss v O'Toole*[29] six people who were residents of Tuam sought an order restraining the respondents from carrying out an unauthorised split-level car park in their locality. In *Bailey v Kilvinane Wind Farm Ltd*[30] the applicant sought an injunction requiring the respondent not only to cease operating a wind farm on its lands, but also to remove the wind turbines, because he believed they had been erected in contravention of planning permission. In *Esso Ireland Ltd v Nine One One Retail Ltd*,[31] after an agreement by the parties for the provision of snack services in petrol stations had run its course, and the defendant asserted a right to a tenancy, Esso sought and received an order directing the defendant to vacate the premises and remove its equipment, and a permanent injunction restraining any further encroachment.

Injunctions are sometimes sought in a work context. If an employee is dismissed from her position, she may apply for an injunction to set aside the dismissal, or to be reinstated at least for the purpose of receiving her salary (*Hartnett v Advance Tyre Company*[32]). It is rare for an injunction to be

---

[28] [2012] IESC 47.
[29] [2013] IEHC 570.
[30] [2013] IEHC 509.
[31] [2013] IEHC 514.
[32] [2013] IEHC 615.

granted in an employment case to restrain dismissal, however.[33] The reason for this is that it is not usually of much benefit to force people to continue working together when trust and confidence has broken down. As McMenamin J said in *Joyce v HSE*[34]: "It is a question of trust, authority, loss of confidence and I think plain common sense".

An injunction might be sought in a "passing off" case. Passing off is where one party has earned a reputation in a particular area and has a recognisable brand, and feels that another party is using such a similar name that people may get confused and that the party which put all the work into creating its reputation would lose business to the newcomer. An example of this is *BMW v Roynane t/a BMWcare.*[35] The defendant, Mr Roynane, was a mechanic in the west of Ireland. He loved BMW cars and specialised in them. He began using the name "BMWcare" in his e-mail address and he bought the domain name "BMWcare.com". On his website he wrote that he was independent, but BMW felt that the use of "BMWcare" was a trademark infringement and constituted the tort of passing off. The court awarded BMW injunctions restraining Mr Roynane from using the "BMWcare" name, because all Mr Roynane had done was add a common descriptive word – "care" – to an internationally known identity.

---

[33] See *Maha Lingam v HSE* [2006] ELR 137.
[34] [2005] IEHC 174.
[35] [2013] IEHC 612.

PROFESSIONAL NEGLIGENCE

Introduction

The law of negligence is a vast area and a whole book could be written on it alone: because this book focuses on business law, we have decided to outline the general principles in the area but concentrate on negligence in a professional context. In law, where so much is defined, some things are left undefined because it just seems more sensible to leave some room for manoeuvre. So, when considering "professional negligence", you do not have to define what a profession is. The Irish courts do not do so. The English courts said, long ago, that

> "[t]he line of demarcation may vary from time to time. The word 'profession' used to be confined to the three learned professions, the Church, Medicine and Law. It has now, I think, a wider meaning".[1]

That statement was made in 1919. So, rather than try to define what a profession is we would do better to simply look at the kinds of cases that come before the courts under this heading. Professional negligence can take many forms. An auctioneer can make a mistake in the valuation of land. A doctor, carrying out surgery, can negligently injure a patient. A solicitor may fail to obtain security for a loan which its client, a bank, is giving, and this may be very bad news for the bank if the borrower defaults. In *Roche v Peilow*, for example, the plaintiffs engaged the defendant solicitors to act for them in the purchase of their house. The Supreme Court stated that Mr and Mrs Roche

> "were entitled to believe that their interests would be protected by the defendants with the degree of care to be expected from a reasonably careful and competent solicitor. That duty of care may be said to arise either as a matter of contract, by reason of an implied term to that effect in the contract of retainer, or alternatively, as an aspect of the tort of negligence arising out of the proximity of the relationship between solicitor and client".[2]

Contained in this quotation are the key elements of professional negligence: the existence of a duty of care; the standard of this care,

---

[1] *Commissioners of Inland Revenue v Maxse* [1919] 1 KB 647 at 657, *per* Scrutton LJ.
[2] *Per* Henchy J, *Roche v Peilow* [1986] ILRM 189 at 195.

which is reasonable competence and reasonable care; and proximity of relationship between the people in question.

Negligence in General

As we noted above, the law of negligence is a vast area. There can be negligence in road use, negligence in the care of children, negligently inflicted psychiatric damage, negligence in relation to public authorities, and so on. You could spend a year reading negligence judgments and do a PhD on a discrete area of the law of negligence. This is a business law book, and this chapter is concerned with professional negligence: before we look at this branch of negligence, however, we must look at the principles that unite all the categories of negligence.

You are a plaintiff. You want to sue someone for negligence. What must you prove? You must prove that the defendant was guilty of negligence to you. You must give details of the alleged negligence. You must state the facts which you say give rise to a duty, on the part of the defendant, to you, and then explain how the defendant breached that duty (for example, that an employer allowed an unsafe system of work to exist). Finally, you must prove that you suffered loss, injury or damage. You must prove your case on the balance of probabilities (not beyond reasonable doubt, which is the burden of proof in criminal cases).

Let's say you are the director of a company which is carrying out an engineering project – a three-storey development over a one-storey car park. Just before the project is completed, structural defects emerge. It becomes clear that the reason you have a problem is that your engineers made inadequate structural plans. Fixing the problem causes delays and costs a lot of money (for example, loss of rental for the car parking spaces, €6,500; loss of rental on the apartments, €65,000; construction costs, €169,000; professional fees, €28,000; bank interest on the extended loan period, €134,500). It would be open to the company of which you are a director to sue the engineering company, either for professional negligence or for breach of contract (or both).[3] As director of a company which finds itself in this situation, the first thing you should consider is

---

[3] This was the scenario in *Woodquay Properties Ltd v Leo W. Wilson Associates Ltd* [2011] IEHC 23.

the steps listed in the paragraph above: details of the engineer's negligence; the reason why the engineer had a "duty of care" to you; how the engineer breached that duty; and how your company suffered loss as a result.

It might be the case that you would sue for breach of contract and not sue in negligence (sometimes the only avenue is to sue for breach of contract because there can be complications in trying to recover for negligently caused pure economic loss[4]). For example, in *James Elliott Construction Ltd v Irish Asphalt Ltd*[5] the plaintiff was awarded damages for breach of contract, not negligence. The defendant was found liable "for the ruination" of the Ballymun Central Youth Facility building.[6] The Centre was built in 2004–2005. The defendant had supplied stone infill, which had expanded. This caused a condition known as "pyrite heave". The judge said that the building "could have been expected to last for up to 100 years in the form in which it was handed over"[7] but soon after its completion cracks began to appear in the ground floor walls. They began as hairline cracks and continued to grow and expand until the building was unusable, and Elliott Construction had to spend €1.55m in fixing the building. Was the material supplied by Irish Asphalt of merchantable quality? It was not, and this was a breach of contract. There was an implied condition which said the material should be fit for purpose. Thus, this case came down to simple contract principles, and the law of negligence could be ignored. In practical terms, cases will often be pleaded on contract and negligence bases, with the plaintiff hoping to succeed under whichever heading is easier to prove.

Medical Negligence

In *Scott v Macey*[8] the plaintiff sued two defendants (Dr Macey, a consultant orthopaedic surgeon in Sligo General Hospital, and the HSE) for negligence in a hip replacement operation. A complication can occur in this operation. It is rare, but it is well known to practitioners. When the

---

[4] See *Glencar Explorations plc v Mayo County Council (No. 2)* [2002] 1 IR 84.
[5] [2011] IEHC 338.
[6] *Per* Charleton J, at 1 of [2011] IEHC 338, the decision on costs; the decision in the case itself is [2011] IEHC 269.
[7] [2011] IEHC 269 at 1.
[8] [2012] IEHC 416.

complication did arise, the question for the court was whether Dr Macey fell below the standard to be expected of a consultant orthopaedic surgeon carrying out a procedure of this kind. The answer was no, partly because it was not obvious that the use of the medical device in question (something called an 'A' profiler) was dangerous or likely to cause injury.

The courts do not use hindsight to judge the conduct of a person accused of negligence. Judges put themselves in the shoes of the person in question, as the situation appeared at the time, and weigh up the avenues open to him or her, always asking whether or not the course of action taken was reasonable. A plaintiff might say that a surgeon was negligent if, during an operation, the surgeon suspected that a bone fracture had taken place, but did not carry out an X-ray to confirm whether it had happened. Then again, it might be the case that this was not negligent, because there are risks associated with carrying out an X-ray in such a situation (such as the lengthening of the procedure and the increased risk of infection), and a surgeon is entitled to take those risks into account. Did the surgeon do what no other medical practitioner would have done in the situation? Did the surgeon take the ordinary care required of a person of his or her level of qualification? If the surgeon were following a standard practice, was it a practice that had inherent defects which should have been obvious if some thought had been given to it? Considering the operation prospectively – i.e. as if you were in the midst of it now, rather than looking back on it with hindsight – ask whether the risks of an adverse event occurring would be "very unlikely to the point of being almost remote or negligible"?[9] These are the kinds of questions the law asks.

In *Kinsella v Rafferty*[10] the defendant was a consultant obstetrician and gynaecologist in Mount Carmel Hospital in Dublin. Mrs Kinsella suffered from a condition called menorrhagia, which, among other things, causes exhaustion, and the medical advice she received was that, having tried other avenues, she should undergo a hysterectomy. During the course of the operation the plaintiff's bladder was snagged by a misplaced suture due, the judge found, to "inadequate care by the defendant," because he had allowed the bladder too remain to close to the field of operation

---

[9] [2012] IEHC 416 at para [45].
[10] [2012] IEHC 529.

when carrying out the suturing work. In this case negligence was established, partly because expert evidence said that "attempting to dissect the bladder off the uterus all the way down before the body of the uterus was removed was a dangerous procedure", i.e. one that no medical practitioner of like specialisation and skill would have followed had he been taking ordinary care. Thus, negligence was established and damages were awarded.

Contributory Negligence

In *Brownrigg v Leacy*[11] a farmer took a case against his auctioneer because he believed that the valuation made by his auctioneer, Mr Leacy, was made negligently. There is an objective way of making valuations. All Irish valuers need to be in compliance with what is known as "the red book", an internationally accepted standard for valuation. There was no real information in Mr Leacy's documentation which showed how he came to his valuations; he was unable to show "any real effort…to produce a true and reliable valuation of the lands". The judge said, for example,

> "[n]o warning of uncertainty of valuation was provided. No warning was given of the risks attendant upon the zoning or non-zoning of the lands or any part of them".[12]

The expert witness considered the valuation "totally out of keeping with the standard valuation", and gave evidence that he would have valued the land at €2.2m as opposed to the assessment of €10m made by Mr Leacy. The judge found that

> "[t]he overwhelming impression created by [Mr Leacy's] evidence was that he hazarded a guess backed up by a vague general knowledge of the value of properties in the immediate area".

Mr Brownrigg went on to rely on Mr Leacy's valuations and it caused him loss. So, did Mr Leacy have to cover all of Mr Brownrigg's loss? The judge said that some of Mr Brownrigg's loss could be laid at the door of Mr

---

[11] [2013] IEHC 434. Mr Leacy wrote Mr Brownrigg a letter which said "[i]n my opinion, I would estimate these lands to have a current open market value in the region of €220,000 to €240,000 per acre".
[12] [2013] IEHC 434 at 15.

Brownrigg's own decision to buy before he sold, so that Mr Leacy's valuations were "only partly responsible for the unfortunate consequences of that decision". This is what is known as "contributory negligence". It means that the plaintiff contributed to some degree to his own misfortune. The judge will measure that degree, and in this case he said Mr Brownrigg was 50% responsible for his loss, and Leacy was responsible for the rest.[13] Thus, where a plaintiff has been in some way to blame for the loss that he has suffered, the defendant can argue that he contributed to the negligence; this is what we mean when we speak of contributory negligence.

"Statute Barred"

Can a person take an action for professional negligence at any time, or must the person take it reasonably quickly? The answer will vary depending on the nature of the case. If a plaintiff is suing for defamation, he must do so within one year. If a plaintiff is suing for breach of contract, he must do it within six years. These periods are known as the "limitation periods". They are set out in statute (the Statute of Limitations 1957) Once they elapse, a case will be "statute barred" – the proposed plaintiff will not be able to take the case. The general period of limitation for a tort action is six years from the date on which the cause of action accrued.[14] If an action claims damages for negligence, nuisance, or personal injuries, then the plaintiff must sue within two years from the date of accrual or the "date of knowledge".[15] *Hegarty v D & S Flanagan Brothers Ballymore Ltd*[16] is an example of the Statute of Limitations in action. The plaintiff entered into a contract that would see the defendant construct a house in Roscommon. When she moved into the house she noticed cracks on the walls; that was in 2002. She didn't think much of them at first, but by 2007 she had issued proceedings against the builders. The case moved along slowly, and it was not until 2012 that the plaintiff sought to join the engineer as a defendant. She said that the certificate he issued, which

---

[13] The measure of damages was €590,000 plus interest.

[14] Statute of Limitations 1957, s 11(2)(a).

[15] For example, an injury may have taken place on 1 October 2015, but the plaintiff only realised he was injured – because the injury didn't manifest itself right away – until 1 November 2015. In this case, the time begins to run from the date of knowledge – 1 November 2015. (Statute of Limitations (Amendment) Act 1991 as amended by the Civil Liability and Courts Act 2004, s 7).

[16] [2013] IEHC 263.

stated that the foundations of the house were adequate, was issued negligently. She said she had relied on this certificate and had suffered loss as a result of his negligence. She sought damages from the engineer. The judge said that the cause of action accrued in January 2002, when the plaintiff first noticed the cracks. The cause of action accrues – i.e. the clock starts to run – from the time of the breach of contract, or when the negligence takes place. From that time, the plaintiff had the usual six years to issue proceedings against the engineer. But she never did. Now she was trying to do so in 2012. The judge had no doubt that if the plaintiff's case against the engineer went ahead it "would be dismissed as being manifestly statute barred".[17] What this means is a plaintiff can not argue that the clock started to run from the time he discovered the wrong. A plaintiff can only make this argument in personal injury claims.

Can a plaintiff argue that they did not discover the negligence until a later time? For example, you purchase a property in 2015. You notice cracks beginning to appear in 2018, but you take no action. You learn in 2020 that remedial works had been carried out on the property in 2014. In 2021 – i.e. seven years after the remedial works were carried out – you issue proceedings in negligence against the builder who carried out the 2014 works, saying that, because you only discovered the cracks in 2018, you are not statute barred. The better view seems to be that your case will be struck out because it is statute barred.[18] There is no discoverability test in Irish law, other than in cases of personal injuries (a topic that is not addressed in this book).

Another example of a professional negligence case that was statute barred is *Irish Equine Foundation Limited v Robinson*.[19] An equine centre was built in Kildare and the final architect's certificate had issued in November 1987. Water seeped in through the ceiling in 1991. Proceedings were issued in January 1996. In contract law the limitation period begins on the date on which the contract is breached (not on the date on which the damage is caused). The plaintiffs also pleaded negligence – which is a tort – and said the time limit started to run from the time that the damage manifested

---

[17] [2013] IEHC 263 at 4, citing *Hynes v Western Health Board* [2006] IEHC 55 (Unreported, High Court, Clarke J, 8 March 2006) and *Barry v Buckley* [1981] IR 306.

[18] *Murphy v McInerney Construction Ltd* [2008] IEHC 232 (Dunne J).

[19] [1999] IR 442, [1999] IEHC 150.

itself (i.e. from 1991, when the water came through the ceiling). That would mean the claim was not statute barred. The judge found that the defects had made themselves known from the beginning, and not just from 1991, and so the six-year period ran from 1987, making the claim statute barred. The Irish Supreme Court has – except in cases of fraud – rejected the "discoverability test", which would say that the time period runs from the time that the damage is discovered.[20]

Negligent Misstatement

What is a negligent misstatement? Will a professional be liable for giving one? The classic case is *Hedley Byrne & Co. v Heller*,[21] which involved a tussle between ad men and merchant bankers. The ad men were the plaintiffs, referred to for convenience as "Hedleys". They had a client called Easipower. They placed orders for advertising time in newspapers and on television for Easipower, and they did so on credit. The agreement between Hedleys and Easipower was that Hedleys would be personally liable to the newspapers and the TV companies if Easipower failed to pay. The ad men started to wonder if Easipower was good for the money. Easipower was a customer of Heller & Partners Ltd, a bank, so the ad men decided to make inquiries, through their own bankers, as to the state of Easipower's finances.

One bank (Hedleys' bank) was asking another bank (Easipower's bank, which was Heller & Partners) a question about a customer. Heller & Partners did not have to answer. But banks seem to cooperate with each other on these kinds of things. Heller didn't spend hours trawling though records, weighing and considering the features of Easipower. Hedleys' bank – and probably Hedleys themselves – did not expect that much from them. Heller & Partners got back to Hedleys' bankers saying there was no need to worry about Easipower's credit-worthiness (they added that they

---

[20] Geoghegan J stated that it was "quite clear" from *Hegarty v O'Lougran* [1990] 1 IR 148, a decision of the Irish Supreme Court, that the House of Lords' decision in *Pirelli v Oscar Faber & Partners* [1983] 2 AC 1 represented Irish law. Constitutional challenges to this situation—as in *Tuohy v Courtney* [1994] 3 IR 1—taken on the basis that the position is unfair to plaintiffs, have been rejected, because it is a matter of being fair to the defendant as well as to the plaintiff.

[21] [1964] AC 465.

made this statement "without responsibility"). Relying on this reference, Hedleys didn't cancel the ad space they had booked for Easipower.

It turned out that Heller & Partners were wrong, and the plaintiffs should have cancelled the ads. The ads ran, Easipower did not pay for them, and the ad men found themselves on the hook for the money. They sued Heller & Partners, saying that the replies to their questions about Easipower's credit-worthiness were given negligently and in breach of Heller's duty of care to them. At the heart of the case was misjudgment, not negligence (in the ordinary sense of carelessness).[22] Mr Heller honestly tried to give a fair assessment of Easipower's credit-worthiness, but he made a statement which "gave a false and misleading impression". As one of the judges put it, in order to succeed, Hedleys had to "establish that the bank owed them a duty, that the bank failed to discharge such duty, and that as a consequence Hedleys suffered loss".[23]

That same judge said:

> "The bank must have known that the inquiry was being made by someone who was contemplating doing business with Easipower Ltd and that their answer or the substance of it would in fact be passed on to such person".

It seemed to the court, as a matter of principle,[24] that if one person assumes a responsibility to another to tender deliberate advice, there could be a liability if the advice was negligently given. It was a long-established principle that a professional person, when exercising his professional service, skill or knowledge, would be guilty of negligence if the service, skill or knowledge were exercised below his normal ability.[25]

Is it any argument to say there is no consideration, therefore no enforceable contract, and therefore there can be no duty of care between the parties?

---

[22] *Per* Lord Reid at p 489. Lord Reid says the case is "nearly indistinguishable" from *Robinson v National Bank of Scotland Ltd* (1916) SC (HL) 154, and he discusses it from 489 to 491.
[23] *Per* Lord Morris of Borth-y-Gest, at 493.
[24] The emphasis is on the principle. The court was clear in saying that the principle didn't mean that legal obligation would attach to every kindly and friendly act. If that were so it would make "the ordinary courtesies and exchanges of life" impossible.
[25] [1964] AC 465 at 495; *Banbury v Bank of Montreal* [1918] AC 626, 689; *Shiels v Blackburne* (1789) 1 HBl 158; *Wilkinson v Coverdale* (1793) 1 Esp 75.

No. An example of a duty of care in the absence of consideration and contract is the duty of care a road user owes towards other road users. Every driver is the next driver's "neighbour". The bank – Heller – knew that some person, unknown to it, was going to rely on what it said and so the bank owed a duty of care to that person.

The duty the bank had to the ad men was to reply honestly. They specifically said that they replied "without responsibility" – an express disclaimer of responsibility. This meant, in this case, that there was a duty of honesty but no duty of care. The phrase "without responsibility" saved them. The court stated: "If the inquirers chose to receive and act upon the reply they cannot disregard the definite terms upon which it was given".[26] Therefore, the ad men failed in their attempt to win damages. Had there been no express disclaimer, the situation would have been different because the court had no difficulty with the principle that a duty could exist irrespective of a contract – the law will imply a duty to use one's professional care and skill when giving professional advice.

Barristers and Professional Negligence

In the past it was not possible to sue barristers for negligence. There is no contract between a barrister and a client (the contract is between the solicitor and the barrister): however, this became a much weaker consideration after the *Hedley Byrne & Co. v Heller* case, when the court held that a contractual relationship was not necessary for there to be negligence in the giving of professional advice. Another consideration has always been the fact that a barrister owes a duty not just to his or her client, but to the court as well. An example of how this can play out in practice is this: a barrister must tell the court if there is a case (also called a "precedent") which goes against his client. If one High Court judge has already decided a similar matter, another High Court judge will usually follow that decision. This may be something the client would prefer not to have brought to the judge's attention, but the barrister has a dual duty to client and to court.

---

[26] Lord Morris of Borth-y-Gest at 504.

In England the immunity from suit was removed from barristers in *Arthur JS Hall & Co. v Simons*.[27] Why could a barrister not be sued in negligence for strategic decisions made in the course of the trial, or for turning up to court unprepared? The Irish courts have not given a definitive answer on this issue. The leading Irish text on the subject says that the Irish courts have shown "positive interest" in the *JS Hall* case that nevertheless "fall[s] short of unambiguous embrace".[28] In *Behan v McGinley* a barrister was sued in negligence and not found liable, but in the course of the judgment the judge stated that that barristers

> "do not enjoy a blanket immunity from suit and can be sued in relation to their management of litigation on behalf of their clients either in respect of their preparatory work or indeed in respect of their management of the trial itself".[29]

Conclusions

- The courts do not use hindsight to judge the conduct of a person accused of negligence.
- A key consideration in deciding whether there was negligence is whether the person in question acted reasonably.
- Where a plaintiff is partly responsible for his loss, this is known as contributory negligence.
- The Statute of Limitations 1957 states that a person must take a negligence action within six years of the date of accrual of the cause of action.
- The cause of action accrues – i.e. the clock starts to run – from the time of the breach of contract, or when the negligence took place.
- There is no discoverability test in Irish law, other than in cases of personal injuries.
- If one person assumes a responsibility to another to tender deliberate advice, there could be a liability if the advice is negligently given. This is called negligent misstatement.

---

[27] [2002] 1 AC 615.
[28] McMahon & Binchy, *Law of Torts*, 4th ed., Bloomsbury Professional 2013, at para 14.249.
[29] *Per* Irvine J, *Behan v McGinley* [2008] IEHC 18; [2011] 1 IR 47 at 69.

PASSING OFF

What is Passing Off?

"[N]o man may pass off his goods as those of another"[1]

This quote essentially sums up the definition of the tort of passing off. Passing off is a tort that attempts to protect the "goodwill" of businesses. The goodwill of a business is an intangible asset that arises from the commercial reputation of the business. It can be established through use of a name, a trademark, packaging, design or an advertisement in connection with a business's goods. Thus, if you are claiming that another business has *passed off* their product or service as yours, you must show that a name, a trademark, packaging, design or an advertisement has become distinctive of your goods and that a reputation has attached thereto, so that use by the defendant would be likely to cause confusion, resulting in damage to your business's goodwill as a result of the other business's packaging and presentation of the product in question. Passing off is classified as an economic tort, as the resultant harm does not cause actual physical loss, but rather economic loss to the business that has lost a customer.

In *Polycell Products Ltd v O'Carroll & Others*[2] Budd J outlined the rationale of the tort as follows:

> "To establish merchandise in such a manner as to mislead the public into believing that it is the merchandise or product of another is actionable. It injures the complaining party's right of property in his business and injures the goodwill of his business. A person who passes off the goods of another acquires to some extent the benefit of the business reputation of his rival trader and gets the advantage of his advertising."

Although passing off may now be a less commonly used tort because of the development of copyright, trademark and intellectual property protections, it still provides a vital protection for businesses, in a way that these legislative regimes do not: for instance, in a passing off action, the registration of trademark is not relevant. The tort is solely based on

---

[1] *Per* Lord Oliver of Aylmerton in *Reckitt & Colman Products Ltd v Borden Inc. and Others* [1990] 1 WLR 491.
[2] *Polycell Products Ltd v O'Carroll & Others* [1959] Ir Jur 34.

property rights and the goodwill acquired by use of the mark/name/ packaging of the product. In the case of a passing off action, the defendant's goods or services need not even be the same as that of the plaintiffs: they may be allied or even different.

Elements of Passing Off

As with every tort, it is up to the plaintiff to prove her case on the balance of probabilities. The test is made up of three elements which must each be proved to the court before a plaintiff can be successful in a claim.

(a) The existence of a reputation or goodwill in the claimant's product including, where appropriate, in a brand name or get-up;

(b) The risk of confusion between what is alleged to be the offending product and the claimant's product; and

(c) Whether damage to the claimant's goodwill by virtue of any such confusion has been established.[3]

What can make a passing off claim complex is that the plaintiff has to submit market survey evidence to prove her goods or services have acquired goodwill and reputation in the relevant marketplace. The survey evidence submitted is subject to cross-examination and challenges. A defendant may also submit market surveys to try to show the contrary. The plaintiff may also have to provide information on her advertising and promotional budget and her sales revenue to support her claim regarding the acquired goodwill and reputation. If, on the other hand, a claimant has a registered trademark, there is no need to show goodwill or market reputation.

(a) Goodwill/Reputation

Goodwill has been defined by the courts as the "attractive force that brings in custom".[4] Goodwill or reputation can be established by showing that you have a distinctive name or distinctive branding, packaging, advertising, etc. that is recognised by the public as attaching to your particular good or service.

---

[3] *Jacob Fruitfield Ltd v United Biscuits (UK) Ltd* [2007] IEHC 368.
[4] *Per* Lord MacNaughton in *Inland Revenue Commissioners v Muller & Co. Margarine Ltd* [1901] AC 217.

Packaging and Design

In *Reckitt & Colman Products Ltd v Borden Inc.*, the House of Lords affirmed a permanent injunction preventing Borden from marketing a lemon-shaped container to sell lemon juice. The plaintiff had marketed their product Jif Lemon Juice in a lemon-shaped container for a number of years. The defendant created a product in a similar container and the plaintiff sought an injunction on the basis that the defendant's product was too similar and therefore liable to confuse customers. Survey evidence was used by Reckitt & Colman to establish confusion on the part of potential customers. This case established the above-mentioned three-part test for the tort of passing off and the House of Lords granted the injunction to prevent the defendants marketing their lemon juice in a similar container.

The Jif Lemon Juice product had been sold since 1956 but it wasn't registered as a trademark: why? The answer is that, had the company applied to register the Jif *lemon* as a trademark, the registrar would have rejected the application. This is because a mark that is a symbol of the goods or services it promotes does not qualify for registration. So, because the Jif lemon is a symbol of lemon and lemon juice, it could not be registered, and the only available remedy was the tort of passing off.

Two fairly recent Irish cases on this issue have further dealt with the issue of packaging and design. In *Jacob Fruitfield Food Group Ltd v United Biscuits (UK) Ltd*[5] Jacobs sought an injunction preventing the distribution of United Biscuit's products — McVitie's fig rolls and cream crackers in packaging which they argued was confusingly similar to that of their own product. Ultimately they were successful in obtaining an injunction in relation to the fig rolls, but they lost their bid in relation to the cream crackers. In this case the court paid particular regard to the fact that the similarity between the two products should be judged, to a significant extent, as a matter of first impression.

In *McCambridge Ltd v Joseph Brennan Bakeries*[6] Brennans did not deny that the packaging of its brown bread (re-sealable bags, very similar green colours, similar sizes and a depiction of wheat) resembled that of

---

[5] *Jacob Fruitfield Food Group Ltd v United Biscuits (UK) Ltd* [2007] IEHC 368.
[6] *McCambridge Ltd v Joseph Brennan Bakeries* [2011] IEHC 433, [2012] IESC 46.

McCambridge's wholemeal bread. It argued that the resemblances between the two packets were common to the trade, or "generic", and that McCambridge could not enjoy any goodwill in them. Brennans also sought to rely on the fact that its name was displayed on the top part of the packaging in red and yellow, the traditional company colours, and that any customer who picked up the bread could not fail to see this. Peart J in the High Court, and followed on appeal by the Supreme Court, looked at the manner in which products which are initially presented in an orderly way in supermarkets get tossed around, such that a manufacturer's name or other distinguishing feature may ultimately be obscured from view.

Having heard evidence from both experts and consumers, Peart J concluded that even prudent shoppers do not frequently closely inspect the product they take from the shelf of the supermarket and place in their trolley. He had found that there was a likelihood that a shopper would in fact end up with a Brennan's as opposed to a McCambridge's wholemeal bread product due to the high turnover of products in a supermarket, where the process of inspection is not particularly close or frequent. The consumer buying in a supermarket undertakes a quick exercise where visual clues rather than close scrutiny are relied on. This view was upheld on appeal by Brennans to the Supreme Court.

Name

The name of a business usually serves to distinguish it from its competitors, but business names can also be easily used to misrepresent the defendant's business as the plaintiff's. In *C & A Modes v C & A (Waterford) Ltd*[7] the plaintiff company carried on a retail clothing business in a chain of 65 shops throughout Britain and Northern Ireland. The Belfast shop attracted customers from the Republic, who travelled up regularly by train, and the company advertised extensively on television and in newspapers which reached people from the Republic. (It did not actually carry on a business in the Republic.) In this case the letters in the defendant company's name bore no resemblance to the names of the individuals involved in the company. The plaintiff was successful in their claim for passing off, despite the fact that they had no stores in the Republic.

---

[7] *C & A Modes v C & A (Waterford) Ltd* [1976] IR 198.

In *Guinness Ireland Group v Kilkenny Brewing Company Limited*,[8] the name 'Kilkenny Brewing Company Limited' had been chosen by the defendant without any deliberate consciousness of the possibility of confusion being created in consumers' minds of a connection between the defendant and the plaintiff. However, the High Court held that the tort of passing off includes the incorporation of a company with a name likely to give an impression to the public that it is a subsidiary, or is associated or connected with, another company that has an established goodwill. Whether the name was intentionally or innocently chosen simply does not matter, and in this instance it was established that Guinness had established goodwill in the name "Kilkenny" when used in connection with beer.

Goodwill in a name can also be based on past trading, as in the "Liberty" case, *Sutherland v V2 Music Limited*,[9] where the pop group "Liberty" from the 1980s took an action against another pop group known as "Liberty X" which had been created out of a UK TV programme in 2001. The court held that, despite the fact that the first band, Liberty, had since split, goodwill, where it exists, may be based on past trading activities and can also have a prospective nature. Future business opportunities could arise, and the potential goodwill the first band, Liberty, could have in the view of the public and music industry could be protected for five years after the band had ceased to perform. However, in this particular instance a sufficient amount of time had passed for there to be no confusion between the two groups but the decision does raise interesting questions in the current climate where many pop groups have reformed years after splitting up, and go on to have successful tours.

Advertising

Advertising techniques can also give rise to a sufficient misrepresentation on which an action may be based – provided the advertisements generate a sufficient association with the plaintiff to make them distinctive of the plaintiff's product or services. In the American case of *Coca-Cola Company v Gemini Rising Inc.*[10] the court held that the use of the plaintiff's descriptive script on T-shirts bearing the logo "enjoy cocaine" mimicked the plaintiff's

---

[8] *Guinness Ireland Group v Kilkenny Brewing Company Limited* [1999] 1ILRM 531.
[9] *Sutherland v V2 Music Limited* [2002] EMLR 28.
[10] *Coca-Cola Company v Gemini Rising Inc.* 346 F Supp 1183 (EDNY 1972).

"enjoy Coca-Cola" advertisements and therefore was held to involve a sufficient misrepresentation.

In the recent Irish case of *Allergan Inc. & Anor v Ocean Healthcare Ltd*[11] Allergan claimed that its BOTOX product had become a household consumer name and that the defendant's BOTOINA product infringed its trade mark BOTOX and amounted to passing off of its BOTOX product. Unlike the BOTOX product, the defendant's product is not injected into the skin but is applied to the surface of the skin by a patented precision applicator in the shape of a syringe. McGovern J, in assessing the similarity, placed emphasis on the first four letters of the respective marks – "BOTO" – holding that the marks were visually and aurally similar. He also had regard to the press release to be issued on the launch of BOTOINA in Ireland and a manual produced for pharmacies, which contained numerous references to BOTOX and its active ingredient Botulinum Toxin Type A. The judge also took account of the overall "get-up" of the BOTOINA product and its marketing with particular emphasis placed on a syringe-like applicator. As a result, it was held that the BOTOINA product was likely to cause confusion and that the sale and/or marketing of that product was being done in such a manner as was likely to cause confusion and to mislead the public into believing that the product sold by the defendant had some connection with the plaintiffs and their BOTOX product.

(b) Risk of Confusion

There is no need to prove an *intention* on the part of the defendant to deceive. The legal test of the risk of confusion is normally whether a casual customer is *likely* to be misled. As seen from the *McCambridge* case, the courts have recognised that customers do not examine products in meticulous detail before buying, so passing off may occur even though careful scrutiny would enable the consumer to discover the distinction. There is no general tort of unfair competition, in the sense that that term would be understood in continental Europe.[12] The "classic" type of passing

---

[11] *Allergan Inc. & Anor v Ocean Healthcare Ltd* [2008] IEHC 189.
[12] Article 10b of the Paris Convention provides that the Convention countries should provide an effective protection against unfair competition. Irish law purports to comply with the Convention requirements through passing off, malicious falsehood and certain criminal statutory offences relating to trade descriptions.

off case was concerned with deception but this was never held to be a *deliberate* deception. For example, in *Hodgkinson Corby Ltd v Wards Mobility Services Ltd*,[13] Jacob J said:

> "There is no tort of copying. There is no tort of taking a man's market or customers. Neither the market nor the customers are the plaintiff's to own. There is no tort of making use of another's goodwill as such. There is no tort of competition... At the heart of passing off lies deception or its likelihood, deception of the ultimate consumer in particular. Over the years passing off has developed from the classic case of the defendant selling his goods as and for those of the plaintiff to cover other kinds of deception, e.g. that the defendant's goods are the same as those of the plaintiff when they are not...or that the defendant's goods are the same as goods sold by a class of persons of which the plaintiff is a member when they are not...Never has the tort shown even a slight tendency to stray beyond cases of deception. Were it to do so it would enter the field of honest competition, declared unlawful for some reason other than deceptiveness..."

However, the boundaries of the tort of passing off have been extended beyond this purely "classic case". Passing off now includes cases where the misrepresentation is that the defendant's goods have the same kind of distinct and recognisable qualities as a particular class of products (e.g. champagne, Swiss chocolate or vodka).

(c) Damage to Good Will

The element of damage to goodwill is crucial in order to succeed in an action for passing off. The fact that a misrepresentation has occurred is not enough if the plaintiff cannot prove that her goodwill is endangered/damaged by that misrepresentation, or will probably be so — if the goods are released onto the market.

Difficulties can arise when the plaintiff and the defendant are not engaged in the same line of business and the courts have to consider whether a passing off action can succeed where the parties to the action are not in direct competition concerning the same goods or business. The general

---

[13] *Hodgkinson Corby Ltd v Wards Mobility Services Ltd* [1955] FSR 169, at 175

position is that the plaintiff will succeed where a false suggestion by the defendant — that the businesses are connected with each other- could damage the plaintiff's goodwill.

It is never a defence to an action in passing off that the defendant's goods are cheaper or that competition in the marketplace is beneficial. However, where the parties operate in different fields of activity, there is usually less danger of confusion and thus less danger of damage to the plaintiff, and this will be reflected in any award of damages. The fact that the plaintiff's business does not trade in the State will not suffice to prove a lack of goodwill within that particular jurisdiction, because goodwill does not necessarily stop at a border. Where the plaintiff's reputation lies in a business which is run abroad, and the defendant starts using a similar name or mark within this State, this will suffice for a claim irrespective of the fact that the plaintiff has no business in the State.[14]

Remedies

Generally in tort law the remedy is the payment of damages. However, in the tort of passing off the plaintiff may seek other remedies depending on what stage of the distribution chain the offending product is at. Available remedies for passing off include injunctive relief, delivery up of the offensive goods, and damages to the owner of the rights or an account of profits by the defendant.

Relationship with Trademark Law

There is no statutory cause of action for passing off and the law has developed through case law; however, as there is now extensive trademark legislation, some would ask if the tort of passing off is still relevant. A claim to passing off may arise out of the use of a sign which is the same as, or confusingly similar to, a registered trademark. Accordingly, there can be considerable overlap of factual circumstances in claims for trade mark infringement and in passing off. Given this overlap, many plaintiffs asserting registered trade mark infringement will also rely upon a claim in passing off. In most instances, the passing off claim is included as a

---

[14] See *Sheraton Corporation of America v Sheraton Motels Ltd* [1964] RPC 202 and also *C & A Modes v C & A (Waterford) Ltd* [1976] IR 198.

secondary claim in order to bolster the trade mark claim (particularly where the claim is based on a likelihood of confusion), rather than one which is included on its own merit. However, in some cases, the passing off is a standalone claim arising out of a different factual and legal analysis then a trademark action.

Generally, passing off is a much broader and more flexible claim than trade mark infringement, as it can cover a potentially wider range of situations, including unregistered marks, get-up and other matter that might not be registerable under the Trade Marks Act 1996.[15] Whilst passing off can, therefore, "fill some of the gaps" in terms of protection, it should be borne in mind that the evidential burden will inevitably be higher in a passing off claim, as under the statutory trademark regime there is no requirement to prove any goodwill in the mark. This, however, is key to a successful passing off claim.

Conclusions

- Passing off is a tort that attempts to protect the "goodwill" of businesses. The goodwill of a business is an intangible asset that arises from the commercial reputation of the business.
- There are three elements which must each be proved to the court before a plaintiff can be successful in a claim:
  (a) The existence of a reputation or goodwill in the claimant's product including, where appropriate, in a brand name or get-up;
  (b) The risk of confusion between what is alleged to be the offending product and the claimant's product; and
  (c) Whether damage to the claimant's goodwill by virtue of any such confusion has been established.[16]
- Goodwill or reputation can be established by showing that you have a distinctive name or distinctive branding, packaging,

---

[15] The Act does provide for registered protection for matter associated with the get-up of a product and its packaging such as colours, shapes, sounds, smells etc., provided that they are capable of graphical representation and capable of distinguishing the goods or services of one undertaking from those of others. However, it is often difficult to obtain registration for such matters because of the requirement to show distinctiveness.

[16] *Jacob Fruitfield Ltd v United Biscuits (UK) Ltd* 2007 IEHC 368.

advertising, etc. that is recognised by the public as attaching to your particular good or service.

- The usual remedy to an action in passing off is that of damges although if taken in time injunctions can be useful in order to prevent passing off occuring in the firstplace.
- Passing off is a much broader and more flexible claim than trade mark infringement, as it can cover a potentially wider range of situations, including unregistered marks, get-up and other matter that might not be registerable under the Trade Marks Act 1996

OFFER AND ACCEPTANCE

Definition of an "Offer"

For a contract to be binding a number of factors must be in place. There must be offer, acceptance, consideration and intention to create legal relations. We deal with the first two in this chapter, and the second two in Chapter 6. These terms – "offer" and "acceptance" – may seem straightforward but they must be carefully defined because situations can arise where a person will say that, in fact, no offer was made, or no acceptance was given. One judge has defined an offer as

> "an expression of willingness to contract, made with the intention that it shall become binding upon the person making it, as soon as it is accepted by the person to whom it is addressed".[1]

The courts generally apply an objective test. If you made an offer to someone, which was clear and unambiguous, it is no use to later say that you did not intend to be bound by it. There should be no vagueness or uncertainty. Nor would you be allowed to say: "I did say that, but it was subject to a condition which I didn't mention".

"Offer" Contrasted with an "Invitation to Treat"

It is vital that you are able to contrast an offer with what is called an "invitation to treat". The key characteristic of an offer is that it is capable of being accepted once it is made. An invitation to treat will fall short of this: invitations to treat come before the making of an offer. For example, when two companies are negotiating a contract, various matters may be discussed, questions asked and preliminary inquiries made. A price list might be sent from one company to the other. One company might invite the other to make an offer. One company might e-mail the other giving a lot of detailed information but saying, at some point, "we may be prepared to sell…" One company may ask another company for their lowest quotation on certain material; a reply containing the price and the earliest time when delivery could take place will not be an offer to sell, but merely a quotation of terms on which an offer might be made to

---

[1] *Air Transworld Ltd v Bombardier Inc.* [2012] All ER (D) 193 (Mar), *per* Cooke J, at para [75]; also reported at [2012] 1 Lloyd's Rep 349.

them.[2] Documents may be drafted during negotiations which are merely designed to invite further negotiation. None of these things can be characterised as offers. They fall short of that status because when communicated, they are not – to use the terminology above – "made with the intention that [they] shall become binding upon the person making it, as soon as [they are] accepted by the person to whom it is addressed". It is always the substance of the communication that matters: if the word "offer" is used but the *substance* of the communication is that it is an invitation to treat, the courts will find that an invitation to treat was made.[3]

When considering an invitation to treat versus an offer, think of an auction. This is a scenario that often confuses students, because they initially think that the auctioneer is making an offer when he calls out a figure. In fact, that auctioneer is inviting you to treat; if you make a bid, you are the one making the offer. The law says that the auctioneer is not bound to accept your offer. Your offer also lapses once another bidder makes a higher bid.

What about advertisements? Usually, an ad you see in a paper or on television will be deemed to be an invitation to treat, because if it was deemed to be an offer, the person or company who placed the ad would be liable to everyone who accepted the offer, and we know from common sense that there might be only a limited number of items which were earmarked to be sold at a sale price. It would be impractical and unfair to the seller for a potential purchaser to arrive in stating that he or she had accepted the offer and was entitled to the fridge, coat or pair of shoes in question. The courts have decided that

> "when one is dealing with advertisements and circulars, unless they indeed come from manufacturers, there is business sense in their being construed as invitations to treat and not offers for sale".[4]

---

[2] *Boyers & Co. v D&R Duke* [1905] 2 IR 617.
[3] It is often the case that the words used by the parties do not reflect the essence of the situation, and where this happens, the courts usually find that the substance trumps the words used. For example, in company law, if the parties both agree that a fixed charge was created, but the substance of the charge is that it is a floating charge, the courts will rule that a floating charge was created.
[4] *Partridge v Crittendon* [1968] 2 All ER 421, *per* Lord Parker CJ at 424.

The same is true of items in a shop window which have a price tag: that is an invitation to treat – and this also applies to online transactions, where a supplier indicates the availability of goods or services (when you click the appropriate button, that is *you* making the offer, which the supplier can reject or accept). In *Fisher v Bell*[5] a shopkeeper displayed a flick knife in the window with a price tag behind it. At the time, the sale of flick knives was illegal. The shop keeper pleaded not guilty because the knife in the window did not constitute an offer to sell the knife – which was prohibited: it was only an invitation to treat. The same logic applies to a menu in a restaurant: the restaurateur may accept your offer to order a lobster raviolo with samphire, peas and carrots, or may tell you he has run out of lobster and the dish is off the menu. The menu is an invitation to treat. In one well-known case – *Pharmaceutical Society of GB v Boots Cash Chemists (Southern) Ltd*[6] – the question was whether a customer who took products off a pharmacy shelf had accepted the pharmacist's offer, or was making an offer when presenting the products to the cashier. The court held that taking the items off the shelves was an offer by the customer to buy, and was not acceptance by the pharmacist to sell. The court said that the contract was not completed until the customer had indicated the article which he needs and the shopkeeper or someone on his behalf accepted that offer.

Acceptance of an Offer

Chitty provides the following definition of acceptance: it is "a final and unqualified expression of assent to the terms of an offer". These words should always be in your mind when considering whether an acceptance has been made: can you see a final and unqualified expression of assent? For example, if a person merely acknowledged the offer, this would fall short of acceptance. Another point to note is that silence will not constitute acceptance. An offer can, on the other hand, be accepted by conduct: if one company offers to sell airplanes to Ryanair, and sends them, and Ryanair uses them, this conduct will amount to acceptance by Ryanair of the offer to sell them. *Parkgrange Investments v Shandon Park Mills*[7], an Irish case,

---

[5] [1960] 3 All ER 731.
[6] [1953] 1 All ER 482.
[7] Unreported, High Court, Carroll J, 2 May 1991.

says that there must be an intention to accept, otherwise the contract will not have become binding.

A vital point is that acceptance should be communicated. This factor used to bring with it a difficult set of questions that turn on the issue of communication: questions that related to the posting and receipt of letters, or the printing of telex communications (for example, a court once had to answer the question of whether there had been acceptance by telex where the ink on the teleprinter failed at the receiving end and the offeree's clerk did not ask for the message to be repeated, so the person accepting reasonably thought he had communicated acceptance, but the offeree claimed not to have received the acceptance).[8] There are a number of cases on these points, but in an introductory work like this, where we are all aware that most communication now happens via e-mail as opposed to letter or telex, what you need to know is the essence of the modern rule, and the essence of it is that acceptance takes place when the other party receives the e-mail, which will be deemed to be instantaneous upon sending it. The question of sending the acceptance within business hours may arise, and business hours will depend on the circumstances of the case. Acceptance would not have taken place if the sender of the e-mail knew that the e-mail had failed to deliver.[9] There is no hard-and-fast rule, but the courts have said in the past that where "the condition of simultaneity is met, and where it appears to be within the mutual intention of the parties that contractual exchanges should take place in this way",[10] then the contract is formed when acceptance of an offer is communicated by the offeree to the offeror and the contract is formed in the place where acceptance is communicated to the offeror.

What if, in the course of long negotiations, one side claims that no contract was formed, while the other claims that a contract was formed? If Apple and Microsoft were involved in negotiations involving many twists and turns, offers and counteroffers, concessions and demands, there might be controversy about whether an offer was actually made and accepted; the courts would look at all the e-mails and documents

---

[8] *Entores Ltd v Miles Far East Corporation* [1955] 2 QB 327.
[9] For a discussion of this, see Beale, *Chitty on Contracts, Vol. I, General Principles*, 31st ed., Sweet & Maxwell 2012, at paras 2-050 and 2-051.
[10] *Brinkibon Ltd v Stahag Stahl* [1983] 2 AC 34 at 41–42.

between the two to decide the question. If Apple had performed some act for Microsoft, and Microsoft was trying to say there had never been proper offer and acceptance, the courts would be keen to hold that a contract had been made.

What if some difficulty arises in the performance of the contract and both companies argue that the question must be decided by reference to their own standard conditions? Usually the argument will turn on the small print of a company's terms. An important case from this point of view is *Butler Machine Tool Co. Ltd v Ex-Cell-O Corpn (England) Ltd.*[11] The case involved a machine tool called a double column plano-miller. Ex-Cell-O Corp was buying it, Butler's was selling it. On 23 May Butler's responded to an inquiry by Ex-Cell-O, saying that they would sell the machine tool for £75,000 and deliver it in ten months' time. Butler's said that the offer was "subject to certain terms and conditions which 'shall prevail over any terms and conditions in the Buyer's order'". When Butler's came to deliver the machine they claimed that the price had increased by £2,892. Ex-Cell-O refused to pay the increase in price. Butler's said the price variation clause in their terms allowed them to charge the extra £2,892. The Court of Appeal did not agree, because when Ex-Cell-O placed their order on 27 May they had said that the order was subject to *their* terms and conditions, and the Court of Appeal held that this amounted to a counter-offer by Ex-Cell-O. When Butler's completed and signed the acknowledgement of this and returned it to Ex-Cell-O, they accepted the terms of the counter-offer. Butler's thought they had protected themselves because they had also included a letter which said that the order was being entered into in accordance with their quotation letter of 23 May. The court held that this letter did not have the effect of incorporating Butler's terms back into the contract, because it said that the order was being entered into in accordance with the quotation of 23 May, and said nothing about the small print conditions on the back of the quotation. This area of contract law is sometimes called the "battle of the forms", i.e. the question is whose form will prevail. It is also sometimes called the "last shot" doctrine. The judge in the Butler's case said:

> "In some cases the battle is won by the man who fires the last
> shot. He is the man who puts forward the latest term and

---

[11] [1979] 1 All ER 965.

conditions: and, if they are not objected to by the other party, he may be taken to have agreed to them".[12]

Certainty of Terms

There should be no vagueness or uncertainty in the terms of a contract. If two parties purported to agree to something but one company had inserted into the contract the phrase "subject to our satisfaction", that contract would be struck down as being too vague. The courts will accept language that might seem vague to the average person, if the phrase in question has a specific meaning to a given industry – for example, butchers, metal workers, estate agents and so on might use terminology which would not have meaning to an outsider but which makes sense within the industry. Terms must be reasonable. Terms should not contradict one another, but if they do the courts will either try to make them fit in with the general meaning of the contract, or may sever them in order to keep the rest of the contract alive.

Termination of an Offer

When may an offer be terminated? "The general rule is that an offer may be withdrawn at any time before it is accepted".[13] Strangely, this even applies if the offeror promised to keep the offer open until a certain time.[14] For example, in *Dickinson v Dodds*[15] Dodds signed a note on Wednesday 10 June and gave it to Dickinson. In the note he had written that he would sell Dickinson a certain property for a specified sum. He also wrote that the offer would be "left over until" Friday 12 June at 9 a.m. Dickinson decided to accept the offer on Thursday morning but he did not communicate this to Dodds, because he thought he had until Friday morning. On Thursday afternoon Dickinson was told by someone that Dodds had either offered or agreed to sell the property to another man. When Dickinson caught up with Dodds on Friday morning he handed him a note of acceptance. Dodds was getting on a train and said: "You are too late. I have sold the property". The court decided the case

---

[12] *Per* Denning LJ at [1979] 1 All ER 965 at 968.
[13] *Chitty on Contracts*, at para 2-088.
[14] The reason for this is that the promise is not supported by consideration.
[15] (1876) 2 Ch D 463.

in favour of Dodds, because it said that the offer was capable of being withdrawn at any time. Importantly, the withdrawal should normally be communicated by the offeror to the offeree, but in this case, Dickinson learnt on Thursday evening that Dodds no longer intended to sell the property to him. So the rule is: communication of withdrawal is generally necessary – you cannot normally withdraw an offer simply by acting inconsistently with it – but the communication does not have to come from the offeror.[16]

The second way an offer may be terminated is if it is rejected. If you reject an offer, you cannot later accept it. If an offer is rejected in e-mail number one, it cannot be accepted in e-mail number two.[17] If someone offers to sell you something for €10,000 and you reply saying you will buy it for €9,000, you have rejected the offer and made a counter-offer.[18] If you mull it over, and decide that, in fact, you would like to buy the item for €10,000 and you send an e-mail saying, "I've reconsidered and will pay the €10,000 you asked for", this will not amount to acceptance, because your counter-offer killed the original offer of €10,000.

The third way an offer can be terminated is by lapse of time. If a time is specified, the offer cannot be accepted after that time. If no time is specified the courts will infer that a reasonable time was intended. What is reasonable will depend on the circumstances: for example, if the goods are perishable, a reasonable time for acceptance of an offer will be a lot shorter than if the goods were pieces of machinery. There are other ways in which an offer may be terminated – by the death of the offeror, the supervening mental incapacity of the offeror, or corporate incapacity – but they are beyond the scope of this introductory work.[19]

"Subject to Contract"

You might have heard of the phrase "subject to contract". What effect does it have to include this phrase in the body of a contract? Generally, it means that the agreement is not complete, and that a formal contract has

---

[16] A similar case is *Routledge v Grant* (1828) 4 Bing 653, where a promise to give someone six weeks to think about an offer was reneged on.

[17] *Grant v Bragg* [2010] 1 All ER (Comm) 1166.

[18] This was the case in *Hyde v Wrech* (1840) 3 Beav 334.

[19] For a detailed analysis see *Chitty on Contracts*, at paras 2-099 to 2-110.

yet to be finalised. The phrase often appears in contracts for the sale of land by private treaty and in contracts for the supply of goods.[20]

Conclusions

- Can you define an offer?
- When the courts consider whether an offer has been made, do they use a subjective or an objective test?
- What is the key characteristic of an offer?
- Can you give examples of an invitation to treat?
- Are advertisements offers or invitations to treat?
- Can you define acceptance?
- What is the "last shot" doctrine?
- If terms of a contract were vague, what effect might that have?
- When may an offer be terminated?
- Name three ways in which an offer may be terminated.

---

[20] See *RTS Flexible Systems Ltd v Molkerei GmbH* [2010] 1 WLR 753 at para [48].

CHAPTER SIX

CONSIDERATION AND INTENTION TO CREATE LEGAL RELATIONS

Why Consideration?

For a contract to be binding there must be an exchange of what is called "consideration". Consideration simply means something of value. It is usually money, but as we will see below it can take various forms. But first we must ask why is there a need for consideration if offer and acceptance have taken place? Without consideration, offer and acceptance are merely promises between two parties.

For example:

(i)   Anthony promises to give me his i-pad and I accept that offer. Anthony then decides not to give me his i-pad.

(ii)   Anthony agrees to sell me his i-pad for €250 and I accept. Anthony then decides not to go through with the sale.

In the first example there is *no contract* as there is no consideration. The law takes the view that, as I was getting something for nothing, I should not have a legal remedy to enforce a mere promise. In the second example a valid contact has been formed. Both parties give consideration and I can enforce the contract. By withdrawing from the contract, Anthony is breaching it.

Definition of Consideration

Consideration is something of value. It is usually money, but it can also be an item or a promise to do something or to forbear from doing something. Forbearance is the promise to not do something that the promisor has an entitlement to do. The classic case is *Hamer v Sidway*.[1] In this case an uncle promised his nephew $5,000 if he refrained from liquor, tobacco, swearing, cards and billiards until he was 21. The nephew carried out his part of the deal and when he was 21 his uncle's estate would not pay him the money, alleging there was no consideration from the nephew. The court held that the nephew had a legal right to drink and smoke, and that by refraining from doing these things, he had given valid consideration for the uncle's promise of money.

---

[1] *Hamer v Sidway* (1891) 124 NY 538.

Adequacy and Sufficiency of Consideration

The general rule regarding consideration is that it must be sufficient but need not be adequate. Sufficient means that there must be some monetary value to the consideration and that it must be capable in law of amounting to consideration. In other words, it is not necessary for each party's consideration to be equal in value. This is based on each party's freedom of contract. The courts will not investigate the adequacy of the consideration as long as it is sufficient. Thus, as long as the bargain is one made honestly and with no allegation of undue influence or duress, it will be enforced by the courts even if one party gets more out of the deal than the other. For example in *Thomas v Thomas*[2] a house was promised to a widow for a rent of £1 per year. This was binding upon the parties: the consideration had value although it was inadequate.

As we have seen, forbearance has been held to be sufficient consideration. Loss of privacy has also been held to be sufficient consideration. In *O'Keefe v Ryanair*[3] the plaintiff was the one-millionth Ryanair passenger, and was offered free flights for life in return for participation in certain promotional activities including television appearances. Ryanair later tried to terminate the arrangement claiming there was no consideration. It was held that the loss of privacy was sufficient consideration.

Past Consideration

Past consideration is never valid consideration. This is consideration for an act that has already been performed before the other party gives her promise. The logic here is that the act of past consideration was done independently of the contract, and therefore had no bearing on the contract. There is no causal link between the act of consideration and the promise of the other party. For example, in *Re McArdle*[4] a woman sued on foot of a promise made by her brother-in-law that he would repay her for certain improvements she made to her mother-in-law's house. However, the promise to pay was made by the brother-in-law some time after the woman had already completed the repairs. The court held that the improvements were not made in response to the

[2] *Thomas v Thomas* (1842) 2 QB 851, 114 ER 330.
[3] *O'Keefe v Ryanair* [2002] 3 IR 228.
[4] *Re McArdle* [1951] Ch 669.

promise to pay as they were in the past and could not be valid consideration.

Illegal Acts

An illegal act is insufficient to amount to consideration.

Performance of an Existing Statutory Duty

Performance of an existing statutory duty is not consideration. The party was under an obligation to carry out the act anyway, so it cannot be said to have been done as a result of the contract. In *Collins v Godefroy*[5] a witness was promised payment if he attended court and gave evidence. This could never amount to consideration, as he was legally required to attend court.

However, any act that goes beyond the call of this existing duty can be valid consideration. In *Glasbrook Bros Ltd v Glamorgan*[6] the plaintiff requested that police provide a full-time guard for their mine during a strike and offered money in return. Here, because the police already had a statutory duty, it was argued that this could not be valid consideration. However, their statutory duty did not extend to providing a full-time guard. The provision of a full-time guard was valid consideration, and thus the police were entitled to the money promised.

Performance of an Existing Contractual Duty

For the same reason as above, the performance of an existing contractual duty is not sufficient consideration. Two sailing-related cases illustrate the point. In *Stilk v Myrick*[7] two sailors deserted a ship and the captain offered the remaining nine sailors their wages if they continued to work on the ship. The court held that the nine remaining sailors were not entitled to the extra money as they merely did what they had already contractually agreed to do – sail the ship home. There had been no extra consideration from the seamen. However, as with a statutory duty, if the

---

[5] *Collins v Godefroy* (1893) 1 B & Ad 950.
[6] *Glasbrook Bros Ltd v Glamorgan* [1925] AC 270.
[7] *Stilk v Myrick* (1809) 2 Camp 317.

existing contractual duty is exceeded, there is then sufficient consideration. In *Hartley v Ponsonby*[8] a high number of desertions from a merchant ship rendered the vessel dangerous and unseaworthy, since it was undermanned. Extra pay was then offered to the crew if they remained loyal. The promise of extra money was enforceable by the seamen as they were working in dangerous conditions not contemplated by their original contract.

Just when the law seemed clear and easily understood, the decision of the Court of Appeal in *Williams v Roffey Brothers & Nicholls (Contractors) Ltd*[9] threw it into confusion in the early 1990s. Here the plaintiff (a sub-contractor) had agreed to refurbish a roof and the interior of 27 flats for the defendant (the main contractor) at an agreed price of €20,000 by an agreed date. The plaintiff seriously underestimated the cost of carrying out the work and approached the defendant seeking additional payments. The plaintiff received additional payments and then further agreed with the defendant that upon completion of the work he would be paid a further £10,300. If the work had run late then the defendant would have been penalised under his own contract with the owner of the flats. The plaintiff then brought the defendant to court seeking the further £10,300, which the defendant had refused to pay. The defendant argued that the plaintiff was only promising to do what he was bound to do anyway and that there was no additional consideration.

Here the court held that even though the plaintiff was doing no extra work, there was a new contract for the £10,300, and that both the plaintiff and the defendant benefited from that contract. The defendant avoided the penalties under his contract with the owner, and also the cost and aggravation of employing a substitute contractor. The plaintiff had provided consideration by giving the defendant grounds for believing that the work would be completed without interruption by reason of insolvency or other difficulties. The court stressed that the defendant's promise of an extra payment was not extracted by fraud or pressure.

This case shows the Court of Appeal using a somewhat pragmatic approach to consideration on this occasion. It has proven a controversial

---

[8] *Hartley v Ponsonby* (1857) 7 E & B 872.
[9] *Williams v Roffey Brothers & Nicholls (Contractors) Ltd.* [1990] 1 All ER 512.

approach and Clark suggests that it makes the boundary between promissory estoppel and consideration difficult to draw.[10] However, it demonstrates an approach by the courts that recognises the commercial realities and difficulties that arise in certain contractual relationships.

The Rule in *Pinnel's* Case

If I am owed €10,000 by Anthony and I accept from him €8,000 in full and final payment of the debt, can I then sue him for the remaining €2,000?

The rule in *Pinnel's* case (1602) states that payment of a smaller sum does not discharge a debt of a greater amount.

However, there are a number of exceptions to the rule in *Pinnel's* case:

- Where part payment is made by a third party.
- Where something else of value along with the part payment is given. It is sufficient for payment to be made early, or in a more convenient form.
- In a situation where the debtor is bankrupt, a composition of creditors can agree to a lesser payment.
- The doctrine of promissory estoppel.

Promissory Estoppel

The English word "estoppel" is probably derived from the French word "estoupe" (meaning stopper or bung). Estoppel, simply put, means this: say a woman made a promise or representation to another person, who, based on that promise or representation, altered her position or situation. The promisor shall be estopped in law from going back on her promise or representation.

Promissory estoppel then prevents a person from going back on her promise. Thus, by making a promise, the promisor is prevented from asserting her strict legal rights. In *Jorden v Money*[11] the promisor led the promisee to believe that she would not seek to recover a debt. Mr Money

---

[10] Robert Clark, *Contract Law in Ireland*, 6th ed., Round Hall 2008, at 62.
[11] *Jorden v Money* (1845) 5 HL Cas 185.

had borrowed £1,200 pounds from Marvell, who died. Mrs Jorden took the bond as successor. Mr Money was about to marry and this debt caused him concern. But Mrs Jorden then promised that she would never enforce the bond. Mr Money, taking Mrs Jorden at her word, went ahead and married. However, after five years Mrs Jorden sought to enforce the bond. Mr Money defended the action, pleading that she be estopped. The House of Lords held that he was liable, as estoppel works only in respect of a statement of existing fact and not in relation to representations about the future.

This strict view of estoppel was threatened by a line of cases taking a more "equitable" view of the doctrine, which commenced after a decision of Lord Denning in *Central London Property Trust v High Trees House*.[12] In this case a property (High Trees House, a block of flats) was let during World War II to the defendant, who in turn sublet it. Due to the war the defendant could not get tenants and the plaintiff promised not to charge full rent for duration of the war. The terms of the agreement stated that the full rent would become payable when the war conditions ended. By the beginning of 1945 all the flats were leased and the landlord sought to recover rental arrears for the last half of 1945. Lord Denning held that even if the terms of the agreement meant that the landlord was entitled to succeed for the last half of 1945, he would not be able to succeed in a claim for the rest of the rent during the war years. Although the plaintiff had a legal right to the money, he could not resile from his promise. It was legally binding, despite the fact that the defendant had given nothing of value in return.

As a result of the *High Trees* case there are four necessary conditions before promissory estoppel can exist:

- There must be a valid contract between the parties;
- The plaintiff must voluntarily promise to limit her rights under the contract;
- There must be an intention that the defendant should rely on the promise; and
- The defendant must alter her legal position because of the promise.

---

[12] *Central London Property Trust v High Trees House* [1947] KB 130.

However, the doctrine has limitations:

- It is a shield and not a sword. In other words, it can be used as a defence, but not as a way to initiate a case; and
- The party seeking to use it as an equitable defence must also have acted fairly in their dealings with the claimants.

Intention to Create Legal Relations

This principle is tied into the central concept in contract – the freedom to contract – that is, that parties are free to negotiate and to enter into agreements, and yet to declare that these arrangements are to be free of legal contractual force. Thus, in order to create an enforceable contract, both parties must intend to enter into a legal relationship. The general rule is that all parties are presumed to have the intention to enter into a contract if it appears to a reasonable observer that they have entered into the contract. If there is an offer that has been accepted by the offeree then the state of mind of the parties is irrelevant. This is known as the rule of objective intent.

However, in certain circumstances the courts will presume that the parties do not intend to enter into a legally binding contract, despite it appearing to a reasonable observer that there is a contract. This usually arises in family or domestic arrangements.

Family Arrangements

The courts recognise that family members can enter into transactions for reasons other than commercial advantage and the courts generally dislike interfering in family relationships, where a large number of non-commercial transactions can take place. However, it has been stated that the presumption against an intention to create legally binding arrangements is linked to very close family relationships such as parent and child or spouses.[13] The presumption can be rebutted if the parties made formal or detailed financial arrangements, or if the family agreement was made in a business context.

---

[13] *Leahy v Rawson*, Unreported, High Court, O'Sullivan J, 14 January 2003.

Commercial Agreements

It is presumed that there is an intention to create legal relations when two companies or commercial entities enter into a transaction, unless it can be shown otherwise. This is a presumption that can only be rebutted by strong evidence to the contrary.

Conclusions

- Consideration means something of value, and need not necessarily be money. For a contract to be binding, consideration must feature as well as offer and acceptance.
- Consideration can also take the form of forbearance or an agreement to a loss of privacy.
- Consideration does not have to be adequate (i.e. it does not have to equal the value of the thing bargained for), it just must be adequate (i.e. it must have some value in the eyes of the law).
- Past consideration is never valid consideration, nor is the performance of an existing statutory or contractual duty.
- Acceptance of part of a debt as "full and final" payment of the debt does not prevent the creditor from seeking the rest of the money, because Pinnel's case says that a payment of a smaller sum does not discharge a larger debt.
- Promissory estoppel is a doctrine which states that a person will be prevented from going back on his promise, if the person to whom the promise was made altered their situation to their detriment, on account of the promise.

CHAPTER SEVEN

THE SALE OF GOODS AND SUPPLY OF SERVICES

Introduction

This chapter focuses on "consumer law" in the context of contracts. What once took up a very minor section dealing with the Sale of Goods and Supply of Services Acts in contract law books now could make up a book in its own right.[1] Consumers have used the law by various means to obtain protection, whether through tort law or contract law, but since the 1970s, mainly as a result of Ireland joining the European Union (then the European Economic Community), Irish consumers have been protected under numerous pieces of legislation. Consumers are also somewhat protected under various criminal statutes dealing with food safety,[2] medicines,[3] agriculture,[4] and more recently the Consumer Protection Act 2007, which has both civil and criminal enforcement mechanisms. This chapter will outline in brief the main pieces of civil legislation at play and the type of contracts affected.[5]

The Legislative Framework

(i) The Sale of Goods Act 1893 and the Sale of Goods and Supply of Services Act 1980

The Sale of Goods Act 1893 was the mainstay of Irish sales law for over a century. Many of its provisions take the form of default rules. As originally enacted, the Act gave contracting parties a free hand to waive or alter the terms that it inserted into contracts of sale. However, an amendment was made by the 1980 Act, and these terms cannot now be altered in the case of consumer sales and can be altered only where shown to be "fair and reasonable" in commercial sales. Key to legislation in this area is the principle that parties to *commercial* contracts are still afforded a substantial degree of latitude to decide their own terms.

---

[1] And now does; see Donnelly and White, *Consumer Law, Rights and Regulation*, Round Hall 2014.

[2] The Food Safety Authority of Ireland Act 1998.

[3] The Irish Medicines Board Act 1995.

[4] The Registration of Potato Growers and Packers Act 1984 and the Diseases of Animals Act 1966.

[5] For more on this area generally see Donnelly and White, *Consumer Law*.

The purpose of the passing of the Sale of Goods and Supply of Services Act 1980 was to strengthen the protections available to *consumers*.[6]

The most significant sections of the Acts are ss 12–15, as amended by the 1980 Act. These sections imply various terms into contracts and can only be avoided by express agreement where the buyer is not a consumer and where the provision is fair and reasonable.

Section 12(1)

This section sets out two obligations:

   (a) an implied condition in a contract of sale that the seller has the right to sell the goods and, in relation to an agreement to sell, that the seller will have the right to sell the goods, at the time property is to pass; and

   (b) an implied warranty that the goods are, and will remain free until the time when the property is to pass from any encumbrances not disclosed to the buyer and that the buyer shall enjoy quiet possession except in relation to encumbrances disclosed at the time of sale.

This section works as a condition and so if it is breached the buyer has the right to reject the goods and claim the purchase price back.

Section 13

This section implies a condition that where goods are sold by description, they will correspond to that description. Section 13(3) provides further that a description extends to a reference to goods on a label or other descriptive matter that accompany the goods. As long as you are relying on the description you can have the benefit of s 13.

---

[6] Unfortunately, the 1980 Act took the form of additions and amendments to the 1893 Act rather than repealing it and replacing it with one consolidated and consumer-friendly piece of legislation. Therefore, in order to understand the statutory rules governing contracts of sale, it is necessary to read the original Act of 1893, the sections substituted in the 1893 Act by the 1980 Act, the textual and non-textual amendments to the 1893 Act made by the 1980 Act and other enactments, as well as the provisions of the 1980 Act.

Section 14

Section 14 of the 1893 Act, as amended by the 1980 Act, provides protection in relation to the quality of the goods. Section 14(2) provides an implied condition that the goods are of merchantable quality apart from defects brought to the attention of the buyer before contracting or defects which ought to have been revealed by examination prior to contracting.

Section 15

This section remains as enacted by the 1893 Act. It provides for three implied conditions in consumer contracts:

(i)   If sold by sample that the bulk will correspond to the sample.
(ii) The buyer must be given a reasonable opportunity to inspect the sample.
(iii) If the goods supplied match the sample in every way but the sample and the bulk are defective (therefore unmerchantable), there is liability in relation to the bulk (if it would not be apparent on inspection of the sample).

As stated above, contracting out of the implied terms inserted into consumer contracts is controlled by the legislation itself, in s 55(4). If the buyer is a consumer, the implied terms as to description, merchantability and fitness for purpose cannot be contracted out of. The other terms can only be contracted out of by consumers if the terms are "fair and reasonable".[7]

(ii) The Unfair Terms Regulations 1995

From the mid-1980s, change in Irish consumer legislation was driven by the European Union, which adopted a number of directives in the area of consumer contract law. One of the more notable pieces of legislation in this area is the European Communities (Unfair Terms in Consumer Contracts) Regulations 1995, which transposed Directive 93/13 into Irish law *via* statutory instrument. These Regulations recognise the weak position of the consumer versus the seller in terms of bargaining power

---

[7] See Clark, *Contract Law in Ireland*, 7th ed., Round Hall 2013, at 283–290.

and level of knowledge.[8] The 1995 Regulations apply to any term in a contract between a consumer and a seller of goods or supplier of services which has not been individually negotiated. A "consumer" is defined in regulation 2 as a "natural person who is acting for purposes which are outside his business".

Under s 3(2) of the 1995 Regulations, a contractual term shall be regarded as unfair (and thus void) if, contrary to the requirement of good faith, it causes a significant imbalance in the parties' rights and obligations under the contract to the detriment of the consumer, taking into account the nature of the goods or services for which the contract was concluded and all circumstances attending the conclusion of the contract and all other terms of the contract or of another contract on which it is dependent.

Section 5(1) provides that where contracts are offered (either in whole or in part) to consumers in writing, the seller or supplier is obligated to ensure that terms are drafted in plain, intelligible language. Further, s 5(2) provides that if there is any doubt as to the meaning of a term, the definition more favourable to the consumer must be applied.

Determining what unfairness in a contract means is up to each national court of the EU member states. The Court of Justice of the European Union (CJEU) has in fact declined to rule on specific terms in contracts and has decided its role is to interpret general criteria of the EU legislation in order to define the concept of unfair terms.[9] In determining whether a term is unfair, the CJEU has stated that the national courts are to consider what rules would apply in the absence of the contractual agreement and then ultimately must ask the question: "whether the seller or supplier, dealing fairly and equitably with the consumer, could reasonably assume that the consumer would have agreed to such a term in individual contract negotiations".[10]

---

[8] See *Oceano Grupo Editorial SA v Rocio Murciano Qintero* (C-240/98 to C-244/98) [2000] ECR I-4941.

[9] *Freiburger Kommunalbauten GmbH Baugesellschaft & Co. KG v Hofstetter* C-237/02 [2000].

[10] See *Aziz v Catalunyacaixa* C-415/11 (30 April 2013): this case concerned the validity of certain terms in a mortgage loan agreement entered into by the parties, and whether they were contrary to the Directive. The CJEU held that Spanish law contravened EU law, as it impaired the protection sought by the Directive, by making it impossible for a debtor to object to mortgage enforcement proceedings on the ground that a term of the relevant mortgage agreement was unfair.

(iii) The Consumer Protection Act 2007 and The EU Unfair Commercial Practices Directive

The Consumer Protection Act 2007 provided for the establishment of the National Consumer Agency (NCA). Under the Competition and Consumer Protection Act 2014, the National Consumer Agency and the Competition Authority were replaced by the Competition and Consumer Protection Commission (CCPC). The Commission took over the functions of these two agencies. The 2007 Act also brought the EU directive on unfair commercial practices into national law. The 2007 Act is vast and somewhat complex; the more notable aspects are dealt with here.

The Competition and Consumer Protection Commission

The Competition and Consumer Protection Commission was established in 2014 and took over the functions and powers of the National Consumer Agency. It has a general function of promoting consumer welfare and is responsible for investigating, enforcing, and encouraging compliance with, consumer law.

Unfair Commercial Practices

The EU Unfair Commercial Practices Directive (Directive 2005/29/EC of 11 May 2005) deals with unfair business-to-consumer commercial practices. It was transposed into Irish law via the Consumer Protection Act 2007.

Commercial practice is defined as "any conduct (whether an act or omission), course of conduct or representation by the trader in relation to a consumer transaction, including any such conduct or representation made or engaged in before, during or after the consumer transaction". This definition is a broad one that includes advertising, marketing, sales promotions, discounts, competitions and use of vouchers, but also goes beyond these examples.

The Act provides that a range of unfair, misleading and aggressive trading practices are banned if they would be likely to cause appreciable impairment of the average consumer's ability to make an informed choice in relation to the product or transaction concerned. Both offline and online transactions, and both goods and services, are covered by the legislation.

The legislation deals with three distinct types of unfair commercial practices: misleading practices, aggressive practices and prohibited practices. A commercial practice is misleading if it contains false or untruthful information or in any way deceives or is likely to deceive the "average consumer", and causes or is likely to cause him/her to take a transactional decision that he/she would not otherwise have taken. The "average consumer" is one who is "reasonably well informed and reasonably observant and circumspect, taking into account social cultural and linguistic factors".

In the context of determining whether a trader has engaged in a misleading practice, two considerations must be taken into account:

- whether the action would cause the "average consumer" to take a decision that he/she would not otherwise have taken – the "average consumer test";
- the trader's professional diligence, i.e. the general requirement to act with good faith in the trader's field of activity and the expected standard of skill and care.

The "average consumer" test also applies in the context of aggressive practices; the second test does not apply. In the context of assessing actions relating to prohibited practices, no test is required; these practices are considered unfair in all circumstances. A "black list" of 31 practices prohibited in all member states has been drawn up and includes such practices as: emotional pressure, inertia selling, pyramid schemes, false claims about curative capacity and aggressive doorstep selling.

Enforcement

Sections 71–73 of the Consumer Protection Act 2007 provide for civil enforcement mechanisms to be available to the CCPC, such as injunctions, prohibitions and compliance orders. Section 74 deals with individual cases of consumers' right to damages. The Central Bank of Ireland also has a role in enforcing the provisions of the Consumer Protection Act 2007 in the financial services area. The CCPC and the Central Bank are required to have a cooperation agreement setting out their respective roles.

Sections 76–84 deal with criminal proceedings for certain breaches of the Act, with a range of penalties set out for the various offences. The maximum fine for a first offence is €3,000 for summary convictions and €60,000 for convictions on indictment.

Whistleblowers

Section 87 of the Act provides protection for people who report breaches of the legislation to the CCPC.

Conclusions

- Consumers have many remedies available to them in law to enforce their rights, including contract law, tort law, criminal law and various specific statutes that offer them protection.
- The Sale of Goods and Supply of Services Acts imply various terms into contracts which cannot be contracted out of, for example: fitness for purpose, merchantability, good title and distance selling terms.
- Consumers also receive protection via the Unfair Terms in Consumer Contracts Regulations 1995, which recognise the weak position of the consumer versus the seller in terms of bargaining power and level of knowledge.
- The 1995 Regulations provide that where contracts are offered to consumers in writing the seller or supplier is obligated to ensure that terms are drafted in plain, intelligible language.
- The 1995 Regulations also provide that if there is any doubt as to the meaning of a term in a contract, the definition more favourable to the consumer must be applied.
- The Consumer Protection Act 2007 established the National Consumer Agency, now the Competition and Consumer Protection Commission. The 2007 Act also brought the EU directive on unfair commercial practices into national law.
- The 2007 Act provides that a range of unfair, misleading and aggressive trading practices are banned if they would be likely to cause appreciable impairment of the average consumer's ability to

make an informed choice in relation to the product or transaction concerned.

- The legislation deals with three distinct types of unfair commercial practices: misleading practices, aggressive practices and prohibited practices.

CHAPTER EIGHT

CONTRACTUAL TERMS AND EXEMPTION CLAUSES

Introduction

Two things at the outset: contractual stipulations carry different weight and they are not always referred to by a consistent terminology (for example, a stipulation which is referred to by some as a warranty may be referred to by others as a term, though the words may have the same meaning). What we can say with certainty is this: if a stipulation is essential to the contract, it will be referred to as a condition. If a condition is breached, the injured party can end the contract and sue, or affirm the contract and sue. The great thing about a term which is a condition is that you have certainty. The party affected by the breach knows where he stands. It does not matter how trivial the breach of condition is, the injured party has the choice just outlined. If a term or a warranty is breached, the injured party is not in as strong a position if they want to simply put the contract to an end (this issue is dealt with in detail in Chapter 13, Remedies for Breach of Contract).

Sometimes cases appeared before the courts where a party said that the stipulation which had been breached was a condition, and the courts decided it was in fact a term; the other side would have argued that the stipulation was merely a term and therefore the right to end the contract and sue for damages was not available. An important case in the 1960s – *Hong Kong Fir v Kawasaki*[1] – held that sometimes contractual undertakings are very complex, and cannot easily be categorised as being "conditions" or "warranties". It was for the courts to decide how fundamental the stipulation was. They decided to call these complex stipulations "intermediate terms"[2], a name which emphasises that, until the court decides, the term is somewhere in the middle. The legal test for deciding what weight to give to a stipulation is to ask whether or not the breach deprived the injured party of "substantially the whole benefit which it was intended that he should obtain from the contract". So, where the nature of a stipulation is a matter of debate, of uncertainty, it will be a matter of interpretation, which falls to the courts.

---

[1] [1962] 1 All ER 474.
[2] Sometimes referred to as "innominate terms".

Express Terms

In order to determine what rights and obligations parties have under a contract, the first thing you look at are the terms that are written down (or "reduced to writing" as the legal phrase has it). These are called the express terms. It is no defence to say "I signed the contract but I did not understand the legal effect of every single clause"; parties are bound by what is written and signed up to. If contracts only consisted of express terms it would be a lot easier to interpret them, but often questions will turn on implied terms and even on terms made orally. This is an important lesson: the express terms can carry implied terms, and the written agreement may not reflect the entirety of the contract because part of the agreement was made orally and not reduced to writing.

Where a key part of the agreement is not written down, what happens where one side says "this part was a term of the contract" and the other side says "that was only a statement I made on the way to agreeing the contract"? This latter kind of statement is called a "representation", i.e. something falling short of a term of the contract. Whether it was merely a representation or it became a term/warranty is decided objectively, and by considering whether there is "evidence by one or both parties that there should be contractual liability in respect of the accuracy of the statement".[3] In *McGuinness v Hunter* (1853) a person who was selling a horse said "[the] horse is alright and I know nothing wrong with him"; this was held to have been a warranty and so damages were awarded because there was something wrong with the horse. *Schawel v Reade*[4] was another horse case. The defendant said to the man who was inspecting the stallion: "you need not look for anything; the horse is perfectly sound. If there was anything the matter with the horse, I should tell you". The horse in fact had moon-blindness. The court held that the defendant had warranted the horse (even though the *word* warranty did not appear anywhere in the agreement). In *Routledge v McKay*[5] a motorcycle was sold where, unknown to either side, certain statements in the registration book were false, because the motorcycle had passed through a number of hands before it came to Routledge and McKay. Had

---

[3] [1913] AC 30 at 51.
[4] [1913] 2 IR 64.
[5] [1954] 1 All ER 855.

the seller warranted the correctness of the entries in the book (which would make him liable in damages)? Or had the seller merely made an innocent misrepresentation (which would not make him liable in damages)? The court said that the seller could not be deemed to have warranted the accuracy of the book unless he expressly made himself responsible for it. *Hummingbird Motors v Hobbs*[6] was a similar case involving the mileage of a car, as recorded by the odometer. The key thing was that the defendant had honestly said that the mileage was correct to the best of his knowledge and belief.

In *Oscar Chess v Williams*[7] a car was sold on the basis that it was a 1948 model; it was in fact a 1939 model. The court said that the defendant was not liable for breach of warranty because: (1) both he and the plaintiffs knew that the defendant had no personal knowledge of the date of the car's manufacture; and (2) the plaintiffs – who were motor dealers – had enough experience to form their own view on that question. An innocent misrepresentation had occurred. If, on the other hand, as happened in the *Dick Bentley* case,[8] a seller states something which is within his own knowledge, and not within the buyer's, and the statement is intended to induce the buyer to buy, then this will be "ample foundation for the inference of a warranty", which will mean a buyer will succeed in damages against the seller.

In *Carey v Irish Independent Newspapers*[9] the plaintiff, who was a journalist, accepted a promotion on the basis that she could work from home during the early morning shift because of family commitments. The paper's editor had given her an assurance that this would be okay, but he had talked to a member of senior management about it, and that person had serious reservations. The editor did not put the assurance in writing so that the paper could review the situation at some later stage. When that editor was replaced, the plaintiff was asked to work the early morning shift in the paper's offices. She said she could not and her employment came to an end. She took an action under a number of headings, arguing that the agreement about working from home during the early morning

---

[6] [1986] RTR 276; [1986] BTLC 245.
[7] [1957] 1 All ER 325.
[8] *Dick Bentley Productions v Harold Smith (Motors) Ltd* [1965] 2 All ER 65.
[9] [2004] 3 IR 52.

shift was a fundamental term of her contract. She had relied on the representations of the editor and was induced by them to enter the contract. She won her case, the judge deciding that a negligent misrepresentation had been made to her.

Implied Terms

Sometimes the written contract will set down only the most important aspects of the agreement, but many other aspects of it are understood to be included. These are known as implied terms. This is a tricky area for the courts, because one side is saying that a certain matter has to be *read in* to the contract. The court has to consider what was the commercial *purpose* of the contract, and the background to it. The courts always say, essentially: "We're not going to make a contract for you – all we can do is imply a term if it arises from the language and the circumstances of the agreement". There are two occasions where they will be very ready to imply a term: (1) where it makes commercial sense (the "business efficacy test"); and (2) where the implied term "represents an obvious but unexpressed intention of the parties".[10] These two occasions are treated by the courts as guiding principles rather than "tests" per se.[11]

Certain terms are implied by law. Contracts involving landlord and tenant, employment, sale of goods, package holidays, transport of goods – these always have terms implied into them because many rules are set out in relation to them in statute.[12] The only way to prevent all those rules being implied into those kinds of contracts is to expressly say in the contract that they will not have effect.

The key rule to remember is that the courts will not imply a term into a contract merely because to do so would be reasonable; it would have to be necessary. For example, in *Dakota Packaging v Wyeth Medica*[13] the two companies had a course of dealing for a number of years and the defendant gave six months' notice terminating their business relationship. The plaintiff company argued it was entitled to a minimum of eighteen

---

[10] Beale, *Chitty on Contracts, Vol. I, General Principles*, 31st ed., Sweet & Maxwell 2012, at para 13-004.
[11] *AG of Belize v Belize Telecom Ltd* [2009] 1 WLR 1988.
[12] See *Liverpool City Co. v Irwin* [1977] AC 239.
[13] [2005] 2 IR 54.

months' notice because of the length of their business relationship. The court said it had no broad discretion to imply terms into contracts, and that the court could not do so simply because a term was fair or reasonable; it had to be necessary to do so. Crucially, in this case no term could be implied because there was no contract between the two companies – there was only an understanding between the two that they would conduct certain business together.

Exclusion Clauses

You will have come across exclusion clauses: gyms that say you leave things in the locker at your own risk; hotels that say the same about things you leave in your room; car parks that claim to take no responsibility for any damage to your car, and so on. There is such a thing as a limitation clause; it seeks to put a cap on a party's liability, after a certain figure. The courts do not frown upon limitation clauses as much as exclusion clauses, because an exclusion clause is such an extreme thing. One objection made against them is that there is inequality of bargaining power involved – but this will not always mean the clause is not valid. It is a basic rule of contract law that parties should be allowed to contract with each other on whatever terms they see fit. And there is a particularly good case to be made for allowing exclusion clauses to prevail, no matter how harsh the result, where both parties have equal bargaining power, something that will often exist in the commercial world.

The key thing is that the exclusion clause should be expressed clearly and should be brought to the notice of the other side. If you wish to rely on it, you should take all reasonable steps to bring it to the attention of the other side. As the judge in *Spurling v Bradshaw*[14] put it:

> The more unreasonable a clause is, the greater the notice which must be given of it. Some clauses which I have seen would need to be printed in red ink on the face of the document with a red hand pointing to it before the notice could be held to be sufficient.

---

[14] [1956] 1 WLR 461; see also *Western Meats Ltd v National Ice and Cold Storage* [1982] ILRM 99.

The law in relation to exclusion clauses (sometimes referred to as "exemption clauses") can be summarised in the following eight rules.

1. *L'Estrange v Graucob*[15] says that once you have signed the contract, it does not matter if you read the terms or not. You will be bound by the small print if you have *signed* the contract (as long as there is no fraud or misrepresentation). This would not necessarily be the case if you were issued with a bus or train ticket, or some other document which you did not sign.

2. *Richardson, Spence & Co. v Rowntree*[16] says that if you are handed *a folded up ticket* when you board a ship and you injure yourself, and there is a clause exempting the ship-owners from liability for loss or injury to passengers, you can successfully argue that you did not know that the writing or printing contained conditions relating to the terms of the contract of carriage, and that the shipping company did not do what was reasonably sufficient to give you notice of the conditions.

3. *Early v Great Southern Railway*[17] says that if you buy a train ticket and it says "see back" and you do not bother reading it, it is tough luck for you: the notice will have been sufficient.

4. In *Olley v Marlborough Court Ltd*[18] it was held that if you go to a hotel, pay and check in at the desk, and later find terms on the back of your hotel room door, those terms will not bind you. An exclusion clause will not operate in those circumstances. The clause must be brought to your attention at the time of the entering into of the contract, i.e. when you are checking in at the desk.

5. *Thornston v Shoelane Parking*[19] is similar to *Olley*. Thornston drove into an automatic car park. At the entrance he took a ticket which had small-print wording on it indicating that somewhere in the car park – he would have had to go looking for it – he would find a full version of the conditions. The court said that to rely on their exclusion clause, the car park owners must show they have done what is reasonably necessary to draw the exclusion clause to the driver's

---

[15] [1934] 2 KB 394.
[16] [1894] AC 217.
[17] [1940] IR 409.
[18] [1949] 1 KB 532.
[19] [1971] 2 QB 163.

attention. The issuing of the ticket at the entrance is an irrevocable step and conditions cannot be incorporated after that point.

6.   In *Spurling v Bradshaw*[20] it was held that if you have a course of dealing with a company and you don't bother to read some of the original contract terms, you will be stuck with them. They will have been incorporated by the course of dealing.

7.   The courts will try to uphold whatever the main purpose of the contract is, so if an exclusion clause tries to exclude something very basic, it will not have force. For example, in *Sze Hai Tong Bank Ltd v Rambler Cycle Ltd*[21] one party sought to exclude liability in a case where it delivered the goods in question to the wrong person. Delivery to the right party was deemed to be so basic that the exclusion clause could not cover it.

8.   In *Photo Production Ltd v Securicor Transport Ltd*[22] the court decided that it is possible to include an exemption clause which excludes liability for fundamental breach, but an important factor will be whether both parties were commercial entities who had similar bargaining power. In such cases the parties are free to apportion the risks as they see fit. In *Photo Production* the words of the clause were very clear.

Conclusions

- Contractual stipulations carry different weight.
- Terms which are reduced to writing are known as express terms.
- Whether a statement was a warranty/term or a representation will be judged objectively, by evidence from one or both parties that there should be contractual liability in respect of the accuracy of the statement.
- A breach of warranty that occurred because of an innocent misrepresentation will not entitle an injured party to damages.
- A negligent misrepresentation of a fundamental term will found a case for damages.
- When considering whether to imply a term into a contract, the court will look to the purpose of the contract and to the background

---

[20] [1956] 1 WLR 461.
[21] [1959] AC 576.
[22] [1980] 2 WLR 283.

facts. It will seek to establish whether the term suits the business efficacy test or whether the term would represent the obvious but unexpressed intention of the parties.

- The courts will not imply a term into a contract merely because to do so would be reasonable; a term will only be implied if it is necessary.
- The key thing about exemption clauses is that the party seeking to rely on the clause should have taken all reasonable steps to bring it to the attention of the other side.

CHAPTER NINE

Misrepresentation

Introduction

One of the leading textbooks on contract law says of the area of misrepresentation that it is "a complex amalgam of rules of common law, equity and statute law"—and the complexity does not end here. For a business student, that is an intimidating beginning. The good news is that, as a business student, you do not need to be able to handle this area as someone with legal training would be expected to. Instead, you should be aware that there are three categories of misrepresentation—fraudulent, negligent and innocent misrepresentation—and you should be able to distinguish between the three. This is useful, because if you know the three kinds of misrepresentation you should be able to avoid making them yourself in a work context. Another very important aspect of the law on misrepresentation is insurance contracts—an area every business needs to have some understanding of.

First of all, for the representation to give rise to legal consequences, it must normally be a representation of fact and not of law.[1] This means we are not talking about scenarios where a person is giving his or her opinion, or informing someone of an intention they have. Whether someone is making a statement of fact or is giving an opinion is not always going to be a clear-cut matter, so the key thing to keep in mind is whether the person giving the statement intended it to be relied on by the person listening, and gave it with an eye to inducing the listener to enter the contract.

We find an example of a misrepresentation in *Cramaso LLP v Ogilvie-Grant*.[2] The defendants owned a grouse moor which formed part of the grounds of a Scottish castle, Castle Grant. People would pay to use the grounds for shooting. The owners of the grouse moor recognised that the business needed investment. It was decided to lease the moor to someone who would invest in it. The key thing about the case is that in the course of negotiations, an inaccurate number was given for the grouse population of the moor. For example, when someone asked for a total figure for the grouse, they were e-mailed a figure which was only representative of the parts of the moor which were considered to be the most heavily populated by grouse. That meant that the figure for estimated grouse population far

---

[1] *Per* Keane J, *Doolan v Murray* (Unreported, High Court, 21 December 1993), at 37, citing *Cooper v Phibbs* (1867) LR 2 HL 149.
[2] [2014] UKSC 9.

exceeded the actual population. This is what is called a "material misrepresentation"—"material" simply means "relevant". If it was given without checking the facts beforehand, it was given negligently. The purpose of the representation was to give reassurance to the purchaser of the lease that there was a substantial surplus of birds on the moor; therefore, the representation induced the purchaser to enter into the contract. When the courts find that such a misrepresentation has occurred, they may set aside the contract, saying it is vitiated by error or fraud. In the *Cramaso* case the representation was made to a Mr Erskine, who went on to form a limited liability partnership—Cramaso—to take over the lease. The defendants tried to argue that the misrepresentation had not been made to Cramaso; it had only been made to Mr Erskine. This argument might have succeeded if the misrepresentation had been withdrawn or lapsed, or because Mr Erskine discovered the true state of affairs before the contract was concluded; in such a case the misrepresentation could not have induced Mr Erskine or his company, Cramaso, to enter into the contract. But this was a case of a continuing misrepresentation. The discrepancy was never discovered before the contract was concluded.

If a person innocently makes an inaccurate representation and later discovers the true state of affairs, that person may be liable in damages if he fails to disclose the inaccuracy.[3] If a person makes a representation which is true at that moment, but which has become false by the time the contract is being entered into, that person has a responsibility to bring to light the true state of affairs.[4] Both of these cases illustrate the continuing responsibility on the person making the representation, and the rule of law which says that pre-contractual representations can have a continuing effect. In the *Cramaso* case the representation, made to Mr Erskine and relied on by his company, had a continuing effect. A negligent representation gives rise to a remedy in damages.

It is important that the representation, made in the course of dealings for a contract, was *made to induce* the other party to act on it, and *actually does*

[3] *Brownlie v Miller* (1880) 7 R (HL) 66, 79; *Brownlie v Campbell* (1880) 5 App Cas 925, 950 *per* Lord Blackburn.
[4] *Shankland & Co. v Robinson & Co.* 1920 SC (HL) 103, 111 *per* Lord Dunedin.

induce the other party to enter the contract.[5] For example, in *McCaughey v IBRC*[6] Mr McCaughey said "I would not have invested" in a certain project had he known certain information, but the court did not accept this evidence; the court believed he would have invested anyway. The courts will not assume that a person would have done the reasonable thing because judges have often seen "instances where people react to particular developments in ways which are irrational, exaggerated, unduly bellicose or unduly timid, or otherwise improbable".[7] Likewise, in *Intrum Justitia BV v Legal and Trade Financial Services*[8] the plaintiff agreed to buy the defendant company. The plaintiff company carried out due diligence. Before it did so, the chairman of the defendant told the financial director of the plaintiff that the defendant had "no skeletons in the cupboard". The defendant also said in an e-mail that a very extensive due diligence was not necessary because there was nothing wrong with the company. It was subsequently discovered that a large embezzlement had taken place in the defendant company. The plaintiff said that the statements about "no skeletons", and so on, had been a misrepresentation. The court found that the plaintiffs had not relied on those statements; they had relied on their own due diligence process. The court said that the misrepresentations did not have to be the "main or paramount consideration" in the mind of the plaintiff, but they did have to be part of the underlying basis on which the plaintiff proceeded— and here they were not.

In *Walsh v Jones Lang LaSalle*[9] David Walsh bought a commercial property. The defendants calculated the floor area—but they miscalculated it by 20% and published the miscalculation in their sales brochure. The defendant argued that it had no duty of care to Mr Walsh to ensure that the details in its brochures were accurate, and that he should have checked himself. The court awarded Mr Walsh €350,000 in damages because he had relied to his detriment on the misrepresentation made by the defendants. The judge held that the information in the brochure was directed at potential buyers and was there to influence

---

[5] *Per* Denning LJ in *Bentley (Dick) Productions Limited v Harold Smith (Motors) Limited* [1965] 1 WLR 623 .
[6] [2013] IESC 17.
[7] *Per* Hardiman J, [2013] IESC 17 at 47.
[8] [2009] 4 IR 417; [2005] IEHC 190.
[9] [2009] 4 IR 401; [2007] IEHC 28.

them to buy, and there for them to rely on. The court held that there was a duty on the defendant to ensure that the information it provided was reasonably accurate.

Fraudulent Misrepresentation

In Northern Bank Finance Corporation v Charlton[10] the Supreme Court stated: "Where a fraudulent misrepresentation has induced a transaction, the rule is that the person deceived has the right to rescind the entire transaction; but the right must be exercised *in toto* so that every part of the transaction, and everything given or obtained under it, is cancelled or restored". *Fenton v Schofield*[11] is an Irish case which offers the perfect example of a fraudulent misrepresentation. Fenton bought lands from Schofield, who told Fenton that the fishery was worth £27,000. In fact, he had lied about the amount of fish, and because of this the true value of the property was only £22,000. This was a fraudulent misrepresentation—because Schofield knew his statement was false when he made it—and Fenton was entitled to damages in the sum of £5,000. The old case of *Derry v Peek*[12] gives guidance when considering fraud: it was said there that "fraud is proved when it is shown that a false representation has been made (1) knowingly, or (2) without belief in its truth, or (3) recklessly, careless whether it be true or false". It is important to remember this third factor: making a representation in a careless or reckless manner. In *Keegan Quarries Ltd v McGuinness*[13] a representation was made that the property in question had been used continuously as a quarry since 1 October 1964 and this was false. It was a false statement made recklessly by Mr McGuinness and it was intended to be relied upon and to induce the purchaser to complete the sale. For this reason Keegan Quarries was entitled to judgment against Mr McGuinness in the sum of €5.5m.

---

[10] *Per* O'Higgins CJ, [1979] IR 149 at 183.
[11] (1966) 100 ILTR 69.
[12] (1889) 14 App Cas 337.
[13] [2011] IEHC 453.

Negligent Misstatement

The area of negligence is a tort. Negligent misstatement is a branch of the tort of negligence.[14] Even if there is no contract between two parties, the court can hold one party liable if it made a negligent misstatement to the other and the party to whom the statement was made relied on it. The most important case in this area—the one which began the modern case law—is *Hedley Byrne v Heller*[15], and its facts are neatly summarised in Clark: "in *Hedley Byrne v Heller* a bank negligently represented a company to be on a sound financial footing. This caused [Hedley Byrne & Co.] to invest in the company, which later collapsed".[16] The House of Lords said that Hedley Byrne and Co.—an advertising firm—was entitled to damages for financial loss caused by their reliance on the misstatement, even though there was no contract between them and the bank, because the courts will imply a duty of care whenever a person seeks the special knowledge and skill of an expert, and the person seeking the advice places reliance on that skill and judgment. One Irish judge summarised this point thus:

> "Circumstances may create a relationship between two parties in which, if one seeks information from the other, and is given it, that other is under a duty to take reasonable care to ensure that the information is correct".[17]

What this means is that a party can be liable for purely economic loss which was caused by a negligent misstatement.

In *Thomas Witter v TBP Industries*[18] the defendants were selling a carpet manufacturing business and they furnished an interested person with audited management accounts for the previous year, which gave an estimate of profits for the year to come. The person who was interested in buying the business bought it, but took a case against TBP Industries the following year on the basis that they had misrepresented the situation to

---

[14] According to Clark—*Contract Law in Ireland*, 7th ed., Round Hall 2013, at 382—"the boundary between negligent misrepresentation and negligent misstatement is uncertain", and business students need to worry about the nuances between the two—which can sometimes puzzle lawyers.

[15] [1964] AC 465.

[16] Clark, *Contract Law in Ireland*, 7th ed., Round Hall, 2013, at p 377.

[17] *Per* Davitt P in *Securities Trust Ltd v Hugh Moore and Alexander Ltd* [1964] IR 417.

[18] [1996] 2 All ER 573.

him with regard to a particular figure—£120,000—in the accounts, and with regard to the use of a "deferred pattern book expenditure", which meant that the profit projections should have been less than the purchaser was told. The plaintiff alleged that the misrepresentations were negligent and that he relied on them. The plaintiff wanted to rescind the contract: this was not possible, because it was impossible to restore the two sides to the position they occupied before the contract. The court found that the misrepresentations were negligently made and the plaintiff was entitled to damages for this.

Darlington Properties v Meath County Council[19] is another example of negligent misrepresentation: Meath County Council—bungling and inept, according to the judge—represented to the plaintiff that certain land would be serviced by a distributor road, something which was of major importance for the plaintiff. The plaintiff bought the land on this basis, but the distributor road never materialised. The court held that the plaintiff was induced to enter into the purchase of the land on foot of negligent misrepresentations made by the County Council in the brochure, tender documents and conditions of contract, and awarded the plaintiff €4m in damages. The judge noted that the duty of care is not confined to professionals: "a vendor has a duty to take reasonable care so as to ensure that statements he makes in seeking to induce a sale are true".[20] One of the earliest cases where this was held to be true was *Esso Petroleum Company Limited v Mardon*[21], where incorrect information about the annual turnover was given to the purchaser of a petrol station. When it became clear that the figures given were drastically at odds with the reality, the purchaser successfully sued for damages.

Innocent Misrepresentation

An innocent misrepresentation is not made fraudulently or negligently, and the general rule used to be that no damages could be recovered where a person has relied on an innocent misrepresentation. Section 45 of the Sale of Goods and Supply of Services Act 1980 changed that. It provided that a person who had been induced to enter a contract by a

---

[19] [2011] IEHC 70.
[20] *Per* Kelly J, at 36, citing *Doran v Delaney* [1998] 2 IR 61.
[21] [1976] QB 801.

misrepresentation could claim damages "if the person making the misrepresentation would be liable to damages in respect thereof had the misrepresentation been made fraudulently" unless the maker of the misrepresentation can prove that he had "reasonable ground to believe and did believe up to the time the contract was made that the facts represented were true".

Exclusion Clauses Relating to Misrepresentation

A party to an agreement might try to exclude or restrict liability for misrepresentation made before the contract was entered into, and to exclude or restrict the other side from pursuing any remedy that would be normally available to them in those circumstances. If such a provision is included in a contract, Section 46 of the Sale of Goods and Supply of Services Act 1980 ("SGSSA 1980") says that it will not be enforceable "unless it is shown that it is fair and reasonable".

When deciding whether a term is fair and reasonable the test is

> "that it shall be a fair and reasonable one to be included having regard to the circumstances which were, or ought reasonably to have been, known to or in contemplation of the parties when the contract was made".[22]

The courts have regard to the relative bargaining positions of the parties, inducements made to secure agreement to a term and the extent to which the customer knew about the existence of the term.

Remedies

When a misrepresentation is discovered, the party who was given the inaccurate information will often want to rescind the contract. The right to rescind is lost in a number of cases. If the misrepresentee[23] becomes aware of the misrepresentation and continues with the contract, this is called affirmation: once a contract is affirmed in these circumstances the right to rescind is lost. The right to rescind can also be lost if the misrepresentee

---

[22] Definition provided in the Schedule to Sale of Goods and Supply of Services Act 1980.
[23] The person who has had some element of the contract misrepresented to them.

delays in seeking rescission.[24] The right to rescind will be lost if at the heart of the matter there is an asset or piece of property which has been bought by a third party—known in law as "the bona fide purchaser for value without notice"—who was unaware of any problems and who purchased the asset for good consideration. Finally, it might be the case that the court thinks it a fairer outcome to award damages instead of granting rescission.[25]

Insurance Contracts

The final part of this chapter is concerned with insurance contracts. These are known as contracts of *"uberrimae fidei"*, a Latin phrase which means "of the utmost good faith". When you enter into a contract with an insurance company, there is an imbalance of knowledge. You may know everything about your health; the insurance company, in asking you to fill out various forms, has to take your word. The danger is that you might be flexible with the truth—something the insurance company would refer to as "non-disclosure". That is why these contracts are *uberrimae fidei*: you have a *duty* to make full disclosure; if you do not, the contract is voidable. This means that, if the insurance company finds out about your material non-disclosure, it can *there and then* inform you that it has no more obligations under the contract, and does not have to honour any of its side of the deal. It will repudiate the contract. It will not usually be entitled to damages.

When you think of insurance contracts, you should think not just of health insurance, but of contracts to insure company property—against fire, water-damage, burglary, and so on. One well-known Irish case—*Chariot Inns Ltd v Assicurazioni Spa*[26]—arose out of a fire which damaged a cabaret premises in Ranelagh, Dublin, known as the Chariot Inn. The principal shareholders in Chariot Inns Ltd—the plaintiff company—were a Mr Wootton and his wife. When Mr Wooton was filling in the form to insure the Chariot Inns premises, he ticked the box "none" in answer to a question as to whether he or his company had claimed for loss over the

[24] *Leaf v International Galleries* [1950] 2 KB 86.
[25] s 45(2) of the SGSSA 1980.
[26] [1981] IR 199.

previous five years. In fact, he had claimed two years previously, when a fire had damaged a Leeson St property belonging to Chariot Inns Ltd. Mr Wootton warranted expressly that the statements made on the proposal form were true and complete. Less than three months later, the Ranelagh premises were destroyed by fire and the plaintiff claimed from the defendant insurer. The insurers argued there had been a material non-disclosure and repudiated liability in respect of the fire. The Supreme Court held that the plaintiff, who was trying to enforce the insurance contract, had failed to make a material disclosure and so the defendant was able to avoid liability. The test, when considering whether a fact is material or not, is whether, if the insurer knew it, the insurer would still decide to take the risk; the courts speak of "that which would influence the mind of a prudent insurer in deciding whether to accept the risk or fix the premium".

It was stated in *Pan Atlantic Insurance Co. v Pine Top Insurance Co.*[27] that the test is not whether a prudent insurer would have "wanted to know" or would have "taken into account" the undisclosed fact even though it would have made no difference to his acceptance of the risk or the amount of premium, because this idea "would give carte blanche to the avoidance of insurance contracts on vague grounds of non-disclosure supported by vague evidence even though disclosure would not have made any difference".[28] If an expert said to the court "I would have wanted to know but the knowledge would not have made any difference" there would be no objective way of testing this statement.

In *Aro Road v The Insurance Corp of Ireland Ltd*[29] the court stated that: "Good faith requires candour and disclosure, not…accuracy in itself, but a genuine effort to achieve accuracy… If the duty is one that requires disclosure by the insured of all material facts which are known to him, then it may well require an impossible level of performance".[30] This "genuine effort to achieve accuracy" is extremely important. In *Keating v New Ireland Assurance*[31] a Mr Keating admitted to "epigastric discomfort" when filling out a life insurance form but was not aware he was suffering

---

[27] [1994] 3 All ER 581.
[28] *Per* Lord Templeman, [1994] 3 All ER 581 at 585.
[29] [1986] IR 403.
[30] *Per* McCarthy J [1986] IR 403 at 414.
[31] [1990] ILRM 110; [1990] 2 IR 383.

from a heart condition. He died from angina. The insurer tried to repudiate its liability under Mr Keating's life insurance. The question was not whether Mr Keating ought to have known that he had a heart problem; the question was whether he did know. The court said: "One cannot disclose what one does not know". The question may be decided differently where the ignorance was wilful, but that was not the case here. Mr Keating had answered all the questions "to the best of his ability and truthfully". Mr Keating had made a genuine effort to achieve accuracy.

In *Coleman v New Ireland*[32] Ms Coleman was diagnosed with multiple sclerosis. She was seeking payment of a sum of €95,000 from the defendants, with whom she had an insurance policy. The defendant argued that Ms Coleman had not disclosed material matters, because eight years previously she had been tested for an inflammation of the eye, and her consultant had told her that there was a possibility that "this or other neurological symptoms could trouble her in the future, but that this would hopefully not be the case". The court decided that the consultant did not express himself in terms which might have caused Ms Coleman alarm and that: (1) there had been no occurrence of the symptoms; (2) there was a time lapse of eight years; and (3) Ms Coleman "had put the entire incident out of her mind on the basis that it did not appear to have been significant". The court held, therefore, that New Ireland had come to an incorrect view as to its entitlement to avoid the policy.

"Basis of Contract" Clause

There is one way for the insurer to protect itself to the utmost: it can include a "basis of the contract" clause, which will mean that total disclosure by the insured is the basis of the contract, and anything short of that will result in the contract being repudiated by the insurer.[33] There was such a clause in *Keenan v Shield Insurance*,[34] and the insurance company was able to repudiate the contract even though Mr Keenan's omission was

---

[32] [2009] IEHC 273.

[33] This might take the form of a declaration at the foot of the proposal form that the particulars therein contained are "true and complete in every respect and that no material fact has been suppressed or withheld", and a further clause stating that the declaration and the answers given on the proposal form should be the basis of the contract between the parties.

[34] [1987] IR 113; see also *Farrell v South East Lancashire Insurance Co Ltd* [1933] IR 36.

very small: he had not mentioned that the previous year he had been paid £53 in respect of fire damage to a pump.

Conclusions

- For a representation to have legal consequences, it must be a representation of fact and not of law. It is not an expression of opinion or intention, but the communication of a fact.
- The representation must be intended to be relied on by the representee, and must induce the representee to enter the contract.
- A person claiming misrepresentation must show that the misrepresentation was relied on.
- If a person innocently makes an inaccurate representation and later discovers the true state of affairs, that person may be liable in damages if he fails to disclose the inaccuracy
- A fraudulent misrepresentation will have been made knowingly or without caring whether the statement is true or not.
- One company may be liable to another where it has negligently given inaccurate information.
- Recission is a commonly sought remedy in cases of misrepresentation but the right to rescind can be lost in a number of ways.
- Insurance contracts are contracts "of the utmost good faith" which require full disclosure from the insured if the contract is not to be repudiated at a later stage by the insurer. The courts have come up with a "prudent insurer" test.
- While the courts will not always insist on accuracy in itself, they will always insist on "a genuine effort to achieve accuracy".

CHAPTER TEN

MISTAKE

Introduction

If two parties make a contract and one of them later says that there was a mistake in it, and litigates this point, the court must ask: "What was the contract intended to be?" In *Kramer v Arnold* it was said that where the parties are in disagreement as to what a particular provision of a contract means "the task of the court is to decide what the intention of the parties was, having regard to the language used in the contract itself and the surrounding circumstances".[1] When the courts are looking at a commercial agreement, the judge will try to give the contract a commercially sensible construction. One well-known English judge, Lord Diplock, said that

> "if detailed semantic and syntactical analysis of words in a commercial contract is going to lead to a conclusion that flouts business common sense, it must yield to business common sense".[2]

The court's task is "to discover what the parties meant from what they have said" and not to force a meaning onto the words which would have the effect of remaking the contract, of giving the contract a meaning which was not intended, or of giving the contract a meaning that a judge thinks would have been better. It was said in *Charter Reinsurance v Fagan* that to do this would be "an illegitimate role for a court. Particularly in the field of commerce, where the parties need to know what they must do and what they can insist on not doing, it is essential for them to be confident that they can rely on the court to enforce their contract according to its terms".[3]

There are three categories of mistake. It would be convenient if they had names that made them readily understandable. But they do not. And on top of that, the courts have recognised that the terminology is not always consistent.[4] The three categories of mistake are as follows:

---

[1] [1997] 3 IR 43 at 55, per Keane J.
[2] *Per* Lord Diplock in *Antaios Compania Naviera SA v Salen Rederierna A.B.* [1985] AC 191 at 201; approved by Clarke J in *BNY Trust Co. (Ireland) Ltd v Treasury Holdings* [2007] IEHC 271.
[3] Lord Mustill in *Charter Reinsurance v Fagan* [1997] AC 313 at 388; approved by the Irish Supreme Court in *Marlan Homes Ltd v Walsh & Ors* [2012] IESC 23.
[4] Costello J, *O'Neill v Ryan (No. 3)* [1992] 1 IR 166 at 183–184.

Common mistake
Mutual mistake
Unilateral mistake

Common Mistake

Common mistake means that the parties have made the same mistake. Mutual mistake means both sides have made a different mistake. And unilateral mistake means that the mistake has only been made on one side.

In *O'Neill v Ryan (No. 3)* an Irish judge gave the following examples of common mistake. He said it would be a common mistake

> "where both parties agree on the purchase and sale of a painting believing it to be a Gainsborough and it is subsequently established that this is not so, or where both parties agree on the sale of tenanted property and both believe that the tenant is protected by the Rent Restrictions Act and subsequently ascertain that this is not so".[5]

Mistakes in contracts are rare enough—McDermott says "the cases in which a party successfully asserts a mistake are relatively rare"[6]—and for this reason a good deal of the examples of mistakes in contracts are quite old. The basic idea is that a contract must be the result of an agreement. A contract will be held to be void where, unknown to the parties, the subject matter no longer existed at the time that the contract was concluded.[7] This was set out in statute in section 6 of the Sale of Goods Act 1893:

> "Where there is a contract for the sale of specific goods, and the goods without the knowledge of the seller have perished at the time when the contract is made, the contract is void".

One example of this is *Couturier v Hastie*,[8] which involved the sale of a cargo of Indian corn; neither party to the contract realised that at the time of the contract, the corn, which was supposed to make its way from

[5] Costello J, *O'Neill v Ryan (No. 3)* [1992] 1 IR 166 at 184.
[6] McDermott, *Contract Law*, Butterworths 2001, at 526.
[7] *Great Peace Shipping v Tsavliris International* [2003] QB 679 at para [51].
[8] (1856) 5 HL Cas 673.

Salonica to the UK, no longer existed. Another old example of a common mistake (one which may sound silly to modern ears) is *Strickland v Turner*[9]; the parties agreed to the sale and purchase of an annuity on the life of a person who, unknown to them, had already died.

So, the rule is clear: if something is expressly identified as being the subject of the contract, and that thing in fact does not exist (or no longer exists), the effect is that the contract cannot be performed. It will be void. Only in rare cases, however, will the court find a contract to be void for this reason. In *Fitzsimons v O'Hanlon* the court said that

> "[w]hile a fundamental mistaken assumption can nullify consent so as to make a contract void, this rule is confined within very narrow limits. It is in the interest of commercial convenience that, in general, apparent contracts should be enforced".[10]

One of the most famous cases of common mistake was *Bell v Lever Bros Ltd*[11], "a vitally important case" in the words of one English judge.[12] Mr Bell and Mr Snelling had been working in the West African cocoa part of the company's business. Lever Bros gave these two employees golden handshakes of £30,000 and £20,000 in consideration of the early termination of their service contracts. Afterwards, Lever Bros discovered that the two employees had breached their fiduciary duties to the company by trading on their own account and making secret profits. If Lever Bros had known about this, they could have saved £50,000 by simply firing them. Lever Bros was under the misapprehension that Bell and Snelling had been keeping to the terms of the contract, and had believed that they were only able to end their contracts if Bell and Snelling agreed to end them. They took a case to recover that golden handshake money, arguing that the contracts which terminated the employment of the two men were void for common mistake. The House of Lords did not side with Lever Bros. Lord Atkin stated that Lever Bros got "exactly what [they] bargained for", i.e. the termination of their employees' contracts.[13] Lord Thankerton said that common mistake

---

[9] (1852) 7 Exch 208.
[10] [1999] 2 ILRM 551 at 558–559.
[11] [1932] AC 161.
[12] *Per* Steyn J, *Associated Japanese Bank v Credit du Nord SA* [1988] 3 All ER 902 at 910.
[13] [1932] AC 161 at 223–224.

"can only properly relate to something which both must necessarily have accepted in their minds as an essential and integral part of the subject matter".[14]

Decades later Lord Steyn said "in my view the principles enunciated in that case clearly still govern mistake at common law".[15]

A good summary of the principles of common mistake can be found in *Associated Japanese Bank v Credit du Nord SA*, where the court made the following statements:

1. The law will try to uphold rather than destroy apparent contracts.
2. The common law rules as to a mistake regarding the quality of the subject matter are designed to cope with the impact of unexpected and wholly exceptional circumstances on apparent contracts.
3. If a mistake is to attract legal consequences it must be shared by both parties, and must relate to facts as they existed at the time the contract was made.
4. The mistake must render the subject matter of the contract *essentially and radically different* from the subject matter which the parties believed to exist (the *Bell v Lever Bros Ltd* point).[16]

Mutual Mistake

As stated above, mutual mistake means that both sides have made a different mistake. In *Mespil Ltd v Capaldi*[17] proceedings for possession of land and the recovery of arrears of rent were settled between the parties. The settlement, however, was made quickly and the barristers who carried it out did not get to write it down in unambiguous terms. It rested on a mutual mistake. The court decided that "the two [barristers] left court that day, each with a genuine but opposite belief as to what the settlement had achieved".[18] This meant that there was no consensus and the settlement was a nullity (practically, this meant that instead of being settled, the proceedings went on to be heard by a judge). The key thing missing in a

---

[14] [1932] AC 161 at 235.
[15] [1988] 3 All ER 902 at 911.
[16] [1988] 3 All ER 902 at 912.
[17] [1986] ILRM 373.
[18] *ibid* at 376.

case of mutual mistake is the meeting of minds, referred to sometimes by the Latin term *consensus ad idem*. A meeting of minds is essential for an enforceable contract; if it is not present, the contract is a nullity.

In *Clayton Love v B & I Steampacket Co.*[19] the plaintiff sought damages for breach of contract when the plaintiff's frozen scampi, which were being transferred from Dublin to Liverpool on the defendant's ship, arrived in bad condition because they had been stored at room temperature. The shipping company said that it would never have agreed to a term of the contract stipulating that the scampi had to be transported under refrigeration, because none of its men worked in refrigerated holds when making the crossing. The plaintiff company was certain that it had requested specific freezing temperatures for the storage. The agreement was made between Miss Heidorn for the plaintiff and Mr Hailes for the defendant. The judge said

> "I believe that Miss Heidorn was contracting in the belief that the food would be loaded into a hold already refrigerated, while Mr Hailes was contracting on the basis that they would be loaded into the hold at atmospheric temperature…. It seems to me that this is a case of mutual mistake".[20]

In this case, the court found that the service the plaintiffs got was so radically different from the one they had contracted for that there had been a breach of a fundamental term, and damages were awarded to the plaintiffs. Why did the court not simply say the contract was a nullity? Perhaps because the plaintiff had suffered damage. The company which was to receive the scampi in Liverpool rejected them. The court found that—leaving aside the question of mutual mistake—certain terms of the contract, which were made over the phone, were fundamental. These terms were that the scampi would be loaded last and that the hold would be shut quickly after loading. The breach of fundamental terms entitled the plaintiffs to damages.

[19] (1970) 104 ILTR 157.
[20] (1970) 104 ILTR 157 at 162.

Unilateral Mistake

A unilateral mistake is where the mistake is one-sided. *Lewis v Averay*[21] is an excellent example of this. Keith Lewis was a post-graduate chemistry student. He had an Austin Cooper "S" which he decided to sell. A man rang him up and asked if he could see the car. When the man came, he gave it a test drive and said he liked it. The judge refers to this man as the "rogue", because we never find out who he was. This rogue told Keith and his fiancée that his name was Richard Green. He led them to believe he was the Richard Green who played Robin Hood in a television series. The rogue wrote out a cheque for the car and signed it "R.A. Green". He said he wanted to take the car right away. Lewis wanted to wait until the cheque cleared and tried to fob him off by telling him there were one or two jobs he wanted to do on the car before letting him have it. The rogue told him there was no need to worry about that. It was late now, eleven o'clock at night. Lewis asked the rogue for ID. The rogue whipped out a special admission pass to Pinewood Studios. It had the official stamp on it, the name "Richard A. Green" and the rogue's photograph. So, finally, Lewis let him have the car. The cheque was worthless; the cheque book had been stolen. In the meantime the rogue sold the car to a twenty-year old music student, Anthony Averay.

Was there a contract between Lewis and the rogue? Even if there were, and even though it would be voidable because of the fraud, Anthony Averay would still get good title to the car because he was an innocent purchaser who had paid good money; he had no notice of the scam. If there was no contract between Lewis and the rogue then the property would not pass from Lewis to the rogue and Averay could not get good title (because the rogue would have no property which he could pass to Averay). So what was the effect of Lewis's mistake?

The judge in *Lewis v Averay* held that: "When two parties have come to a contract—or rather what appears, on the face of it, to be a contract—the fact that one party is mistaken as to the identity of the other does not mean that there is no contract, or that the contract is a nullity and void from the beginning. It only means that the contract is voidable, that is, liable to be

---

[21] [1972] 1 QB 198.

set aside at the instance of the mistaken person, so long as he does so before third parties have in good faith acquired rights under it".[22] Keith Lewis did make a contract that evening. He made it with the very person who was standing in front of him—the rogue. If he found out in time, he could avoid the contract, i.e. get his car back. But finding out later, if some other person has bought the car in the meantime, means finding out too late. The court would not require the music student to "give back the car" to Lewis. It was the same in *Phillips v Brooks Ltd*[23], where a swindler pretended to a jeweller to be Sir George Bullough of 11 St James's Square. The jeweller checked the directory—this was Edwardian England, old sport—and found there was such a man living at that address. The rogue in that case disappeared with the diamonds, leaving a dishonoured cheque. In *Phillips v Brooks Ltd* the ultimate buyer was also held to be entitled to the ring; tough luck on the jeweller.

In *Hartog v Colin and Shields*[24] the defendants contracted to sell Monsieur Hartog, a Belgian national, 30,000 Argentine hare skins. These kinds of skins were normally sold at prices per piece. By an alleged mistake, they offered the skins at prices per pound and not prices per piece (the value of a piece was about one-third of the value by pound). The court asked whether Hartog could have reasonably supposed that the offer expressed the real intentions of the seller. Applying this reasonableness test, Hartog must have known that the offer to sell per pound was a mistake—"anyone with any knowledge of the trade must have realised that there was a mistake", the judge said.[25] Because the buyer knew of the mistake, his acceptance of the offer did not make the contract a binding one.

Remedies: *Non Est Factum*

What are the remedies for mistake? One remedy has a Latin name: *non est factum*. This is a defence used by a person who has signed a document—a contract, for example—and wishes to assert that the signature was not theirs, or that they were induced to sign by fraud.

[22] [1972] 1 QB 198 at 207.
[23] [1919] 2 KB 243; see also *Ingram v Little* [1961] 1 QB 31; for a more contemporary rogue, see *Shogun Finance Ltd v Hudson* [2004] 1 All ER 215.
[24] [1939] 3 All ER 566.
[25] *ibid* at 568.

"If a party has been misled into executing a deed or signing a document essentially different from that which he intended to execute or sign, he can plead *non est factum* in an action against him".[26]

The defence has been pleaded quite often—often hopelessly—in cases since the financial crash of 2008. For example, in *ADM Londis v Gibson*[27] the defendants tried to say that they did not know they were signing a guarantee. It is not easy to succeed in this. The judge decided that "[t]here is no conceivable way that a person could sign the guarantee document relied on herein without knowing it was a guarantee". In *Tedcastle McCormack and Co. Ltd v McCrystal*[28] the court said the following three things needed to be established:

"(a) That there was a radical or fundamental difference between what was signed and what it was thought was being signed; (b) That the mistake was as to the general character of the document as opposed to its legal effect; and (c) That there was a lack of negligence. That is, that the person concerned took all reasonable precautions in the circumstances to find out what the document was".

Remedies: Rectification

If the parties have been carrying out oral negotiations and certain terms which were mentioned are omitted from the written contract, the court may rectify the contract. The court will not make a rectification where the parties simply overlooked something, or deliberately left something out. Rectification will only be ordered to carry out the intentions of the parties as they were understood at the time of the making of the contract, and where there is an actual live issue as to the legal rights between them.

Other Remedies

Three other remedies are common. A party can seek to rescind the contract; can seek damages to compensate him; and can ask the court to

---

[26] Beale, *Chitty on Contracts, Vol. I, General Principles*, 30th ed., Sweet and Maxwell 2008, at para 5-101.
[27] [2010] IEHC 432.
[28] Morris P, High Court, 15 March 1999.

order "specific performance", which is an order of the court obliging one side to go through with an agreement in whole or in part. These are dealt with in more detail in Chapter 13.

Conclusions

- Common mistake relates to something which both parties have accepted in their minds as an essential and integral part of the subject matter.
- If a mistake is to attract legal consequences it must be shared by both parties, and must relate to facts as they existed at the time the contract was made.
- The mistake must render the subject matter of the contract essentially and radically different from the subject matter which the parties believed to exist.
- A fundamental mistaken assumption can nullify consent and make a contract void.
- This rule is confined within very narrow limits.
- In general the courts uphold contracts, because this is in the interest of commercial convenience.
- If something is expressly identified as being the subject of the contract and that thing in fact no longer exists, the effect is that the contract cannot be performed. It will be void (*Couturier v Hastie*).
- In *Bell v Lever Bros Ltd* a mistake on the part of the employers as to the situation was not enough to make the contract void because the employers wanted the employees gone, and by giving them golden handshakes they got what they bargained for.
- In *Mespil Ltd v Capaldi* there was a mutual mistake and no meeting of minds. This meant that the settlement could not be enforced and the case had to go to hearing.
- In *Clayton Love v B & I Steampacket Co.* there was a mutual mistake as to how the scampi were to be stored, but the court decided the case on the basis of some of the fundamental terms of the contract.
- If you make a contract with a swindler who is impersonating someone else, you have still made a good contract. If you realise the mistake fast, you can avoid the contract. If the swindler manages to sell the item on—a jewel, a car—to an innocent third party, then

you will have to accept that you have been swindled (*Lewis v Averay, Phillips v Brooks*).

* You cannot take advantage of a mistaken term in a contract where you have good reason to believe that the term in question is a mistake.

CHAPTER ELEVEN

ECONOMIC DURESS AND UNDUE INFLUENCE

Introduction to Economic Duress

If a person is forced to do something against his or her will, the courts may refer to their "apparent consent" and may conclude that the coercion had the effect of making the "consent" meaningless.[1] As far back as 1731, in *Astley v Reynolds*, it was held that a person who had handed over money to another person because they felt under "economic compulsion" could get it back if the compulsion had deprived the person of "his freedom of exercising his will".[2] Slowly, the courts came to recognise that this could happen to companies.

The first thing we can say on this topic is that economic pressure can, in certain circumstances, amount in law to duress. The duress must be proved. If it is, it renders a transaction voidable, and if it causes damage or loss, the injured party can seek damages in tort law.[3] The most common route, however, if a party has been subjected to economic duress, is not to seek damages, but to seek restitution of the property or the money exacted under duress, and for the court to rule that the oppressed party can legitimately avoid the contract.

When will this happen? "There must be pressure, the practical effect of which is compulsion or the absence of choice", and there must be "the victim's intentional submission arising from the realisation that there is no other practical choice open to him".[4] How does a person or a company prove this "absence of choice"? There may be a paper trail of protest; there may be a lack of independent advice; someone may have said "we will resort to the courts to recover the money we transferred to you".[5]

What if there is only silence on the part of the person who felt the pressure? The *Universe Tankships*[6] case was an example of this. There was no protest at the time. What happened was this. Members of a trade union refused to give a particular ship the assistance it needed in order to leave the port. This refusal was instigated by the defendant trade union as part of a

---

[1] "Duress, whatever form it takes, is a coercion of the will so as to vitiate consent". *Per* Lord Scarman, *Pao On v Lau Yiu* [1979] 3 All ER 65 at 78–79.
[2] *Astley v Reynolds* (1731) 2 Stra 915, 93 ER 939, cited in [1989] 1 All ER 641 at 646.
[3] *Barton v Armstrong* [1975] 2 All ER 465 and *Pao On v Lau Yiu* [1979] 3 All ER 65.
[4] *Per* Lord Scarman, [1982] 2 All ER 67 at 88.
[5] *Maskell v Horner* [1915] 3 KB 106.
[6] [1982] 2 All ER 67.

long-running campaign against certain kinds of ships which sailed under flags of convenience. The detention of the ship was causing the shipowning company severe financial loss. Eventually, the shipowning company gave in to the union's demands—one part of the agreement involved a payment of US$80,000—and the ship was allowed to leave the port after its ten-day detention. The shipowning company simply paid up and then sought the return of the $80,000. Was this a case of economic duress? The test applied by the court is whether the alleged victim of the duress had any "practical choice" open to him and the court found that there was no practical choice open to the ship owning company.

Pressure Which is Not Legitimate

In the law of economic duress, we do not ask whether a person or a company knew the precise terms of the contract at the time he or it entered into the contract. We look past the apparent consent and ask whether or not that apparent consent was produced by pressure that was exercised by another, pressure which is not legitimate. The law does not find all kinds of pressure to be wrong. The courts have said that where a party is seeking to prove economic duress "the pressure must be one of a kind which the law does not regard as legitimate".[7] Judges accept that in commercial and financial life many acts are done under pressure—sometimes under overwhelming pressure—but that does not meant they are done under duress.

> "Commercial pressure, in some degree, exists wherever one party to a commercial transaction is in a stronger bargaining position than the other party".[8]

It may be that, in a majority of cases, there is a stronger and a weaker party involved in striking a deal; this power imbalance does not mean that the weaker party should be entitled to redress. When considering whether pressure is legitimate you must ask yourself two questions: (1) what is the nature of the pressure? (2) what is the nature of the demand for which the pressure is being applied?

---

[7] *Per* Lord Wilberforce and Lord Simon in *Barton v Armstrong* [1975] 2 All ER 465 at 476–477.
[8] *Per* Lord Diplock [1982] 2 All ER 67 at 75.

Maskell v Horner[9] is a case that brings to mind a scene from Pat McCabe's *The Butcher Boy*, where Francie insists that "mammy's boy" Philip Nugent pay him what he calls "the pig toll tax" for the privilege of being allowed to continue on his way. The plaintiff in *Maskell v Horner* was a merchant who carried on business near a place called Spitalfields Market. The defendant owned Spitalfields Market and, from the outset, he demanded tolls from the plaintiff. The plaintiff said he should not have to pay any toll because he was not part of the market, and the defendant said toll paying was an "immemorial custom" and that if the toll was not paid he would seize the plaintiff's goods, which had to pass that way. The defendant was as good as his word, and seized the plaintiff's goods. When the plaintiff consulted a solicitor he was told that all the other merchants outside the market were paying tolls, so he might as well pay them; the most he could do was to make the payments under protest. This was a case of duress. The judge said:

> "If a person pays money which he is not bound to pay, under the compulsion of urgent and pressing necessity or of seizure of his goods (actual or threatened), he can recover it".[10]

Decades later, in *B & S Contracts and Design Ltd v Victor Green Publications Ltd* the court said:

> "it is sufficient to say that if the claimant has been influenced against his will to pay money under the threat of unlawful damage to his economic interest he will be entitled to claim that money back".[11]

In that case the plaintiffs had contracted to build stands at a trade exhibition. Their workmen went on strike because the plaintiff had been refusing to pay them severance pay. The plaintiffs told the defendants they could not afford to pay the sum the workmen were seeking so the job could not be finished. The defendants said they would contribute money to pay off the workmen. Were the defendants allowed to deduct that money from the contract price? The plaintiffs said no, and issued

---

[9] [1915] 3 KB 106.
[10] [1915] 3 KB 106 at 118. The judge said the case was very like a duress case but that it technically wasn't duress because the money was paid under the pressure of seizure or detention of goods.
[11] *Per* Eveleigh LJ, [1984] ICR 419 at 423.

proceedings. The court found that the promise was made under duress, i.e. a veiled threat to the defendant's economic interests, where there was no way for the defendant to avoid a bad outcome other than by paying the amount sought by the workmen.

In *Atlas Express Ltd v Kafco Ltd*[12] the plaintiffs entered into a contract with the defendants to deliver cartons of basketware to shops across the country. The plaintiffs' depot manager mistakenly thought that each truckload would carry between 400 and 600 cartons of basketware and a certain price was agreed. In fact, the trucks could only take 200 cartons. The plaintiffs then requested the defendants to pay a minimum price per load which was more than anticipated. The defendants felt they had no choice but to pay this extra money because they had no time to find an alternative carrier and needed to get the baskets to the various outlets of the retail chain which was selling them. So the defendants agreed to the new rate but later refused to pay. The court found that the pressure in the circumstance was illegitimate and that the defendant's apparent consent to the new rates was vitiated by economic duress.

Introduction to Undue Influence

What is undue influence and why should a student of business law know what it is? The reason is this. If a court finds that "undue influence" has taken place, whatever transaction was entered into will be set aside. It will be undone. A lot of people have tried to use the doctrine as a defence in actions taken against them by banks since the financial crash.[13] Take, for example, *Bank of Ireland v Stafford*.[14] Philip and Gerard Stafford entered credit agreements with the plaintiff for over €5m. The two brothers were funding an investment portfolio. They agreed that all correspondence relating to the credit agreement would be sent to Philip's house, because he was the moving spirit behind the business ideas. Philip was the one who took the leading part in the negotiations with the bank. Gerard died

---

[12] [1989] 1 All ER 641. See also Kerr J in *The Siboen and the Sibotre, Occidental Worldwide Investment Corp v Skibs A/S Avanti* [1976] 1 Lloyd's Rep 293 and Mocatta J in *North Ocean Shipping Co Ltd v Hyundai Construction Co. Ltd, The Atlantic Baron* [1978] 3 All ER 1170.

[13] In *Danske Bank AS v Walsh* [2013] IEHC 190 (Herbert J), undue influence was unsuccessfully pleaded by the guarantors of a loan. In *EBS Ltd v Campbell* [2013] IEHC 154 (Birmingham J) a wife was unable to establish undue influence.

[14] [2013] IEHC 550.

in 2008 and his wife, Marian, did not pay his share of the interest to the bank as it arose each month. The bank was able to recover a good deal of the money owing to it, but there was still a €1m shortfall. The bank took proceedings against Philip and against Gerard's widow. Marian made the argument that her husband would not have had the capacity to enter into these financial agreements with the bank and that he must have been subject to the undue influence of Philip. The court heard the evidence of Gerard's housekeeper.

> "She said that when she was asked to witness his signature, the deceased asked her in a perfectly normal manner. She said himself and Philip were there and I just went into the sitting room where they were and they just said 'would you mind signing this as an independent witness?'"[15]

On further questioning, she said that they seemed to be carrying on their business meeting in a normal way. The court also heard that Gerard had taken professional advice before entering the agreement. Gerard did suffer from depression and bipolar disorder, but the judge found that

> "his condition was well managed by medication…. While he undoubtedly had many dark periods in his life when he would not be able to function normally, the evidence from a substantial number of witnesses who dealt with him professionally was to the effect that in his business affairs, he was conscientious and methodical and would take great care to read documents before signing them".

The evidence pointed to a warm relationship between the two brothers and there was no indication that Philip had exerted an undue influence on his brother. The judge rejected the widow's defence of undue influence. If Marian had been successful, the bank's attempt to recover any money from her would have failed. The transaction entered into by her husband could have been set aside.

From the cases dealt with in this chapter, it should become fairly clear what kind of conduct constitutes undue influence. There is no one definition of the term. The courts find it more useful to maintain a

---

[15] *ibid* at 4.

flexible approach, and traditionally they have referred to "unconscionable conduct". In the *Etridge* decision, one judge offered various phrases which flesh out this concept: "the taking of unfair advantage", "misuse" of influence, "abuse of trust and confidence" and a "connotation of impropriety".[16]

It might be said that the doctrine of undue influence is a cousin of the law on duress. If I am seeking to establish undue influence, I will have to prove that there was a relationship of trust and confidence between me and the person who influenced me. I will have to show that that person abused that relationship. A very common example of this is an assertion by a wife that she signed a guarantee at her husband's insistence, without knowing what she was really signing. A transaction of this kind involving family members will give rise to a presumption of undue influence. If the transaction is one that—to use a now well-known phrase from *Royal Bank of Scotland v Etridge (No. 2)*[17]—"calls for explanation", then there will be the presumption that the transaction came about because of one side exerting an undue influence over the other. Sometimes it will be a generous gift—say, for example, between a bachelor uncle and his nephew—which will "call for explanation". Since *Allcard v Skinner*[18] the courts have said they would set aside a gift unless the person who received it could prove that the gift was a result of the giver's free will.[19]

In *O'Flanagan v Ray-Ger Ltd*[20] the son and wife of a deceased man had to take a case against his former business partner, Mr Pope, who, they said, had exerted an undue pressure over the dying man in his last months. The result of the pressure was that Mr O'Flanagan made an agreement which would see his shares in the company transfer to Mr Pope after his death, instead of to his family: clearly a transaction which "calls for explanation". The court set aside the written agreement between the two men. Mr Pope was a very persuasive man and exerted

---

[16] [2002] 2 AC 773 at paras [8], [9], [10], [32]; see also *Chitty on Contracts, Vol. I, General Principles*, 30th ed., Sweet and Maxwell 2008, at p 625.
[17] [2002] 2 AC 773 at para [10].
[18] (1887) 35 Ch D 145 at 171; what is meant by "gift" can be taken to be "an immoderate gift, which bears no proportion to the circumstances of the giver" (*per* Byrne J, *Cavendish v Strutt* (1903) 19 TLR 483).
[19] *M.C. (a ward) v F.C.* [2013] IESC 36 *per* MacMenamin J at para [17].
[20] Unreported., High Court, Costello J, 28 April 1983.

a great influence over Mr O'Flanagan, to the chagrin of Mrs O'Flanagan. The two men used to go drinking three or four times a week together. In the later stages of Mr O'Flanagan's cancer, Mr Pope suggested they go drinking again and discuss the business. Mr O'Flanagan asked instead that they meet in an office beside the company's auditor's office, and that the meeting last no more than half an hour, but Mr Pope's idea prevailed, and they went drinking together twice (Mr Pope claimed they drank coffee in the pub). These sessions produced the written agreement which the O'Flanagans were trying to have set aside. The judge found that the only "conclusion to be reached in relation to this agreement [was] that the defendant must have used undue influence to procure it".

An example of a successful plea of undue influence is *Ulster Bank Ireland Ltd v Roche*.[21] There were two defendants, Louis Roche and Sorcha Buttimer. The two were in a personal relationship. Louis had a motor trade business. Sorcha was a director but she took no part in the business. She signed a €50,000 guarantee over the liabilities of the business, and when the bank tried to enforce it, Sorcha argued that she had been subject to the undue influence of Louis and so the guarantee should be set aside. She also argued that the guarantee appeared to have been witnessed by a bank employee, but that this was not true because she had never met the employee or gone to the bank's premises.

The law says that someone who signs a document which might have significant legal effect without reading it or asking anything about it must take whatever consequences flow from the commercially binding agreement.[22] But to balance this, the law of undue influence steps in to help the vulnerable. Should the bank have asked questions about Sorcha before she signed? Sorcha was not a shareholder in the business, nor was she actively involved in it. The bank had some knowledge that Sorcha and Louis were romantically involved. Circumstances like these mean the bank is "placed on inquiry". It should look into the matter. The court said that the personal relationship takes on a more significant aspect

---

[21] [2012] 1 IR 765.
[22] *ACC Bank plc v Kelly* [2011] IEHC 7 (Unreported, High Court, Clarke J, 10 January 2011); *Irish Bank Resolution Corporation Ltd v Quinn* [2011] IEHC 470 (Unreported, High Court, Kelly J, 16 December 2011).

when those matters are considered and that a bank should take some steps to ensure that such a person, about to give a guarantee, was freely and openly agreeing to do so. The court said that Sorcha was

> "entitled to rely on the undoubted undue influence which Mr Roche exercised over her by virtue of the failure of Ulster Bank to take any steps to seek to ensure that she was acting freely in circumstances where, for the reasons which I have sought to analyse, Ulster Bank was, in my view, placed on inquiry".[23]

The general principle is that a bank must make inquiries where the facts suggest that there may be a non-commercial element to a guarantee.[24] For a bank to defeat a defence of undue influence, a key element is for it to show that the person asserting the undue influence received independent legal advice.

Categories of Undue Influence

There are three categories of undue influence. They were set out in *Barclay's Bank v O'Brien*.[25] The first category is "actual undue influence", where the claimant must prove that the wrongdoer exerted undue influence on him or her to enter into the transaction in question. This is not common because it is difficult to *prove* actual undue influence. We might call this Class 1 undue influence.

The second class of undue influence is called "presumed undue influence", and there are two kinds of this, known as Class 2A and Class 2B. Class 2A says that certain relationships simply raise the presumption that undue influence has been exerted; an example of the kinds of relationships meant are those between a solicitor and client, or a medical advisor and a patient.

Class 2B simply widens the presumption. Maybe the transaction did not involve a doctor and patient, or a solicitor and client, but there was

---

[23] [2012] 1 IR 765 at 781.
[24] The position in the UK is found in *Royal Bank of Scotland plc v Etridge (No. 2)* [2002] 2 AC 773 where Lord Nicholls said that the lender should be regarded as being on inquiry in every case where "the relationship between the surety and the debtor is non-commercial". The Irish position is not as broad.
[25] [1993] 4 All ER 417.

nonetheless the kind of trust and confidence between the parties that you would normally find in a Class 2A relationship. In such cases the key element is the nature of the relationship—the presence of "trust and confidence" between the parties, or, more particularly, whether one party reposed such trust and confidence in the other. A wife might try to establish Class 2B undue influence where she alleges that she placed trust and confidence in her husband in all financial matters; the key element in her defence will be proving the trust and confidence. If the creditor is the bank, the bank will be deemed to have been under a requirement to take reasonable steps to satisfy itself that the wife's agreement to act as guarantor was properly obtained, i.e. that independent legal advice was obtained. Failure to do this will mean the creditor will be unable to enforce the guarantee.

Improvident Transactions

Finally, we might briefly note that there is another branch of the law similar to this. A transaction will be set aside even though no undue influence has been shown if it appears that the two parties have not met on equal terms, and that one has struck a bargain that is of no benefit to him, and of great benefit to the other person.[26] This is called an "improvident transaction", but there is no need to go into it here because it is not usually found in business transactions.

Conclusions

- Apparent consent is meaningless where it has been obtained by economic compulsion.
- A key element in economic duress is that there is "no other practical choice" open to the victim.
- If a court finds that "undue influence" has taken place, it will set aside the transaction in question.
- There is no one definition of undue influence, but *Royal Bank of Scotland v Etridge* gives us some alternative phrases which flesh the term out.

---

[26] *Grealish v Murphy* [1946] IR 35 and *Fry v Lane* [1888] 10 Ch D 312.

- Undue influence is often invoked against banks by the partners of people who are active directors of a business.
- The key element is whether the person in question was allowed to make an independent and informed decision.
- *Bank of Ireland v Stafford* shows us the kind of factors which will lead a court to decide that undue influence has not taken place.
- *O'Flanagan v Ray-Ger Ltd* gives us an example of where a court will set aside a transaction between business partners where one partner has exerted undue influence.
- *Ulster Bank Ireland Ltd v Roche* gives us an example of the doctrine being successfully invoked and tells us that for a bank to protect its position, it should ensure that a guarantor who has a personal relationship with an active director of a company is told to seek independent legal advice.

CHAPTER TWELVE

DISCHARGE

The Four Ways a Contract May Be Discharged

When does the contract come to an end? A contract is discharged in a number of circumstances. The first is the simplest: when it is completed to the satisfaction of both sides. This is called discharge by performance (if the performance is not complete but is substantial, the rule in *Hoenig v Isaccs*[1] says that the work done will have to be paid for). The second is that the parties can agree to the discharge of the contract: for example, there might be a term in the contract which states that if a certain event occurs, the contract will come to an immediate end ("discharge by agreement"). And then there is a whole range of possibilities which can occur where one or both sides are not satisfied. The third is discharge by frustration and the fourth is discharge by breach. We will look at these in more detail.

Frustration

When we talk about frustration in a contract law context, we are talking about circumstances that are beyond the control of the parties. It might be the case that neither of the parties are at fault, like in *Taylor v Caldwell*, where a music hall burnt down and the destruction of the hall discharged the contract (the plaintiff was out of pocket because he spent money advertising the concert; he sued for that money but was unsuccessful because the event had *frustrated* the contract). In *Taylor v Caldwell*[2] the subject matter of the contract was destroyed and the effect of this frustration was that the contract was terminated immediately.

In the *Davis Contractors*[3] case, both sides agreed the work would be done in eight months, but the work took longer, so it was argued that the contract was frustrated. The court decided that this was an example of a contract becoming more onerous, but not being frustrated. One of the judges said that while there was no fault on either side, what had happened was "an unexpected turn of events" which "render[ed] the contract more onerous than the parties had contemplated", and that is not a ground for

---

[1] [1952] 2 All ER 176.
[2] (1863) 3 B & S 826.
[3] *Davis Contractors Ltd v Fareham Urban District Council* [1956] 2 All ER 145.

relieving either side of the obligation it had undertaken.[4] It is important to remember that while both sides may suffer disappointed expectations, "it by no means follows that disappointed expectations lead to frustrated contracts".[5] Another example of events which did not amount to frustration is the *Tsakiroglou* case.[6] Tsakiroglou was a Sudanese company which sold groundnuts. The buyers were Germans based in Hamburg. The nuts were usually shipped to Europe via the Suez Canal but when the Egyptians nationalised the canal, all hell broke loose and normal trade was disrupted. The only alternative was to ship the produce the whole way around Africa, increasing the cost massively, and Tsakiroglou said that the contract had been frustrated. The court said no: it said that the sellers were certainly put to greater cost but that the nature of the contract was not "fundamentally" altered or "radically different". The courts have been relatively consistent in saying that the doctrine of frustration must be applied within very narrow limits.

So, when does frustration take place? The Irish Supreme Court has approved the following definitions:

> "Frustration of a contract takes place where there supervenes an event (without fault of either party and for which the contract makes no sufficient provision) which so significantly changes the nature (not merely the expense or onerousness) of the outstanding contractual rights and/or obligations from what the parties could reasonably have contemplated at the time of its execution that it would be unjust to hold them to the literal sense of its stipulations in the new circumstances; in such cases the law declares both parties to be discharged from further performance".[7]

In a case called *National Carriers*—which is where the foregoing definition comes from—the judges also suggested that the best explanation of the doctrine was given in the *Davis Contractors* case, where one of the judges said:

---

[4] *Per* Viscount Simonds [1956] 2 All ER 145 at 151.
[5] *ibid* at 150.
[6] *Tsakiroglou & Co. Ltd v Noblee Thorl GmbH* [1962] AC 93.
[7] Blayney J in *William Neville & Sons Ltd v Guardian Builders Ltd* [1995] 1 ILRM at 7, where he approved of Lord Simon's definition in *National Carriers Ltd v Panalpina (Northern) Ltd* [1981] AC 675 at 700.

"There must have been by reason of some supervening event some such fundamental change of circumstances as to enable the court to say, 'This was not the bargain which these parties made and their bargain must be treated as at an end'".[8]

Both of these definitions have been accepted by the Irish Supreme Court as being the law in Ireland.

The supervening event cannot be self-induced; this should be an obvious enough point. Once the contract is frustrated, all future obligations are discharged. Whatever loss has occurred to either party must—to use the legal phrase—"lie where it falls".

Interpretation of Contracts by the Courts

The Irish courts have said that in any case where the parties are in disagreement as to what a particular provision of a contract means

"the task of the court is to decide what the intention of the parties was having regard to the language used in the contract itself and the surrounding circumstances".[9]

The words in the contract will be given their ordinary and natural meaning. When they are interpreting a contract, the judges are conscious that their job is to "discover what the parties meant from what they have said" and not to "force upon the words a meaning which they cannot fairly bear" because to do that would be to "substitute for the bargain actually made one which the court believes could better have been made".[10]

Breach of Contract

A contract is not terminated merely because a breach occurs; if that were true, parties who wished to end their obligations could simply breach

---

[8] [1981] 1 All ER 161 at 188. The judge who offered this definition, Lord Radcliffe, then went on to give an even shorter summary of the doctrine, this time in a quotation of five words from the Aeneid: *Non haec in foedera veni.* [It was not the thing I promised to do.]

[9] *Per* Keane J in *Kramer v Arnold* [1997] 3 IR 43 at p 55, approved by McKechnie J in *Marlan Homes Ltd v Walsh* [2012] IESC 23.

[10] *Per* Lord Mustill in *Charter Reinsurance v Fagan* [1997] AC 313 at 388, also approved by McKechnie J in *Marlan Homes Ltd v Walsh* [2012] IESC 23.

the contract. Further to this, certain terms and conditions may be breached and the injured party may not be allowed to terminate the contract because the term may have been a "non-essential" one.[11] But where a serious breach takes place, the injured party has a right to choose one of two paths (called, in law, a "right of election"): the injured party can terminate the contract and claim damages immediately, or can affirm the contract. Whichever path is chosen closes off the right to choose the other path. Affirmation means you are saying:

> "I want to keep the contract alive. I want you to perform what you're supposed to perform and I accept the defective element and I will sue you for the difference".

If a party decides to affirm, it must be done without any ambiguity. The main thing is: do not delay. If an injured party delays, the contract may be taken as having been affirmed, regardless of whether the injured party was mulling over the option of suing for damages. Chitty says:

> "If the innocent party elects to treat the contract as continuing, then it remains in existence for the benefit of the wrong-doer as well as of himself. The wrong-doer is entitled to complete the contract and to take advantage of any supervening circumstance which would...diminish his liability".[12]

If the contract is breached before it is due to begin, this is referred to as "anticipatory breach". If this happens, the rule in *Hochster v De La Tour*[13] says that the injured party can claim damages immediately. The cause of action here is the renunciation of the contract.

Any breach of contract will give rise to a cause of action—i.e. an ability to sue—but not every breach will mean that an injured party is discharged from his contractual obligations. It is not accurate to talk about a contract ceasing to exist once a breach has occurred, because as a result of the contract, a secondary obligation remains: to pay

---

[11] Or as Lord Diplock would say: "Every synallagmatic contract contains in it the seeds of the problem: in what event will a party be relieved of his undertaking to do that which he has agreed to do but has not yet done?" [1962] 1 All ER 474 at 485.

[12] *Chitty on Contracts*, Vol. I, *General Principles*, 31st ed., Sweet and Maxwell 2012, at para 24-011.

[13] (1853) 2 E & B 678.

compensation for non-performance. Nor is it accurate, in most cases, to talk about the contract being "rescinded" (that usually only happens where the contract expressly provides for rescission). One of the tricky aspects about this area of the law is that judges have often used differing terminology to describe the kind of breach that will allow for the right of election, described above. The breaches which allow for this are:

1. A fundamental breach (breach of a "condition").
2. A breach of a term which amounts to a condition.
3. A repudiatory breach.

"Conditions" and "Terms"

The first two points above are discussed in this section. By the late nineteenth century, the two major distinctions made were between "conditions" and "warranties". If a warranty was breached the injured party only had a right to damages. Conditions were usually judged to be stipulations that went "to the root of the matter".[14] We still use the word "condition", but now, in addition to talk of warranties, you will see references to "terms". The important thing to note is what weight each category carries: the graver the category that is breached, the more extensive the remedy for the injured party.

If a condition is breached—regardless of whether the loss to the innocent party was a minor one—then the injured party may treat himself as discharged of his liabilities under the contract.

The courts always pay attention to the substance of the stipulation, and do not decide the question merely on whether the word "condition" has been used. If two parties enter a contract for the transport of tuna from the Indian Ocean to Ireland, and the phrase "time is of the essence in this contract" appears in the contract, that time requirement will be a condition of the utmost importance, one which, if breached, will allow the injured party to terminate the contract. So, the first thing to note is that breach of a condition is a most serious matter.

---

[14] *Bettini v Gye* (1876) 1 QBD 183.

At the other end of the spectrum is the contractual stipulation known as the "term". Terms are usually of a copy-and-paste variety. Breach of a term will not always be as serious, but in commercial contracts the parties can impliedly agree that breach of a term will be as serious as breach of a condition. The courts have allowed this to be the case because it is felt that it adds to the certainty of commercial ventures[15]; they will not, however, construe a term as a condition if to do so would be "contrary to common sense".[16] If a term is descriptive of something—in a sale of goods contract, or a contract for the hire of a ship or a vehicle—it will usually be treated as a condition. You may take this definition as a rule-of-thumb:

> "Where the likely effect of any breach of a contractual term is serious loss or damage to the promisee, this will be a good indication that the term is a condition".[17]

There is a category which lies between conditions and terms: innominate or intermediate terms (this text will use "intermediate terms" because it more clearly signifies an in-between category). When the courts consider an intermediate term, essentially what they are saying is:

> "we're not immediately sure whether the stipulation was a condition or a term. We have to look at the *effect of the breach*. To do that we have to see whether the breach deprives the injured party of substantially all the benefits that were intended by the contract. In answering this question, we will find out whether the stipulation breached was a condition or a term".

The way the judges saw it, too many contractual stipulations were being classed as conditions. This meant that it was too easy to terminate a contract: you could point to a breached condition and it was over. By saying that they would have to consider whether a stipulation was a condition or a term, the courts were trying to encourage parties to perform the contract, something that it was felt was better for commercial life.

---

[15] *Bunge Corpn New York v Tradax Export SA Panama* [1981] 2 All ER 513.

[16] *Hong Kong Fir Shipping Co Ltd v Kawasaki Kisen Kaisha Ltd* [1962] 2 QB 26 at 62.

[17] Bradgate, *The Law of Contract, Butterworths Common Law Series*, Andrew Grubb series editor, 4th ed, Butterworths 2010, at 1603 [para 7.13].

"Substantially the Whole Benefit" Test

The test judges apply was set out in *Hong Kong Fir v Kawasaki*[18]. There, the judges said:

"does the occurrence of the event deprive the party who has further undertakings still to perform of substantially the whole benefit which it was the intention of the parties as expressed in the contract that he should obtain as the consideration for performing those undertakings?"[19]

This is the key phrase: whether a party is deprived of "substantially the whole benefit" of the contract. If the answer is yes, the injured party will be discharged of obligations. This test applies whether or not the event has been caused by the default of one of the parties. If the event has been caused by the default of one of the parties, that party cannot rely on it as relieving him of performing further obligations under the contract (because a person can't take advantage of their own wrong). The innocent party in such a case can, however, treat the event as relieving him of his obligations under the contract, but does not necessarily have to take this attitude.

The *Hong Kong Fir* decision is extremely important because, according to one Irish judge in *Westpark Investments Ltd v Leisureworld Ltd*,[20] it

"emancipated the common law from the stultifying formalism inherent in the distinction between conditions and warranties for the purposes of ascertaining whether a particular contract had been discharged by breach in favour of a test which sought to inquire whether the other party to the contract had been effectively denied the benefits which the contract intended he or she should enjoy".

Repudiatory Breach

According to Clark, repudiatory breach involves "a decision by one party that he will not perform his obligations".[21] The courts have said:

[18] [1962] 1 All ER 474.
[19] *Per* Lord Diplock, [1962] 1 All ER 474 at 485.
[20] [2012] IEHC 343 (Hogan J) at para [21].
[21] Clark, *Contract Law in Ireland*, 7th ed, Round Hall 2013, at 626.

> "Repudiation is a drastic conclusion which should only be held to arise in clear cases of a refusal, in a matter going to the root of the contract, to perform contractual obligations".[22]

In this area, as in the areas we have seen above, the facts of the case will be of the first importance, and the judges will decide what kind of breach occurred based on the facts of the case. As one judge said:

> "there is no magic in the words 'fundamental breach'; this expression is no more than a convenient shorthand expression for saying that a particular breach or breaches of contract by one party is or are such as to go to the root of the contract which entitles the other party to treat such breach or breaches as a repudiation of the whole contract".[23]

Whether this has happened will be decided by a judge, taking into account all the facts and circumstances of the case.

An example of this approach can be found in a recent case heard in the English Technology and Construction Court: *Mayhaven v Bothma*.[24] The case involved a building contract for works on a nursing home between a company called Mayhaven and a company called DAB Builders. A dispute that arose in the course of the work was referred to arbitration and the arbitrator made an award in DAB's favour. DAB honestly believed that Mayhaven had not paid them the sum, so they suspended work on the nursing home. Mayhaven treated this suspension of work as a repudiatory breach and accepted it as terminating the contract. Was Mayhaven correct? The judge said that the answer to the question

> "whether a contractor's wrongful suspension of the works amounts to a repudiatory breach will depend on the terms of the contract, the breach or breaches of contract and all the facts and circumstances of the case. The question is not capable of a simple answer, as a matter of general principle".[25]

---

[22] *Per* Lord Wilberforce, *Woodar Investment Development Ltd v Wimpey Construction UK Ltd* [1980] 1 All ER 571 at 576.

[23] *Per* Lord Upjohn, *Suisse Atlantique Société d'Armement Maritime SA v NV Rotterdamsche Kolen Centrale* [1966] 2 All ER 61 at 86.

[24] *Mayhaven Healthcare Ltd v Bothma and another (trading as DAB Builders)* 127 Con LR 1; [2009] EWHC 2634 (TCC).

[25] *Per* Ramsey J, 127 Con LR 1 at 9.

In this case, the court found that the suspension of works by DAB was wrongful but it did not amount to a repudiatory breach of the contract because there was no absolute refusal or abandonment of the work and because DAB, though its belief was mistaken, was acting *bona fide*.

Fundamental Breach and Exclusion Clauses

Could a company draw up a contract to include a clause which exempted it from any liability for a fundamental breach of the contract? This question was decided in *Photo Production Ltd v Securicor Transport Ltd*.[26] The plaintiffs owned a factory. They employed the defendants to provide security. While on night patrol, an employee of the defendant deliberately lit a small fire. The fire got out of control and the factory and the stock—altogether worth £615,000—were destroyed. The plaintiffs sued the defendants. The defendants said they had an exemption clause which saved them: it said that they would not be responsible for

> "any injurious act or default by any employee…unless such act or default could have been foreseen and avoided by the exercise of due diligence on the part of the [defendants]".

The House of Lords found for the defendants because, first, the exception clause was clear and unambiguous and protected the defendants from liability, and second—and this is a very important point—both parties were commercial entities. The court said that because both were commercial entities and they had equal bargaining power, the parties are to be left "free to apportion the risks as they think fit".[27] It would be different if the exclusion clause was used by a commercial entity against a consumer, but in this case, the equality of bargaining power was a determining factor for the judges.

Conclusions

- A contract can be discharged in four ways: by performance, by agreement, by frustration, by breach.

---

[26] [1980] 1 All ER 556.
[27] *Per* Lord Wilberforce, [1980] 1 All ER 556 at 561.

- The key thing about frustration is that there must be a supervening event which fundamentally changes the circumstances and has the effect of turning the bargain the parties made into something that is fundamentally different from the original agreement.
- A contract is not frustrated merely because it becomes more difficult or more expensive to perform.
- If a contract is frustrated, it is terminated immediately and the loss lies where it falls.
- Not all breaches of contract lead to the termination of the contract.
- The right of election means that the injured party can either terminate the contract and claim damages immediately or affirm the contract. An injured party has the right of election in three circumstances: where there has been a fundamental breach, a breach of a term which amounts to a condition, or a repudiatory breach.
- The language used in contracts—condition, warranty, term—is not the deciding factor for the courts when they are considering whether a stipulation was a condition or a term. The deciding factor is what the substance of the stipulation was.
- If the courts are unsure whether a stipulation is a term or a condition they will ask themselves whether the innocent party is deprived of "substantially the whole benefit" of the contract.
- When two companies are bargaining and one includes a clause which exempts it from liability for even fundamental breach of the contract, that clause will be upheld because both entities are commercial concerns with equal bargaining power.

CHAPTER THIRTEEN

REMEDIES FOR BREACH OF CONTRACT

Introduction to Damages

The fundamental compensatory principle in contract law is to award damages to an injured party, in order to put them in the same position as if the contract had been performed.[1] The next question is: at what stage should the courts pinpoint the injured party's loss? Should the courts decide the loss is to be assessed as of the date when he suffers the loss, or at some time afterward, when more is known? The answer is that they should be assessed on the date when the cause of action arose, i.e. the date of the breach. There is a duty on the injured party to mitigate his loss: for example, if the contract was for the hire of a ship—a charterparty—and the ship in question was withdrawn from use for some reason, in breach of contract, the injured party would have to mitigate his loss by going into the market and getting a replacement "as soon as reasonably possible on the best terms available" for the remaining period of the contract.[2] The courts calculate the extra cost of getting a substitute ship, a variation in the rates, and so on, and will award as damages to the injured party whatever the loss is. The injured party cannot recover damages for anything that could have been reasonably avoided had he taken reasonable commercial steps to mitigate his loss. You might, as the injured party, want to sit on your loss and just try to recover it by suing the repudiator, but the courts frown upon that, because they say that while you do not owe the repudiator any duty, fairness requires that you cannot be allowed to act in an unreasonable and uncommercial way.

Remoteness

The repudiation of a contract might set off a chain of events which will end up causing great loss to the injured party—but should all of this loss be compensated for? Sometimes it will be argued that certain losses are too "remote", a legal use of the word which means that the losses in question did not naturally arise out of the breach and were not within the contemplation of both parties at the time they made the contract. The test for remoteness was set out in the mid-nineteenth century in

---

[1] *Golden Strait Corp v Nippon Yusen* [2007] 2 AC 353 at para [9], *per* Lord Bingham of Cornhill; also, *Robinson v Harman* (1848) 1 Exch at 850, 855.

[2] *Per* Lord Carswell [2007] 2 AC 353 at 389, citing *Koch Marine Inc. v D'Amica Societa di Navigazione Arl (The Elena D'Amico)* [1980] 1 Lloyd's Rep 75 *per* Robert Goff J.

Hadley v Baxendale.[3] The plaintiffs owned a mill. An essential part of the machinery broke. The defendants were employed to bring a replacement. They took a long time, longer than the plaintiffs expected. The plaintiffs sued them for all the money they were not able to make during that "extra" period. The court said that the damages should: (1) arise naturally from the breach; and (2) should have been in contemplation of both parties at the time they made the contract. The *Victoria Laundry* case[4] illustrates the point. The plaintiffs owed a laundry. The boiler broke. The defendants were employed to deliver a replacement; they delivered it months after it was expected. The court said that two kinds of loss had occurred to the laundry owners: (1) the usual loss of the profits from the laundry business that arose naturally from the breach of contract; (2) losses caused by not being able to perform very lucrative dyeing contracts which had come up, which the defendant knew nothing about. These kinds of losses are only recoverable if the defendant had sufficient knowledge of the activity to make it reasonable to fix him with liability for the loss.

Assessing Damages

In *Ruxley Electronics and Construction Ltd v Forsyth*,[5] Mr Forsyth employed builders to install a pool at the back of his house. When it was done, he discovered that it was 6ft 9in at the deep end instead of the 7ft 6in he had asked for. Did Mr Forsyth have the right to the cost of redoing the whole pool (called, in law, "the cost of reinstatement")? Should he be compensated for the loss of value, which would have been a much smaller sum? On the one hand, it could be argued that he should be entitled to the cost of a new pool, because there was no other way of giving him what he contracted for. On the other, it could be argued that the pool he got was a perfectly safe one in general, and perfectly safe for diving: it was just a little shallower at the deep end than he had asked for, so he should be awarded damages for loss of value. One remedy seemed to give too much compensation, the other too little. The House of Lords said it was vital that Forsyth show he had suffered loss because of the breach: if he had suffered none, he could only recover nominal damages.

[3] (1854) 9 Ex 341.
[4] *Victoria Laundry (Windsor) v Newman* [1949] 2 KB 528.
[5] *Ruxley Electronics and Construction Ltd v Forsyth* [1995] 3 All ER 268.

"For the object of damages is always to compensate the plaintiff, not to punish the defendant".[6] The House of Lords said that in many cases, the cost of reinstatement would be the appropriate measure of damages[7], but in this case, it should be the difference in value. This is because,

> "first, the cost of reinstatement is not the appropriate measure of damages if the expenditure would be out of all proportion to the good to be obtained, and secondly, the appropriate measure of damages in such a case is the difference in value, even though it would result in a nominal award".[8]

The key point is whether or not it is reasonable to insist on reinstatement. In *East Ham BC v Bernard Sunley & Sons Ltd*[9], an insistence on reinstatement was reasonable because panels which had been fixed to the external walls of a school fell off because the contractor had put them on in a defective manner. In *G W Atkins Ltd v Scott*,[10] the court found it was unreasonable to award the cost of retiling a whole roof despite the tiling being defective, because the defects were mostly cosmetic and minor. Instead, a small sum was awarded for the bad workmanship. Thus, in the *Ruxley* case, Mr Forsyth was awarded the difference in value between what he bargained for and what he got, because to award the full cost of a new swimming pool would be out of proportion and unreasonable. The court was also able to award modest damages to reflect the fact that the breach had meant Forsyth was dissatisfied with his pool (£2,500 general damages for "loss of amenity").

In *Leahy v Rawson*[11] the plaintiff employed the defendants to build an extension to a cottage. When she moved in to the extension, she felt the work was substandard and incomplete. A technician prepared a report confirming her misgivings. She sued the defendants for the amount it would cost her to demolish and rebuild the extension. The defendants argued that she should have carried out remedial works on the extension.

---

[6] [1995] 3 All ER 268 at 282.
[7] See *East Ham BC v Bernard Sunley & Sons Ltd* [1965] 3 All ER 619, where an insistence on re-instatement was reasonable.
[8] *Per* Lord Lloyd of Berwick, [1995] 3 All ER 268 at 283 following Cardozo J in *Jacob & Youngs Inc. v Kent* (1921) 230 NY 239.
[9] [1965] 3 All ER 619.
[10] (1980) 7 Const LJ 215.
[11] [2004] 3 IR 1.

Instead, she had left the extension as it was and spent her money converting the garage into a living space (she ran a B&B). She said she had been told by one builder that attempts to fix the extension would "only be a patch up job and the walls would be crooked and off-line".[12] What damages were appropriate? The cost of fixing the extension or the cost of demolishing and rebuilding it? The court said that the plaintiff should be entitled to damages measured at the cost of reinstatement "if and only if such measurement of damages is reasonable".[13] The judge took the unusual step of visiting the house and said it was "a depressing and untidy sight and the existence of this incomplete and defective work is a major disamenity".[14] The judge found that the plaintiff had acted reasonably and awarded her the full amount for demolishing and rebuilding the extension: €121,894.85.

Recission

Speaking about rescission, an English judge gave the following pithy definition; he said that with rescission there ought to be "a giving back and a taking back on both sides".[15] If a transfer of land took place following a misrepresentation, the person who procured the land only held it on trust for the transferor. Goods automatically revest in the misrepresentee. The idea is to put the parties in the position they were in before the transaction occurred (the "status quo ante"). If this cannot be done—and it could not be done in the Irish case of *Northern Bank Finance Corporation v Charlton*[16]—then rescission is not an option. If there has been a misrepresentation and the court grants rescission, the contract is deemed to have been void *ab initio*.

A person wishing to rescind has to do it promptly because delay is taken as affirmation. In *Leaf v International Galleries*[17] a man discovered that the painting he bought five years previously was not by the artist he was told had painted it. His delay amounted to acceptance of the painting. Affirmation is the first bar to rescission. Lapse of time is the

---

[12] *ibid* at 14.
[13] *ibid, per* O'Sullivan J, at 16, approving Henchy J in *Munnelly v Calcon Ltd* [1978] IR 387 at 399.
[14] [2004] 3 IR 1 at 24.
[15] *Per* Bowen LJ in *Newbigging v Adam* [1886–90] All ER Rep 975 at 984.
[16] [1979] IR 149.
[17] [1950] 2 KB 86.

second. The third occurs when a third party—someone who was not party to the contract—has acquired rights in the thing which you wish to have returned to you. Inability to achieve the status quo ante is also a bar to rescission.

It was held in *The Great Peace* case[18] that the courts do not have jurisdiction to grant rescission of a contract where there has been common mistake if the contract is valid and enforceable on ordinary principles of contract law.[19] The rule is that a contract cannot be avoided for a common mistake regarding the quality of the subject matter unless the subject matter was "essentially different" from that which the parties believed to exist.

Specific Performance

If you go into court asking for "specific performance", what you are asking the judge to do is order that the other party to the contract carry out whatever obligation has been signed up to. That might mean they have to specifically perform the transfer of a plot of land, the sale of a premises or the delivery of goods. You ask for this when you are more interested in having the contract performed than in seeking damages.

For a court to order specific performance, a number of things need to be in place. The contract must be a valid, enforceable one. If damages would be an adequate remedy, the court will not order specific performance. A piece of land, a premises, an art work, for example, may be unique, so that failure to transfer them on foot of an agreement to do so can not be compensated by damages: specific performance would often be granted. For a different type of contract, however, such as a contract for the sale of commodities, which could be obtained from another supplier, damages will be adequate, so specific performance would not be ordered.

Certain contracts cannot be specifically performed: contracts of employment are a classic example. Where a relationship has broken down between people, it would be fruitless, and probably foolish, to force

---

[18] *Great Peace Shipping Ltd v Tsavliris Salvage (International) Ltd* [2002] 4 All ER 689.
[19] [2002] 4 All ER 689 at 729 (This case ruled that *Solle v Butcher* [1949] 2 All ER 1107, though it gave greater flexibility, was not good law).

them to work together. Company directors and employees may not go to court seeking specific performance of their contract; instead, they should take an action which seeks damages for wrongful dismissal.

Injunctions

An injunction is a remedy that often appears in the newspapers. Sometimes residents who live near stadiums threaten to seek an injunction to prevent a concert. Sometimes injunctions are sought to prevent protests from continuing. To take a few examples from the newspapers: A security company provides services to insolvency practitioners who repossess properties. This activity has irked anti-eviction campaigners, and they have taken to protesting wherever the security company is hired. The company has won a contract to provide security at an awards ceremony. The campaigners say they will be there, protesting peacefully outside. The company says this activity is damaging to its business. It goes to the High Court and seeks an injunction to prevent the campaigners from carrying out their protest.[20] Ryanair feels that its business is being undermined by a company which uses a subdomain name online which includes the Ryanair name, and which invites customers to make bookings through its site rather than Ryanair's. Ryanair seeks an injunction prohibiting this behaviour, and succeeds.[21] A company seeks to appoint a receiver over shares in a private hospital which are owned by the co-founder of the clinic. If the owner of the shares can offer convincing argument why this should not happen, his best course of action is to seek an injunction to restrain the appointment of the receiver.[22]

What are the key aspects of an injunction? First, a definition: it is a court order which compels a party to do or to stop doing something. All of the injunctions above are prohibitory, but a court can order a person to carry out some action, and this is called a mandatory injunction. An injunction is an equitable remedy, which means it is subject to certain rules of fairness (for example, the person seeking it must come to court "with

[20] "Ktech Security wins court order against anti-eviction protest", *Irish Times*, 13 January 2015.
[21] "Ryanair wins legal case against screenscraper site", *Irish Times*, 8 January 2015.
[22] "Larry Goodman firm restrained from appointing receiver over Blackrock Hospital shares", *Irish Times*, 22 December 2014.

clean hands" and must not have delayed). For a person to be able to seek an injunction they must have standing ("*locus standi*"); to show standing, a person must show the court that he has a certain right or interest which is either being breached, or is about to be breached. An injunction which will last forever can be sought (a perpetual injunction), or a party can seek one which will last only a few days (an interim injunction) or until the hearing of the action in order to maintain the status quo (an interlocutory injunction[23]). The person seeking the injunction must swear to their version of events in an affidavit. Also, the person seeking the injunction will usually have to agree to set aside money to compensate the defendant if, at the full hearing, it is found that the defendant was in the right; this is called an undertaking as to damages.

Finally, when considering whether or not to grant an injunction, the courts always consider whether an award of damages at a later date would be adequate, instead of the grant of an injunction. The courts follow "the *Campus Oil* test"[24] which asks three questions: (1) is there a serious issue to be tried? (2) are damages an adequate remedy? and (3) does the balance of convenience lie in favour of granting or refusing the application? This last question allows the judges a lot of room to use their own discretion. The idea is to weigh up the harm or wrong that can be done to a defendant against the plaintiff's need for protection.[25] Put another way, it is the risk of injustice to either side that is considered in this last point.

Quantum Meruit

To sue under the heading of *quantum meruit* means to sue "for the value of services provided". It is sometimes seen as a form of restitution, where a defendant is ordered to pay for a benefit received from the plaintiff. For example, in *Donnelly v Woods*[26] the plaintiff was a financial advisor to two men who bought eighteen acres of farm land. He sued for

---

[23] "Interlocutory relief is granted to an applicant where what he complains of is continuing and is causing him harm or injury which may be irreparable in the sense that it may not be possible to compensate him fairly or properly by an award of damages." *Per* O'Higgins CJ, *Campus Oil (No. 2)* at 105.
[24] *Campus Oil v Minister for Industry and Energy (No. 2)* [1983] IR 88.
[25] *Per* Lord Diplock, *American Cyanamid v Ethicon Ltd* [1975] AC 396 at 406.
[26] [2012] IEHC 26.

quantum meruit, on the basis that he had not been remunerated in consideration for financial and consultancy services. He was unsuccessful for a number of reasons (one of which was that the judge thought it "remains puzzling as to precisely what [he] did") but the judge gave this helpful statement on the topic:

"An entitlement to be paid on a *quantum meruit* basis can be established where it is clear from the course of dealings between the parties that the claimant worked for the defendant on request and on the basis of a mutual understanding that the service provided would be remunerated. If there is absence of agreement as to rate, then despite their failure to conclude a contract, the law will intervene to provide a remedy. This is done on the basis of fairness: where a worker is hired to do a job, that worker is entitled to be paid".[27]

Conclusions

- The principle of damages in contact law is to put the injured party in the same position as if the contract had been performed.
- Damages are assessed as of the date of the breach.
- The injured party has a duty to mitigate its loss.
- Sometimes, it will be argued that certain losses are too "remote". The relevant test in this regard is the one set out in *Hadley v Baxendale*: the damages should (1) arise naturally from the breach and (2) have been in contemplation of both parties at the time they made the contract.
- When a court is asked to award either the sum which is the cost of reinstatement or the sum which represents loss of value, the cost of reinstatement is not the appropriate measure of damages if the expenditure would be out of all proportion to the good to be obtained, and the key point will often be whether or not it is reasonable to insist on reinstatement.
- Rescission is a remedy which is often sought where misrepresentation has occurred. If granted, the contract is deemed to have been void *ab initio*. The idea is to put the parties in the position they were in before the transaction occurred.

---

[27] *Per* Charleton J, [2012] IEHC 26 at para [11].

- Common mistake does not usually lead to rescission.
- If damages would be an adequate remedy, or if the contract is a personal one (like an employment contract), the court will not order specific performance.
- For a person to be able to seek an injunction, they must have standing, they must have come to court "with clean hands", and they must have a right or interest which is either being breached, or is about to be breached. When considering whether to grant an injunction the courts follow "the *Campus Oil* test".

INTRODUCTION TO COMPANY LAW

Sole Traders

There are different ways of carrying on business. You can be a sole trader. You can be in a partnership. Or you can incorporate a private limited company or a public limited company. We'll look at the first two of these first. Sole trader status is the simplest of all. Farmers, carpenters, plumbers, florists, doctors, dentists, barristers: these are all traditional examples of sole traders. The definition of a sole trader is "a natural person who is engaged in a trade, profession or business on his or her own account". A natural person means a human person, as opposed to a company, which is called at law a "corporate person". Some business activities—like selling insurance and driving a taxi—are regulated to protect the public, but nearly anyone can operate as a sole trader. It is easy to start as a sole trader. No annual returns have to be made. There is no supervisory office, like there is for companies, which can strike a sole trader off a register for compliance defaults. The sole trader can take all business decisions without having to consult anyone else. Whatever profit is made belongs to the sole trader. There are two big downsides though: the first is unlimited liability (the debts of the business may lead to the bankruptcy of the sole trader) and the second is an inability to offer floating charges as security when trying to raise finance.[1]

Partnerships

The second way of carrying on business is to be a partner in a partnership. A partnership is "the relation which subsists between persons carrying on business in common with a view to profit"; this definition comes from s 1 of the Partnership Act 1890. Usually a maximum of twenty people are allowed to enter into partnership (solicitors and accountants are exempt from this limit[2]). As in the case of a sole trader, a partnership can be created without a great deal of hassle. It does not have to be registered, or even founded on a written contract (though it is governed by the rules of contract law). Unlike a company, where a group of directors will be appointed to manage the day-to-day business, each partner is entitled to be involved in the management of the partnership.

---

[1] Other disadvantages—which a company does not have—include a less favourable tax code and having to pay higher stamp duty when transferring real property.

[2] As are banking partnerships and partnerships to breed thoroughbred horses.

But, like the sole trader, the biggest disadvantage of carrying on business in this way is the possibility of bankruptcy, because there is no shield between a partner and the debts of the partnership. If one of the partners dies, the partnership comes to an abrupt end (unlike a company, which continues its legal existence even if all the directors and shareholders were to die). The partnership might simply dissolve because one partner decides he wants out.

Companies Limited by Shares

The most popular way to do business in Ireland is to incorporate a private limited company (known either as a "private company limited by shares", or as an "LTD"). According to the most recent statistics, there were 161,071 private companies in Ireland, which accounts for 86.07% of all companies registered with the Companies Registration Office ("CRO"). When we say that a company is "limited by shares" we mean that the liability of the members is limited to what they owe on the shares. You might buy a hundred shares in a LTD. Each share cost €1. You only had to pay 25 cents for each share at the time of purchase, on the understanding that you would pay the rest later. The directors may at some point make what is known as "a call": in order to increase the company's capital they will ask all the shareholders to pay—for example—a further 25 cents on each share. Your only obligation as a shareholder is to pay whatever sum is outstanding on your shares. If the company goes into liquidation and is deep in debt, and you have paid 50 cents in total for every €1 share you own, the most the liquidator can ask you for is the remaining 50 cents on each share. You cannot be asked to pay for any amount of the debt that the failed company owes. You are protected from this by your limited liability.

This rule—that a shareholder's liability is limited—goes hand in hand with the rule that companies have separate legal personality. The idea is this: you have a legal "personality" in the sense that you are a legal person. Companies are "corporate persons". If you are a shareholder in a company, the company's legal personality is separate from your legal personality. If it does something wrong, it may be sued—but you may not. You are simply the shareholder. If it amasses great debts and is put into liquidation by its creditors, the creditors may only seek their money from the company's coffers, not from yours. This rule was established over a hundred years ago in a case called *Salomon v Salomon & Co. Ltd.*[3] At first the point was controversial. Judges in the second-highest court in the jurisdiction thought that the rule allowed dishonest persons to cheat their creditors. For example, you and a friend could set up a company limited by shares, becoming the two directors and only shareholders. You could run it badly, build up debts, and in the end, let the company be wound up, telling the creditors you were sorry but the company was insolvent—knowing that you could not be pursued. Initially it was thought that to allow for separate legal personality would be to create "an instrument for cheating honest creditors".[4] But the House of Lords knew the advantages for the economy of separate personality and limited liability: it encouraged people to take risks, something of the first importance in a dynamic, entrepreneurial society. It recognises the two very important reasons for incorporating a company—to avoid bankruptcy and to make borrowing money easier, both entirely legitimate wishes. To return to the example of you and your friend for a moment: if you were merely shareholders in that situation, it is true that you would not be liable for any of the debts of the company. But if you were the directors as well, as you are in the example, our law provides that you can be made personally liable for the debts of the company in certain circumstances, and trading in a reckless or fraudulent manner is one of them. In this way, the law strikes a balance. It allows companies to have separate legal personalities—and shareholders to have limited liability—while protecting creditors of the company to a certain extent by making directors responsible for reckless trading.

In order to be a LTD, the company must have three characteristics: it must not have more than 149 members (i.e. shareholders); there must be a restriction on the transfer of shares (i.e. the shares cannot be listed on a stock market, the directors may have a discretion to refuse to register a transfer of shares, and only members may have a pre-emption right to buy the shares of a departing member); and the public are not allowed to subscribe for shares, debentures or other securities of the company.

A company limited by shares has a particular advantage over sole traders and partnerships when raising finance: it can offer lending institutions not

---

[3] [1897] AC 22.
[4] [1895] 2 Ch 323 at 339.

only fixed charges, but floating charges as well, something sole traders and partnerships cannot do. Floating charges are dealt with in Chapter 18 (Corporate Borrowing).

LTD Versus DAC

The Companies Act (CA) 2014 was enacted on 1 June 2015. As of that moment, around 85% of companies in Ireland were registered as "private companies limited by shares". The Act does something new in Irish company law. It divides private limited companies into two kinds. First, it provides for a reformed private company limited by shares (which will continue to be known by the shorthand "LTD"[5]). Reforms include endowing the LTD with the contractual capacity of a private person, giving it the ability to dispense with annual general meetings ("AGMs"), providing that only one director is necessary, and providing for a simplified single-document "constitution" to replace the traditional memorandum of association and articles of association. All existing private limited companies are automatically converted to the new model private limited company on 1 December 2016, unless they wish to remain as they are, in which case they must convert to a "Designated Activity Company" ("DAC").[6]

The key features of the new model private limited company are:

1. Only one director is required (but if it has only one director, someone else must be the secretary; if there are two directors, one director can be both director and secretary).
2. It has the same contractual capacity as a natural person.
3. AGMs can be dispensed with if all the shareholders agree to do so.
4. It has a simple, one-document constitution.
5. It can pass ordinary and special resolutions using a written procedure (i.e. it does not need to hold a shareholders' meeting to do so).

---

[5] It seems that at one stage the proposed shorthand was to be "the LTD", the private company limited by shares.
[6] The CRO is charging no fee for conversions. Companies Act 2014 provides for an eighteen-month transition period.

The Designated Activity Company

There are two kinds of DAC: a private company limited by shares and a private company limited by guarantee.[7] Charities, management companies, companies incorporated for a specific purpose, companies limited by guarantee: these kinds of companies are the likely candidates for DAC status. Unlike the new model private limited company, a DAC continues to have an objects clause,[8] must have at least two directors, and cannot dispense with AGMs. A DAC is therefore referred to as a private company limited by shares or by guarantee which only has the capacity to do the acts or things set out in its constitution (i.e. memorandum and articles).[9] If a company is a DAC, its name must end with "Designated Activity Company"[10] unless it qualifies for an exemption (for example, if it is a charity).[11] Existing private companies which wish to convert to DAC status should do so by 1 September 2015.

A DAC's memorandum and articles of association are together referred to as its "constitution".[12] A DAC's memorandum of association must state (a) its name; (b) which type of DAC it is (a private company limited by shares, or a private company limited by guarantee and having a share capital); (c) its objects; (d) that the liability of its members is limited; (e) in the case of a DAC limited by shares, the amount of share capital with which the DAC proposes to be registered and the division thereof into shares of a fixed amount; (f) in the case of a DAC limited by guarantee, a statement of how much the members will contribute to the assets of the company if it is wound up.[13]

---

[7] CA 2014, s 963. Practitioners should note that a DAC limited by guarantee is different from a company limited by guarantee, which is dealt with in Pt 18 of the Act.

[8] A company's objects clause sets out the "objects" of the company, i.e. the objectives for which it was set up. Prior to the Companies Act 2014 all companies were obliged to have such a clause, and could not enter contracts for any matters which stood outside those objects. Any such contract would be beyond the powers of the company ("ultra vires") and void.

[9] Existing Private Guarantee companies are deemed to be DACs.

[10] Or "Cuideachta Ghníomhaíochta Ainmhithe", s 969.

[11] If the DAC's objects are the promotion of commerce, art, science, education, religion or charity or if its constitution requires its profits (if any) or other income to be applied to the promotion of its objects and prohibits the making of distributions to its members—then the DAC will tend toward the exemption; see ss 971 and 1180.

[12] s 967.

[13] For a full list of requirements see Companies Act 2014 ss 967–968 and see Schs 7 and 8 of the Act for guidance on writing the core documents of the DAC.

Key DAC Provisions

1. If a DAC wishes to alter its objects, the company may do so by special resolution.[14]
2. If a DAC wishes to alter or add to its articles, it may do so, also by special resolution.[15]
3. A DAC must have at least two directors.[16]
4. Unless its constitution says otherwise, a DAC can use the unanimous written resolution procedure to pass special resolutions without holding actual meetings.[17]
5. Unless its constitution says otherwise, a DAC can use the majority written resolution procedure to pass ordinary resolutions.[18]
6. In the case of a DAC limited by shares being wound up, members' liability is limited to the amount unpaid on the shares; in the case of a DAC limited by guarantee, the contribution is limited to the guarantee set out in the constitution, and there is an obligation on each member to pay any sums unpaid on any shares.[19]
7. The same examinership rules which apply to LTDs apply to DACs.[20]

Guarantee Companies

The second most popular form of company in Ireland is the company limited by guarantee ("CLGs"). They are usually used where the company in question is not trading for profit. Traditionally, this has meant that three kinds of operations incorporate as CLGs: charities, management companies (of apartment blocks, for example) and sports clubs.

There is no special body of company law which applies only to management companies. The Multi-Unit Development Act 2011 ("the MUD Act") states that owners' management companies ("OMCs") are to be companies which are registered under the Companies Acts.[21]

---

[14] s 974.
[15] s 977.
[16] s 985.
[17] s 193 read with s 989.
[18] s 194 read with s 990.
[19] s 997.
[20] Pt 10 of CA 2014 (particularly s 510) read with s 998.
[21] Multi-Unit Development Act 2011, s 1(1).

Incorporating OMCs became common for solicitors because there are so many multi-unit developments in Ireland, and every multi-unit development is obliged to establish an OMC. Ownership of the common areas of the multi-unit development must be transferred to the OMC.[22] When a person purchases a unit in the development, that person because a member of the OMC. Clarke J stated, in simple language, what the purpose of OMCs was in *Palaceanne Management Ltd v AIB Plc*[23]:

> Under the typical scheme (and again the case here) what was contemplated was that the common areas together with the freehold reversion of the leases would be transferred to the management company when all of the apartments had been sold so that the obligations formerly resting on the developer then passed to the management company. To that extent it was typical (and the case here) that the management company joined in each lease. Thereafter it was for the owners, in their capacity as shareholders in the management company, to make decisions as to the level of upkeep and expenditure consistent with the mutual obligations to which they had committed under the respective leases by virtue of which they held their individual apartments and the constitutional documents of the management company itself.

Most OMCs are incorporated as public companies limited by guarantee not having a share capital (CLGs). Only a minority have been incorporated as private companies limited by shares. If, prior to 1 June 2015, a guarantee company has had a share capital, it will now be considered a private company, and will be considered to be a DAC at the end of the transition period (1 December 2016). The CA 2014 states that, in general, Parts 1 to 14 of the CA 2014—which apply to the new model private limited company—apply to CLGs. Certain provisions in Parts 1 to 14 are disapplied—for example, the doctrine of *ultra vires* is not abolished for CLGs because they retain their objects clause, the two director minimum requirement remains, and so on.[24]

---

[22] Multi-Unit Development Act 2011, s 3.
[23] [2012] IEHC 182 (at para [2.4]).
[24] See table at s 1173.

A "company limited by guarantee" or "CLG" means a company which does *not* have a share capital and the liability of whose members is limited by the constitution to such amount as the members may undertake to contribute in the event of the company being wound up.[25] CLGs are public, not private, companies (which means, amongst other things, that they must have at least seven members, and must hold an AGM). The law in relation to CLGs is set out in Part 18 of the Companies Act 2014.

Public Limited Companies

Aer Lingus, Ryanair, AIB, Bank of Ireland, Diageo, Fyffes, Glanbia, Kerry Group, Paddy Power, Tesco: all of these companies are listed on the Irish stock exchange. All of these companies are public limited companies ("PLCs"). You can buy shares in any listed company. The restriction on buying shares in a private limited company does not exist with PLCs. The LTD in Ireland is often small, tightly knit and run by families or friends, and the shareholders are often involved in the management of the business (i.e. they are directors). The PLC is quite different, in that its shareholders often won't know each other at all and the shareholders won't usually be the directors. PLCs cast their net wide, but there are only around 100 of them in Ireland. In fact, PLCs account for no more than 1% of all registered companies in this country. One reason for this is that it is far easier to set up and run a *private* limited company than it is to set up and run a public limited company. To give four examples of the requirements for PLCs: a PLC must have an allotted share capital of at least €25,000—with 25% of that fully paid up—before it can commence trading; a PLC must have a minimum of seven members; the transfer of shares in PLCs is heavily regulated to prevent market abuse; and a prospectus must be prepared in order to sell shares to members of the public. These matters either do not play a role for a private company limited by shares, or are much simpler, hence the popularity of the LTD.

---

[25] s 1172; the form of a CLG's constitution is set out in s 1176.

Conclusions

Sole trader status is the simplest way of carrying on business, but sole traders are exposed to unlimited liability for the debts of the business.

- Most partnerships are confined to a maximum of 20 people and they too are exposed to unlimited liability for the debts of the business.
- The most popular way to do business in Ireland is to incorporate a private limited company (the LTD or DAC) because the liability of the shareholders is limited.
- Most private companies will be LTDs rather than DACs, under the new regime brought in by the Companies Act 2014 (which came into force on 1 June 2015).

Directors

General Duties of Directors

It has been said that directors have "but one master, the company".[1] This has been the rule for over a hundred years.[2] It still holds good in a strict sense. The idea is that directors should not have a duty to both the company and to shareholders, because this parallel duty could cause conflict or confusion. The interests of the shareholders may be short-term, whereas directors, in considering the interests of the company, should take the long view. The courts in New Zealand and Australia have been willing to say that there can be a duty to both company and shareholder where the parallel duties do not overlap, or where, in the context of a family-run company, the shareholders were dependent on the directors for information and advice, and the directors were trusted with regard to particular transactions, and that trust was taken advantage of.[3] But the Irish courts have not had to consider these possibilities, so while the reasoning of the New Zealand or Australian cases may be followed, it has not been followed yet. The strict rule, therefore, is that directors owe a duty to the company and not to the shareholders.

In two areas, however, the legislature and the courts have stepped in to expand the duties of directors. First, directors have a duty to the company's creditors in one particular case: where the company is facing an insolvent situation. In that case, the courts have held that the interests of the creditors displace the other interests—that their interests "intrude" on the normal hierarchy.[4] Second, directors have a duty to "have regard" to the interests of the company's employees.[5] This duty does not have much force, however, because the duty to have regard to employees is owed to the company, so the employees cannot enforce it in their personal capacity. As such, it is a piece of tokenism.

Company directors have a general duty to ensure that their company complies with the Companies Act 2014.[6] They must deliver to the

---

[1] Per Lord Cullen, *Dawson International v Coats Paton plc* [1989] BCLC 233 at 243.
[2] First enunciated in *Percival v Wright* [1902] 2 Ch 421.
[3] See *Coleman v Myers* [1977] 2 NZLR 225 and *Brunninghausen v Glavanics* (1999) 32 ACSR 294.
[4] *Kinsella v Russell Kinsella Property Ltd* [1986] 4 NSWLR 722 approved in Ireland in *Parkes v Hong Kong & Shanghai Bank Corp* [1990] ILRM 341, *Re Frederick Inns Ltd* [1994] 1 ILRM 387 and *Jones v Gunn* [1997] 3 IR 1.
[5] Companies Act 2014, s 224.
[6] Companies Act 2014, s 223.

Companies Registration Office (CRO) the company's constitution, together with the following statement, signed by them: "I acknowledge that, as a director, I have legal duties and obligations imposed by the Companies Act, other statutes and at common law".[7]

Directors' Fiduciary Duties

Directors have fiduciary duties to the company; for example, a director must:

1. Act in good faith in what the director considers to be the interests of the company.
2. Act honestly and responsibly in relation to the conduct of the affairs of the company.
3. Not use the company's property, information or opportunities for his or her own or for anyone else's benefit (unless this is expressly allowed by the company's constitution or the use has been approved by a resolution of the company in general meeting).
4. Exercise care, skill and diligence in carrying out the role of director.[8]

Directors must disclose an interest in contracts entered into by the company.[9] Directors and secretaries must notify the company in writing of their interests in shares or debentures of the company.[10] If a director acts in breach of any of the duties outlined above, he will be liable either to account to the company for any gain he made, or to indemnify the company for any loss it suffered as a result of the breach.[11] If an action is taken against a director for any such breach, the court may relieve him of liability if it appears that he acted honestly and reasonably.[12]

Company secretaries must also sign up to a written statement acknowledging their duties and obligations.[13] The secretary is the custodian of the company's various registers and the secretary's duties

---

[7] ibid.
[8] For a full list of directors' fiduciary duties see Companies Act 2014 s 228, but note that the list is not intended to be exhaustive.
[9] Companies Act 2014, s 231.
[10] ibid, s 261.
[11] ibid, s 232.
[12] ibid, s 233.
[13] ibid, s 226(5): "I acknowledge that, as a secretary, I have legal duties and obligations imposed by the Companies Act, other statutes and at common law".

are delegated by the board. Directors of a private company limited by shares have a duty to ensure that the secretary has the requisite skill to perform the role of secretary.[14]

Directors and Dividends

The declaration of dividends is a matter for the directors. The shareholders cannot force the directors to declare dividends. In *Scott v Scott*[15] the members instructed the directors to declare an interim dividend. The instruction was invalid because it was an attempt to usurp the powers of directors, in particular in this case, the power to decide the financial direction of the company.[16] If the directors do not want to declare a dividend the shareholders cannot direct them to do so (*Ryanair Ltd v Aer Lingus plc*[17]). Dividends must be declared by the directors and they must be *payable*—that means they can only be distributed to members if the company has distributable assets (i.e. sufficient profits).

Loans, etc. between Directors and Company

If a director receives a loan from his company, the terms of which are not in writing, there is a presumption that the loan is repayable on demand.[18] If, on the other hand, a director—or a connected person—claims they made a loan or a quasi-loan in favour of the company, and the terms are not in writing, (or if they are and the writing is ambiguous), there is a presumption in favour of the company that no loan or quasi-loan was ever made.[19]

Conflict of Interest Transactions

There is a general rule against directors entering in to substantial property transactions with their companies. Directors are not allowed to enter into any "arrangement" with their company whereby they acquire a non-cash asset from the company, or whereby the company acquires a non-cash

---

[14] Companies Act 2014, s 226(2).
[15] [1943] 1 All ER 582.
[16] As to whether the refusal to declare a dividend could amount to conduct that would come within s 212 of the Companies Act 2014,, the only consideration of this point is an English case *Re Sam Weller & Co* [1990] BCLC 80, and the result is not conclusive
[17] [2011] 3 IR 69.
[18] Companies Act 2014, s 236. The rule includes quasi-loans.
[19] Companies Act 2014, s 237.

asset from the director, *unless* the arrangement is first approved by a resolution of the company in general meeting.[20] If the non-cash asset is worth €5,000 or less, this rule will not apply. If the non-cash asset is worth in excess of €65,000, the rule will always apply. And if the non-cash asset is worth 10% of the amount of the company's relevant assets, the rule will always apply; the relevant assets are the value of its net assets determined by reference to the entity financial statements in respect of the last financial year.

There is a general rule that a company is not permitted to make a loan to one of its directors, to enter into a credit transaction as a creditor for a director, or to enter into a guarantee or provide security for a director.[21] The rule does not apply if the value of the arrangement is less than 10% of the company's relevant assets. The rule can also be circumvented. If directors want to carry out any such transactions, they need to use a procedure called the Summary Approval Procedure. This involves the members passing a special resolution and the directors declaring that the company is solvent.[22] Breach of the rule may mean a director will be guilty of a category 2 offence.[23]

Restriction and Disqualification

If a company goes into insolvent liquidation, the liquidator often takes an application to have the directors of that company either restricted from acting as directors for a five-year period, or disqualified from acting as directors. The liquidator must take this application unless relieved of the obligation to do so by the Director of Corporate Enforcement. Restriction lasts five years. The court has no discretion to alter that period. A restriction order applies to all types of company.[24] In resisting a restriction application, a director must show that he acted honestly and

---

[20] Companies Act 2014, s 238 (this rule applies to "connected persons" too, i.e. a company which is "connected" to the director. In such a case the connected company would also need to pass a resolution in general meeting).

[21] Companies Act 2014, s 239. This rule also applies to directors of the company's holding company, and "connected persons". The rule applies also to quasi-loans.

[22] Companies Act 2014, s 202.

[23] Companies Act 2014, s 248. A category 2 offence means: On indictment, maximum fine of €50,000 and/or maximum prison sentence of five years. On summary conviction, maximum fine of €5,000 and/or maximum prison sentence of 12 months.

[24] Companies Act 2014, s 819(6).

responsibly in relation to the conduct of the affairs of the company.[25] The court must also be satisfied that the director cooperated "as far as could be reasonably expected" with the liquidator "when requested to do so by the liquidator". Restriction is just that, a restriction on acting as a director, not an absolute prohibition. A restricted director may act as a director as long as the company which proposes to include him on the board has an allotted share capital of not less than €100,000 in the case of a private company limited by shares (the capital requirement in relation to a PLC is €500,000). If a restricted director wishes to be appointed director or secretary of a company, he must give that company written notice of his status as a restricted director, with the fourteen days immediately before appointment as director or secretary.[26] A company which has a restricted director on its board cannot use the Summary Approval Procedure.[27]

Disqualification is a more serious matter, and carries a greater stigma. The key aspect of disqualification is "unfitness" to be concerned in the management of a company.[28] The court has discretion with regard to the time period: a judge can impose anything from a two-year period to a twelve-year period. It may be that, hearing the evidence, the court will decide that the director's conduct merits a restriction order rather than a disqualification. In *Re Bovale Developments*[29] two directors were disqualified for seven years for "particularly serious" misconduct and fraud (this included "systematic falsification" of books of account, plus a €6 million understatement of their gross remuneration). The disqualification period might have been longer but the two directors made some level of voluntary disclosure to the Revenue which led to their paying €22m in tax, interest and penalties. In *Re CB Readymix Ltd; Cahill v Grimes*[30] a liquidator who was "determined to screw the Revenue no matter what it took" was disqualified for seven years, partly because he destroyed books and records of the company and partly because he failed to understand the gravity of what he had done. In *Official Receiver v Doshi*[31] Mr Doshi was disqualified for twelve years for false invoicing, financing the company's business by

---

[25] Companies Act 2014, s 819(2).
[26] Companies Act 2014, s 825. Failure to do so is a category 3 offence.
[27] (unless it is for a members' voluntary winding up) CA 2014, s 827.
[28] Companies Act 2014, s 842.
[29] [2013] IEHC 561 (High Court, Finlay Geoghegan J).
[30] [2002] 1 IR 372.
[31] [2001] 2 BCLC 235.

retaining a large amount of money from the Revenue, and trading recklessly. In *Re Dawson Print Group Ltd*[32] a director in his mid-twenties was not disqualified, despite having been director of two companies which went into liquidation, the cause of which was partially attributable to his mismanagement, because the judge felt he had learnt his lesson.

A number of behaviours will make disqualification likely: (1) failure to keep proper books of account and failure to make annual returns; (2) trading fraudulently or recklessly; (3) engaging in tax fraud; (4) attempting to shift the assets of an insolvent company to a company newly incorporated by the same directors (the phoenix syndrome).

It is a category 2 offence for a person who is restricted or disqualified to act in relation to a company in a way that he has been prohibited from doing. This means that, at its most extreme, the penalty is a maximum fine of €50,000 and/or maximum prison sentence of five years.[33]

Restriction and Disqualification Undertakings

There is a way a director can avoid the court process in relation to a restriction or disqualification order. He may now make an undertaking, which the Director of Corporate Enforcement ("DCE") may accept, not to act in a way that would be prohibited if the person had been subject to one or other order.[34] If the DCE has reasonable grounds for believing that one or more of the categories for disqualification apply to a person, he may give notice to that person asking whether or not he is willing to give a disqualification undertaking for a proposed period. If the director accepts, the details are sent to the CRO. The same process exists for restrictions. The idea is to save time and money by avoiding court appearances.

Formally Appointed Directors, De Facto Directors, Shadow Directors

A person can become a director in three different ways. The first way is by formal appointment. A LTD needs only one director. In the case of a one-person company, that person will be the "promoter" of the company;

---

[32] [1987] BCLC 601.
[33] Companies Act 2014, s 855.
[34] Companies Act 2014, Pt 14, Chapter 5.

he will get all the documentation ready for the CRO and nominate himself to be director upon the incorporation of the company. In the case of a single-member company, the sole member may appoint a person to be a director of the company by serving notice in writing on the company, which states the name of the person in question. In general, the first directors of a company are the people who are nominated by the subscribers (or a majority of the subscribers).[35] Any subsequent directors must be appointed by the members in general meeting. The existing directors may appoint a person to be a director of the company, but that person will only hold office until the next AGM, when the members can vote on his re-election.

The second and third ways a person may be considered to be a director have one important thing in common: it will be the court that decides that they acted in a certain way which merited the name of director, and the court will be considering this after the company has entered insolvent liquidation. The reason for this is that, if a company goes into insolvent liquidation, it might not just be the formally appointed directors who were responsible. There might be other people who should be made responsible, but who were not formally appointed directors.

The first of these is referred to as a de facto director. The phrase just means that he was a director in *fact*, or "in all but name", though he was not formally appointed. A de facto director is defined as one who "occupies the position of director of a company but who has not been formally appointed as such".[36] The duties which apply to formally appointed directors apply to de facto directors as well. De facto directors can be restricted and disqualified. A test for whether a person was a de facto director was set out in a well-known case, *Re Hydrodam*:

> A de facto director is a person who assumes to act as a director. He is held out as a director by the company, and claims and purports to be a director, although never actually or validly appointed as such. To establish that a person was a de facto director of a company it is necessary to plead and prove that he undertook functions in relation to the company

---

[35] All the rules relating to the appointment of directors are set out in Companies Act 2014, s 144.

[36] Companies Act 2014, s 222.

which could properly be discharged only by a director. It is not sufficient to show that he was concerned with the management of the company's affairs or undertook tasks in relation to its business which can properly be performed by a manager below board level.[37]

The second type of non-formally appointed director is the shadow director. This concept is a recognition by the law that a person may influence the actual directors from behind the scenes. A shadow director is defined as "a person in accordance with whose instructions or directions the directors of a company are accustomed to act". It is important to note, however, that a person who is giving professional advice—an accountant, for example, or a solicitor—will not be deemed to have been a shadow director; such a person may well have been giving instructions to the formally appointed directors, and they may have been accustomed to following them, but the instructions will have been given in a professional capacity. The leading review of Irish law on shadow directors took place in *Re Hocroft Developments*[38] where the judge emphasised that the directions or instructions must have been followed by the directors in a way that was "repetitive, customary and recurring"; the communications must not have been "infrequent, rare or occasional".

General Power of Management and Delegation

Directors are charged with the day-to-day management of the business.[39] This is their exclusive domain. Shareholders cannot interfere with the day-to-day decisions directors make because if they could the business of the company could be paralysed. It would be wrong to think that the exercise of directors' powers is totally unfettered. They are subject to: (1) any regulations in the company's constitution; (2) the provisions of the Companies Act 2014; and (3) any directions given by the members in general meeting, via a special resolution, which are not inconsistent with the regulations in the company's constitution. If directors choose, they may delegate their powers to committees or other persons. A key position is that of Managing Director ("MD"). The Companies Act 2014 recognises that different companies use different terminologies, but an MD will be a

---

[37] *Per* Millett J, [1994] 2 BCLC 180 at 183.
[38] [2009] IEHC 580.
[39] Companies Act 2014, s 158.

person who occupies the role of MD "by whatever name called".[40] The Managing Director, acting alone, has the same powers as the board, acting collectively, to bind the company to contracts. Companies can choose whether to give those powers to an MD for use concurrently with the board, or to the exclusion of the board's powers.

Reckless and Fraudulent Trading

If in the course of a winding up, or in the course of an examinership, it appears that any person was knowingly a party to the carrying on of any business in a reckless manner, the court has the power to declare that such a person shall be personally liable for all or part of the debts of the company.[41] It must be shown that the person was an officer of the company at the time of the recklessness. The inclusion of "knowingly a party" makes it difficult to prove, because a certain element of subjectivity is involved. There is a second provision, however, which is an objective one: in that case it is only necessary to prove that the person ought to have known (by virtue of the general knowledge, skill and experience he had) that his actions would have caused loss to the creditors of the company.[42] As an alternative to that, it could be proven that the person was party to contracting a debt by the company which he did not honestly believe "on reasonable grounds" that the company would be able to repay. The courts have said: "It is not sufficient that there be some worry or uncertainty as to the ability to pay all creditors".[43] Usually the courts will look for willful disregard of a clear risk to creditors. Personal liability can be imposed in both of these alternative cases.

Personal liability can also be imposed for fraudulent trading, but again, the "knowingly a party" element of the definition raises the evidential bar.[44] The kinds of activity that would come under this heading are: tax evasion, attempts to conceal company assets from creditors, siphoning off of assets, dual books of account being kept (a false one for the Revenue, a true one for the directors), stock being transferred to an associated company attempts to avoid stamp duty, false invoicing and under-

---

[40] Companies Act 2014, s 159.
[41] Companies Act 2014, s 610(1)(a).
[42] Companies Act 2014, s 610(3)(a).
[43] *Per* Lynch J, Re Hefferon Kearns [1993] 3 IR 191.
[44] Companies Act 2014, s 610(1)(b).

declaration of taxes. Personal liability can also be imposed for failure to keep proper books and records[45] and for any misfeasance (e.g. misapplication of money, wrongful retention of company property).[46]

Conclusions

- In Ireland, directors owe a duty to the company and not to the shareholders
- Directors have a duty to the company's creditors where the company is facing insolvency
- Directors fiduciary duties are set out in CA 2014, s 228, and you should learn a number of them (at least the four set out in this chapter)
- The shareholders cannot force the directors to declare dividends.
- There are rules which prevent directors from self-dealing – entering in to substantial property transactions with their companies or receiving loans from their companies (sections 238 and 239 of CA 2014)
- If a company is being wound up, a director may face an application by the liquidator that he be restricted from acting as a director for five years. His main defence is to show the court that he acted honestly and responsibly in relation to the conduct of the company's affairs.
- Disqualification from acting as a director is a more serious measure and the court decides how long the disqualification period should last.
- Neither restriction nor disqualification mean the imposition of personal liability on a director for the debts of the company. Such liability may be imposed where a director traded recklessly or fraudulently.
- If a company is being wound up, the court might find that a person who was not formally appointed as a director nonetheless had the responsibilities and obligations of a director, either because they were a director in all but name (a de facto director) or because they gave the properly appointed directors repeated instructions which were carried out.
- Shareholders cannot interfere with the day-to-day decisions of the directors

---

[45] Companies Act 2014, s 609.
[46] Companies Act 2014, s 612.

AGENCY

Definition of Agency

One of the leading texts on agency begins with the following definition:

> "Agency is the fiduciary relationship which exists between two persons, one of whom expressly or impliedly manifests assent that the other should act on his behalf so as to affect his relations with third parties, and the other of whom similarly manifests assent so to act".[1]

There are a number of points to be teased out from this definition. The first is "fiduciary relationship". This means a relationship of trust and confidence. A fiduciary relationship imposes certain obligations.[2] The primary one is loyalty and fidelity, and if this is breached, and a fiduciary makes a secret profit from his or her position, or an unauthorised benefit, that profit or benefit will have to be accounted for (i.e. returned to the rightful owner). If an agent wishes to enter into an agreement which might be inconsistent with his fiduciary duties, he should first obtain his principal's consent. It could be said that out of the duty of loyalty arises the "no conflict of interest" rule. So, this kind of relationship arises between two persons, one of whom—the person known as the principal—says "will you act as agent for me?" and the other who agrees to do so. The agent then has the power to affect the principal's legal relations with third parties, which is legal language for outsiders: people or companies which are not part of the principal.

Actual Authority

When the agent enters into a contract on behalf of the principal, it is as if the principal is entering into it himself (or itself— the principal may be the board of directors of a company). An agent may be instructed to sign a contract on behalf of the principal, but the agent's authority may go beyond this: often agents will be given some level of discretion to carry out acts which are in line with the principal's goals. A key point is

---

[1] Peter G. Watts (ed) *Bowstead & Reynolds on Agency*, 20th ed., Sweet & Maxwell 2014, at para 1-001.

[2] It has been noted—in *Bristol and West Building Society v Mothew* [1996] 4 All ER 698—that "not every breach of duty by a fiduciary is a breach of fiduciary duty". This is just something to be aware of, but for a course like this, which is an introduction to the principles of business law, you don't need to worry about that level of detail.

consensus and agreement: the agent must assent to act in such a way for
the principal, and the arrangement will have come about by consensus.
When this is the case, we refer to the agent having "actual authority".
A short definition was provided by Lord Diplock: "An 'actual' authority
is a legal relationship between principal and agent created by a consensual
agreement to which they alone are parties".[3]

Ostensible Authority

The situation is a little trickier when a person seems to be an agent, and
seems to have the authority of the principal. In such cases, the principal
sometimes seeks to dishonour an agreement entered into by the agent,
disclaiming all responsibility. In cases such as this, the third party will
want to enforce the contract, and so will come to court arguing that
while the agent did not have actual authority, he did have "ostensible
authority" (sometimes referred to as "apparent authority").

The key case is this regard is *Freeman and Lockyer (a firm) v Buckhurst
Park Properties*.[4] Mr Kapoor wanted to be a property developer. He
joined forces with Mr Hoon and they formed Buckhurst Park Properties
("BPP"), and through that company, they bought a large English estate.
Their idea was to do it up and sell it on. Kapoor and Hoon made
themselves directors of BPP and each man nominated a man to be
director. So, in total, the board comprised four people. The company's
articles allowed for the appointment of a managing director (something
that would be done by an ordinary resolution recorded in the minutes),
but the board never made that appointment. They allowed Mr Kapoor
to act as managing director. Acting in that way he hired a firm of
architects, the plaintiffs, to carry out work on the estate. When they did,
they looked to be paid, but Mr Kapoor had disappeared, and the board
of BPP was saying that Kapoor never had the actual authority to hire
the plaintiffs, so it could not be liable to pay their bill. The court decided
that Mr Kapoor had the ostensible authority to enter into the contract
with the architects and that he bound BPP to the agreement. This was
because (1) the board always knew that Kapoor was acting as managing
director, and by knowing this and doing nothing to stop it, they were

[3] [1964] 1 All ER 630 at 644.
[4] *Freeman and Lockyer (a firm) v Buckhurst Park Properties (Mangal) & Anor* [1964] 1 All ER 630.

holding him out to be the managing director; (2) employing the architects was just the kind of thing a managing director would do. The judge set out a four-point test for establishing whether a person has ostensible authority. If each question is answered "yes", then the person has ostensible authority:

1. A representation that the agent had authority to enter, on behalf of the company, into a contract of the kind sought to be enforced must have been made to the contractor;

2. The representation must have been made by a person or persons who had "actual" authority to manage the business of the company, either generally or in respect of those matters to which the contract related (this means that the principal—usually the board—must be the one who has made the representation. An agent cannot make the representation that he has the requisite authority. The agent does not, in theory, even have to be aware of the existence of the representation. The most common form of representation is conduct, i.e. by permitting the agent to act in some way.);

3. The contractor must have been induced by the representation to enter into the contract; and

4. The company must not have been deprived, under its memorandum or articles of association, of the capacity either to enter into a contract of the kind sought to be enforced or to delegate authority to the agent to enter into a contract of that kind.

It is important to be very clear on the first and second points. Lord Diplock, in his speech in *Freeman & Lockyer*, said:

> if in the case of a company the board of directors who have "actual" authority under the memorandum and articles of association to manage the company's business permit the agent to act in the management or conduct of the company's business, they thereby represent to all persons dealing with such agent that he has authority to enter on behalf of the corporation into contracts of a kind which an agent authorised to do acts of the kind which he is in fact permitted to do normally enters into in the ordinary course of such

business. The making of such a representation is itself an act of management of the company's business.[5]

What that means in the context of Mr Kapoor is that Mr Kapoor had ostensible authority because the board permitted him to act as a managing director and to do acts which are the kind of acts a managing director would do. The only way the board could have avoided liability under the contract would have been to say "in the articles of the company, the company was not permitted to enter into a contract like the one in question" or "the articles prevent the delegation of that kind of authority to an agent". When BPP was unable to say that, it was prevented from denying the contract.

Rule in *Turquand's* Case

There is an old company law rule called the rule in Turquand's case. It says that if an outsider consults the company's articles (or "constitution"), and sees, for example, that the company may appoint a managing director by passing an ordinary resolution, and if the outsider believes that all along he has been dealing with the managing director—as the architects in Freeman & Lockyer thought—that assumption is one the outsider is entitled to make. The rule in Turquand is called the "indoor management rule". It says that if the

> "persons conducting the affairs of the company do so in a manner which appears to be perfectly consonant with the articles of association, then those dealing with them, externally, are not to be affected by any irregularities which may take place in the internal management of the company."[6]

In *Biggerstaff v Rowatt's Wharf Ltd* the judge said

> "[t]he persons dealing with him [the apparent managing director] must look to the articles, and see that the managing director might have power to do what he purports to do, and that is enough for a person dealing with him bona fide".[7]

---

[5] [1964] 1 All ER 630 at 645.
[6] *Per* Lord Hatherley, *Mahony v East Holyford Mining Co* (1875) LR 7 HL at 894.
[7] *Per* Lindley LJ, [1896] 2 Ch at 102.

The outsider does not have to look at the articles of association, but if they later find out that the articles conferred no power to appoint a managing director, they "[can]not have been heard to say that the person with whom they contracted had been held out by the company as its managing director".[8]

Ratification

If an agent enters into a contract with a third party, but does not have actual authority to do so, the principal can ratify the act, making it as legitimate and valid as if the agent had the necessary authority from the beginning. This is called ratification (or "agency by ratification"). In such a case, before ratification the principal will not necessarily be liable to fulfill the obligations which the agent has purported to bind him to, but upon ratification the principal becomes liable from the date the agreement was entered into.

Pre-Incorporation Contracts

Section 45 of the Companies Act 2014 allows for pre-incorporation contracts to be ratified by the company. The idea is that, before its formation, the promoters of a company may enter into contracts on behalf of the company, and these can be ratified once the company is up and running. Section 45(2) states:

> "Upon such contract or other transaction being so ratified, the company shall become bound by it and entitled to the benefit of it as if the company had been in existence at the date of such contract or other transaction and had been a party to it".

Agency of Necessity

In some circumstances—in an emergency, for example—a person may be justified in taking action for another's benefit. This is said to be a special category of agency, "agency by necessity". There is no coherent set of

---

[8] *Per* Willmer LJ, [1964] 1 All ER 630 at 637, citing *Biggerstaff v Rowatt's Wharf Ltd, British Thomson-Houston Co. Ltd v Federated European Bank Ltd* and *Clay Hill Brick and Tile Co. Ltd v Rawlings*.

rules on this area, but usually the person acting for another's benefit will already be an agent. Bowstead and Reynolds define it thus:

> A person may have authority to act on behalf of another in certain cases where he is faced with an emergency in which the property or interests of that other are in imminent jeopardy and it becomes necessary, in order to preserve the property or interests, to so act.[9]

The doctrine seems to have been born in nineteenth-century cases involving shipping, where the shipmaster was faced with emergency situations and needed to act to preserve the cargo, and in so acting created contracts which bound the principal. The doctrine is almost obsolete in the modern world, where off-the-cuff decisions are less likely to be necessary due to modern communications. The doctrine still exists, however, in cases where the cargo owner does not answer the ship, or where communication is rendered impossible. The key points are: (1) emergency which requires action; and (2) impossibility of receiving instructions.

Del credere Agent

A *del credere* agent is one who guarantees the price of goods purchased by a third party.[10] This kind of agent does so for a higher fee (called a *del credere* commission).

Special Agent

A special agent only has authority to bind the principal in one designated transaction. It is a well-established contrast to a general agent (discussed at greater length in the early paragraphs of this chapter), but it is now doubted whether it is of "much utility" in the present day, because of the development of the doctrine of ostensible authority.[11]

---

[9] *Bowstead & Reynolds on Agency*, at para 4-001.
[10] *Mercantile International Group Plc v Chuan Soon Huat Industrial Group Ltd* [2002] EWCA Civ 288, at para [40].
[11] *Bowstead & Reynolds on Agency*, at para 1-041.

Duties of an Agent

An agent's primary duty is to perform his contractual obligations and not to exceed his authority. The agent must obey all lawful and reasonable instructions issued by the principal. If instructions could be read in two ways, as long as the agent honestly believes his reading is the correct one (and if it was not reasonable to seek clarification), the principal will not be able to sue him for breach of contract. An agent is obliged to carry out his duties with skill, care and diligence (particularly so where the agent has discretion). Agents have an implied duty to keep their principals in the loop. And finally, as mentioned above, agents have a duty not to enter into any conflict of interest with their role as agent.

Rights of an Agent

Most of the law has historically been on the side of the principal: it is the principal, the courts have said, who needs to be protected. The main right of an agent is to remuneration. The agent may sue the principal in tort,[12] though the rights of the agent are normally based on contract law. The agreement should expressly provide the circumstances in which the agent is to be remunerated. Usually it is advisable for an agent to seek to include a clause in the contract which provides for remuneration on a *quantum meruit* basis (that is, payment for as much work as was done, in cases where the contract does not come to the foreseen conclusion).

Termination of Agency

Agency can be terminated by agreement between the principal and the agent; by revocation by the principal of the authority or by the agent's renunciation of the authority; upon the completion of a particular transaction; by the expiry of a certain time period; or by the happening of a certain event: it will depend on the terms of the agreement.

---

[12] *Henderson v Merrett Syndicates Ltd* [1995] 2 AC 145.

Conclusions

- A "fiduciary relationship" is a relationship of trust and confidence which imposes certain obligations, the main one being loyalty and fidelity.
- If an agent makes secret profit from his or her position, that profit or benefit will have to be "accounted for" (in court, a plaintiff will seek "an account of profits").
- When the agent enters into a contract on behalf of the principal, it is *as if* the principal is entering into it himself.
- The question of whether a person had ostensible authority arises where a third party entered into a contract with a company representative whom the third party believed to have had full authority to bind the company.
- It is important to know the four-point test for ostensible authority which is set out in *Freeman and Lockyer*.
- The rule in Turquand's case says that third parties are not to be affected by any irregularities which may take place in the internal management of the company.
- The Companies Act 2014 allows companies to ratify pre-incorporation contracts.

CORPORATE BORROWING

Introduction to Charges

Key to a company's ability to raise finance is its ability to offer as security to a lending institution not just a fixed charge over its premises or a piece of land, but a floating charge over its assets, which fluctuate and may be altered or replaced in the normal course of business. Only companies can offer floating charges. In exchange for a loan, a lending institution will receive an interest in a charged asset. If the company defaults in servicing its loan, the charge-holder can enforce the charge (often by appointing a receiver over it). Floating charges have this advantage: they allow the company to continue to use the charged asset in the ordinary course of business until some future defined event happens (such as default).

The Floating Charge

There are two main kinds of charges: fixed charges and floating charges. A fixed charge can be given over something that is solid and immovable, like a piece of land, a business premises, a house, or a factory. In the early days of modern commercial life, when companies needed to raise capital they went to lending institutions, borrowed money, and entered agreements that if they were unable to repay the loan, the institution would have recourse to one or more of their fixed assets (these agreements were called "debentures" and "securities").

For over a hundred years the courts have been guided by the three-point test outlined in the *Yorkshire Woolcombers* case.[1] It says that a charge will be a floating charge if

> "(1) it is a charge on a class of assets of a company, present and future; (2) if that class is one which, in the ordinary course of the business of the company, would be changing from time to time; and (3) if you find that by the charge it is contemplated that, until some further step is taken by or on behalf of those interested in the charge, the company may carry on its business in the ordinary way as far as concerns the particular class of assets I am dealing with".[2]

---

[1] [1903] 2 Ch 284.
[2] [1903] 2 Ch 284 at 295.

This test has been approved in Ireland.[3] In this jurisdiction, one judge explained the floating charge thus: "The charge floats over the assets of the company until some act is done which causes it to fasten on to the property and goods of the company".[4]

If a floating charge is to be enforceable, it must be registered with the CRO within 21 days of its creation; if it is not, the charge will be void against the liquidator, i.e. when the charge-holder seeks to join the priority queue in a liquidation, he will find himself at the bottom of the pile with the unsecured creditors. For this reason it is vital that the charge-holder, at least, realises that a charge has been created.[5] The courts say that the right to sell an asset belonging to a debtor, and apply the proceeds to pay the debt, cannot be anything other than a charge. Knowing this, you must ask whether the charge is a fixed or a floating one. If the charge provides for various circumstances—shifting, circulating possibilities—and it allows the chargor to use the asset as if there were no charge on it until some future event, and this situation will pertain until that future event (e.g. default), then it will be a floating charge, and must be registered.

Two Ways of Registering a Charge

It used to be the case that some kinds of charges had to be registered and others did not. Now, all charges must be registered.[6] The Companies Act (CA) 2014 provides two procedures for registering charges, the one-stage and the two-stage procedures.[7] The one-stage procedure consists of sending the prescribed particulars in the prescribed form to the CRO within 21 days of the creation of the charge. The two-stage procedure consists of (1) sending notice to the CRO of an intention to create a charge, and (2) within 21 days of the Registrar receiving that notice, sending the Registrar the prescribed particulars in the prescribed form, stating that the charge previously referred to has in fact been created. If this second step

---

[3] *Re Holidair* [1994] 1 IR 416 at 445.
[4] *Per* Kenny J in *Re Interview Limited* [1975] IR 382 at 395.
[5] For an example of this failure, see the *Cosslett* case, [2002] 1 BCLC 77.
[6] The only exception is any charge which falls under SI No. 1 of 2004 or SI No 89 of 2004. These statutory instruments are enactments of EU regulations which deal with Financial Collateral Arrangements.
[7] CA 2014, s 409.

is not taken, the Registrar of Companies removes the notice of the intention to create the charge. If the second step is taken, the day the Registrar received notice of the intention to create the charge will be—retrospectively—the day of its actual creation. If a charge is incompletely registered, it will only be partially void. Whatever is omitted will have no force. Unless either the one-stage or the two-stage procedure is carried out, every charge created under the new Act will be void against the liquidator (and any creditor of the company).

Duty of the Company to Register Charges

The company which creates the charge is obliged to register it.[8] The reality is that in practice, it is usually the charge-holder who registers the charge, i.e. the bank or its solicitor. The CA 2014 says that any person "interested in the charge" may register it and that this has "the same effect as if the company" had done so.[9] That person may recover the fees incurred in registering the charge from the company.

Priority of Charges

If two charges are registered on one asset, the first in time has first priority. The relevant date for priority purposes is the day the CRO receives the details of the charge; if a party is using the two-stage procedure, the relevant date is the date of the receipt of the *intention* to create a charge.[10] If a number of charges are registered on the same day, the earliest in time has priority. Whenever a charge is registered, the CRO issues a certificate of registration.[11]

The Crystallisation of Floating Charges

Three things cause floating charges to stop floating, to "crystallise". If you ask yourself why a charge would cease to hover above the company, waiting for some future event to take place, you might think the obvious answer is that something has caused the company to stop in its tracks,

---

[8] CA 2014, s 410.
[9] CA 2014, s 410(2).
[10] CA 2014, s 412.
[11] CA 2014, s 415.

with the knock-on effect being that the charges fall to the ground, so to speak. If that is what you thought, your guess was right. If the company goes into liquidation, its life is over, and the floating charge has nothing to float over anymore: it must fall to the ground. It crystallises, and becomes known as a "quasi-fixed charge" (to denote that it did not start off life as a fixed charge). Another situation where the company may shudder to a halt is if a receiver is appointed; this is the second kind of event which crystallises a floating charge. The third is if the company ceases to do business.

Late Registration of Charges

If a charge is not registered within 21 days of its creation, there is scope to apply to court for late registration.[12] Omissions and misstatements can also be rectified using this process. The person asking the court to register the charge late can advance any of the following arguments: (1) that the failure to register was accidental, or due to inadvertence or some other sufficient cause; (2) that late registration would not prejudice the position of creditors or shareholders of the company; (3) that for some other reason it is just and equitable to grant relief in respect of an omission or misstatement. A court will not allow late registration where a charge-holder has delayed for no good reason and late registration would displace other creditors.[13]

Fixed Charges on Book Debts

Given the nature of book debts—always fluctuating and circulating—it may sound strange that a company can create a fixed charge over them. At one point it was thought, logically, that only floating charges could be given over book debts. The courts have since decided that it is possible to create fixed charges over book debts, as long as the book debts are paid into a separate bank account over which the charge-holder has total control, and over which the company can in no way exercise any discretion. A key attribute is that "effective possession" must be given to the bank.[14] If the company has any "free use of the proceeds", then, even

---

[12] CA 2014, s 417.

[13] *Re Resnoid and Mica Products Ltd* [1983] Ch 132.

[14] *Supercool Refrigeration and Air Conditioning v Hoverd Industries Ltd* [1994] 3 NZLR 300 at p 321; see also *Re Spectrum Plus Ltd* [2005] 2 BCLC 269.

if the parties have named it a fixed charge, a floating charge will have been created (in this regard it is always the substance of the charge which is important, as opposed to what the parties have decided to call it).[15] A perfectly drafted fixed charge over book debts would look like this:

> "The company at all times during the continuance of this security shall pay all monies received by it from time to time in respect of book debts into an account with AIB Ltd at 36 Tullow Street, Carlow, designated for that purpose and shall not without the prior consent of the bank in writing make any withdrawal from the said account nor direct any payment to be made from the said account".[16]

Charges on book debts, like all other charges, must be registered with the CRO.

Registration of Title Clauses

A registration of title ("ROT") clause is a clause in a contract for goods which says that the title in goods will not pass to the buyer until the buyer pays the seller for them. In the words of one judge:

> "unsecured creditors…receive a raw deal. It is therefore not surprising that this court looked with sympathy on an invention designed to provide some protection for one class of unsecured creditors, namely unpaid sellers of goods".[17]

There are four different kinds of ROT clauses. Under the CA 2014, all charges must be registered with the CRO, but not all ROT clauses are charges. Two kinds of ROT clauses do not require to be registered and two kinds do. The trick is to know which is which.

The first kind is the simple ROT. The essence of what is happening is that the seller is retaining title in specified goods until the buyer pays the purchase price. One Irish judge explained that in this situation, if the buyer were to go into liquidation, the buyer's creditors could not seize

---

[15] *Re Keenan Brothers Ltd* [1985] IR 401.
[16] This was the clause in *Re Keenan Brothers Ltd* [1985] IR 401.
[17] *Per* Templeman LJ, *Borden (UK) Ltd v Scottish Timber* [1981] 1 Ch 25 at 42.

the goods because they are merely "in the *apparent* possession of the buyer".[18] The simple ROT clause does not require registration.

The second type of ROT clause which does not require to be registered is known as the "current account clause" or "all sums due" clause. They differ from the simple ROT clause only to the extent that they provide that the title in the goods shall not pass until *all* sums due to the seller have been paid—not only the sums due arising from the particular contract at hand. These clauses were upheld in Ireland as non-registrable charges.[19]

The next two kinds of ROT clauses do need to be registered. The first of these is called an "aggregation clause". It begins with the usual ROT stipulation and adds that if the relevant goods are manufactured or processed into some other products, then title in those new products rests with the seller too. It is the safest course of action to assume that this type of clause is a charge that requires registration. Such a clause might fail if the goods are irreversibly mixed with something. For example, *Borden (UK) Ltd v Scottish Timber Products*[20] is famous because the good supplied became irreversibly mixed with a new good and the Court of Appeal held that in this circumstance the ROT right vanished. The defendants made chipboard. The plaintiffs supplied them with resin. Nothing in the contract prevented the defendants from using the resin before they paid for it. The problem was that the resin "became an inseparable component, or ingredient, of the chipboard".[21] The court said:

> "When the resin was incorporated in the chipboard, the resin ceased to exist, the plaintiffs' title to the resin became meaningless and their security vanished. There was no provision in the contract for the defendants to provide

---

[18] Carroll J. The purchaser "is not the maker or giver of the bill of sale. He is the holder or grantee under the bill." See *Re Charles Dougherty* [1985] 1 IR 346. If title passes to the purchaser and only equitable and beneficial ownership remains with the seller, as it did in *Re Bond Worth* [1979] 3 All ER 919, then legal title will have passed to the purchaser, and the purchaser will be the one creating a charge over the goods in favour of the seller.

[19] *Re Stokes & McKiernan* [1978] ILRM 240; the same is true in the UK, see *Armour v Thyssen Edelstahlwerke AG* [1991] BCLC 28.

[20] [1981] 1 Ch 25.

[21] *ibid* at 43.

substituted or additional security. The chipboard belonged to the defendants".[22]

The second registrable clause is the "proceeds of sale clause". If a supplier says that the buyer holds all the proceeds of the sale of the goods in question "in trust" until all the money owed to the supplier is paid, then that is a more complicated idea than the simple ROT, and it steps over into the registrable category.

Conclusions

- A floating charge "floats over the assets of the company until some act is done which causes it to fasten on to the property and goods of the company".
- A vital aspect of the floating charge is that until it crystallises, the company which has granted the charge can continue to deal with the charged assets as if there was no charge over them.
- Under the CA 2014, all charges must be registered and there are two ways of registering a charge.
- The one-stage procedure consists of sending the CRO the details of the charge within 21 days of its creation.
- In the two-stage procedure, if the second step is taken, the day the Registrar received notice of the intention to create the charge will be—retrospectively—the day of its actual creation.
- There is scope for late registration of charges but the court will ask whether other creditors would be prejudiced and whether the company is insolvent.
- ROT clauses are not necessarily charges. They only become charges which require registration if they become more complex in nature. The simple ROT and the "all sums due" clause do not need to be registered.

---

[22] *ibid.*

CHAPTER EIGHTEEN

INSTRUMENTS: BILLS OF EXCHANGE, CHEQUES, PROMISSORY NOTES

Introduction

This chapter deals with three kinds of financial instruments: bills of exchange, cheques and promissory notes. These are referred to as "negotiable instruments". They date back to the Middle Ages, when merchants across Europe came up with a way of trading with one another without having to physically transport money on the occasion of each transaction—but we do not need to go into the history of their development. What matters to us is their use in the modern world. One leading textbook has suggested that with the increase in the digital transfer of money, the use of negotiable instruments must inevitably decline, but since "the advantages of negotiability cannot be denied" these instruments will be with us for at least the foreseeable future.[1]

Bills of Exchange

Bills of exchange are important in international trade. What a bill of exchange does is allow for trade credit by allowing payments to be made on agreed future dates. Banks are usually used as agents for the collection of the bill. It gives the seller—and the bank—a stronger legal position: by using a bill of exchange a seller creates formal evidence of the demand for payment from the buyer. The bank will have a valid legal claim on all parties to the bill, both seller *and* buyer. In the event of non-payment, both the seller and the buyer have easy access to legal remedies.

The law in relation to such bills was codified in the UK and Ireland in the Bills of Exchange Act 1882. Fifteen countries follow the rules as set out in that Act, including India, Israel, Singapore, New Zealand and Australia.[2] Many other countries follow the codification of the rules that was set out in the Geneva Convention of 1930. A bill of exchange is defined in our jurisdiction as:

> an unconditional order in writing, addressed by one person to another, signed by the person giving it, requiring the person to whom it is addressed to pay on demand or at a fixed or

---

[1] Goode, *Goode on Commercial Law*, 4th ed, Lexis Nexis 2009, at 519.
[2] The full list is: UK, Ireland, Cyprus, Hong Kong, India, Israel, Malaysia, Pakistan, Philippines, Singapore, Sri Lanka, Australia, New Zealand, Fiji, Tonga.

determinable future time a sum certain in money to, or to the order of, a specified person, or to bearer.[3]

If an instrument does not comply with this definition, it is not a bill of exchange. A key feature is certainty: you can see the definition says it is *an unconditional order in writing*. It must state a fixed time and a clear money sum. It must be payable to a specified person. The bill of exchange must be a self-contained document; it should not refer to obligations set out in other documents or to any contingent factors. A bill of exchange must be signed; the lack of signatures, too, would make it incomplete.

There are three parties to a bill of exchange: the drawer (usually the seller in the transaction, the person who issues the bill); the drawee (usually the buyer, the recipient); the payee (usually the seller or the seller's banker, the party to whom the bill is payable). The bill of exchange can be payable immediately (referred to as "at sight") or at a specified future date (for example, payable at 30 days sight).

Cheques

"A cheque is a bill of exchange drawn on a banker payable on demand"— this is the definition of cheques set out in s 73 of the Bills of Exchange Act 1882. The provisions of that Act, which apply to bills of exchange payable on demand, also apply to cheques, but "a cheque is a very different kind of animal" to a bill of exchange.[4] The bank may or may not pay on foot of the cheque, depending on whether the account is in funds or an overdraft facility has been agreed. A cheque must be presented for payment within a reasonable time of its issue,[5] and a reasonable time is determined by consideration of the facts of each case and the usage of trade and of bankers. Two aspects stand in particular contrast between cheques and bills of exchange:

> A cheque is a payment direction; it is usually intended to be presented and paid promptly (in the Republic of Ireland cheques usually go out of date after six months from the date of issue).

---

[3] s 3, Bills of Exchange Act 1882.
[4] Goode, *Commercial Law*, at 569.
[5] s 74, Bills of Exchange Act 1882.

The use of cheques creates legal relationships between the collecting bank (whose customer is the payee) and its customer and between the paying bank (where the drawer keeps his account) and its customer.

It normally takes three business days for a cheque to clear in Ireland. The cheque has to travel from the collecting bank's clearing department to the paying bank's clearing department.

Crossing Cheques

A cheque crossing is an instruction made to the bank by the drawer to make payment only to a banker. It means the cheque will be cashed into a bank account, so it is a protection against theft. If the bank is not named, the instruction will be called a "general crossing", because payment can be made to any bank. For a cheque to be crossed, generally it must bear one of two additional things across its face: (1) The words *"and company"* (or any abbreviation of that) between two parallel transverse lines, either with or without the words "not negotiable"; or (2) two parallel transverse lines simply, either with or without the words "not negotiable".[6]

If the crossing bears the name of a specific bank, then the instruction is called a "special crossing". A cheque that is specially crossed will bear across its face the name of the banker, either with or without the words "not negotiable". If a crossing is made, it is unlawful for any person to "obliterate or…add to or alter the crossing".[7]

If a cheque were crossed specially to more than one banker, usually the banker on whom it is drawn must refuse to pay out on foot of it (the exception is when the cheque is crossed to an agent of the bank).[8] An error in this regard can leave the bank liable to the true owner of the cheque for any loss sustained. Bankers can avail of a defence where they have acted "in good faith and without negligence".[9]

---

[6] s 76, Bills of Exchange Act 1882.
[7] s 78, Bills of Exchange Act 1882.
[8] s 79, Bills of Exchange Act 1882.
[9] s 80, Bills of Exchange Act 1882.

Duty of Banks

The relationship between bank and customer is governed by the law of contract. Banks invariably offer retail customers standard terms ad conditions which, when accepted, govern the relationship. One Irish judge described the relationship of banks to customers in this way: "The relation of a bank to its customer is that of debtor to creditor. A bank can, and, indeed must, diminish its indebtedness to the customer by obeying the mandate of the customer to pay away to third parties moneys up to the amount which the bank owes the customer, or, in other words, which is standing to the credit of the customer's current account".[10] Put another way, banks owe their customers the money which the customers have put into their bank accounts, and banks must follow the customer's instructions when it comes to paying that money out. To some, it is initially a startling realisation—perhaps because we used to be taught to think of the bank as a safe haven for our money, and of the bank as the one doing *us* the favour—that "[w]hen a depositor makes a deposit with a bank he is essentially lending the money to the bank".[11]

It is the duty of banks

> "to honour cheques drawn on a given branch provided that the presented cheques are in legal form and provided that the customer's account is in sufficient and available credit to meet the amount of the cheques".[12]

If more cheques are drawn by a customer than his account is able to meet, the bank has a duty "to use discretion, having regard to the interests of the customer, as to which cheques should be paid". This is part of the paying function of the bank, and arises out of the contractual relationship between bank and customer (the drawer of the cheque). The bank has no duty to the payee of one of those cheques (even if the payee happened to be a customer in a different branch of that bank). The reason behind this clear-cut duty to the drawer and not to the payee is to avoid confusion, and to

---

[10] *Per* O'Connor LJ, *Reade v Royal Bank of Ireland* [1922] 2 IR 22 at 26–27.
[11] Breslin, *Banking Law*, 3rd ed., Round Hall 2013, at 125.
[12] *Per* Henchy J (slightly adapted), *Dublin Port and Docks Board v Bank of Ireland* [1976] 1 IR 118 at 135.

avoid bringing into conflict the paying and collecting functions of the bank. If there were a duty to both drawer and payee, the bank, in some circumstances, could not act with an even hand towards both parties: it would necessarily have to prefer one. It could also result in "the unfair preferment of a payee who happened to be a customer in another branch of the bank over a payee who happened not to be a customer".[13]

So, the bank's duty to a customer is to honour cheques which are drawn on accounts which are in credit, and to use discretion. The bank has no duty to give advice to a customer, but if it does give advice, it must give it with reasonable care. A bank has no duty to tell a customer about a better account which is available. A bank also has a duty of confidentiality to its customers. This has been recognised in terms of public interest, rather than simply an element of the contractual duty.[14] The duty and right of confidentiality is not absolute.[15] It can be waived by the customer himself, if the customer asks the bank to provide him with a reference for another lending institution; under compulsion of law, i.e. as a result of some piece of statute (for example, legislation which provides for investigations into companies); as a result of the discovery process in legal proceedings; or by obligations under the money laundering legislation.[16]

A bank may be sued by a customer in tort—for negligence, for example, or in defamation (for example, for mistakenly informing another customer that your cheque could not be honoured because you were indebted to the bank).

The customer has two established duties to the bank (the courts have not expanded these duties over the decades): (1) a duty not to draw a cheque in such a way that would make fraud or forgery easy (like writing it in pencil); (2) a duty to inform the bank of any forgery of a cheque. A third duty has been posited, either as a branch of the duty to mitigate your loss, or a "new duty in the age of electronic banking": the duty to look after one's banking cards and security data (passwords).[17]

---

[13] ibid at 136.
[14] National Irish Bank Ltd v RTE [1998] 2 IR 465 (see Lynch J at 494).
[15] Per Clarke J, Cooper Flynn v RTE [2000] 3 IR 344 at p 351.
[16] Criminal Justice (Money Laundering and Terrorist Financing) Act 2010.
[17] Breslin, Banking Law, at 222.

Promissory Notes

Bills of exchange and cheques are categorised as "orders to pay". There is another branch of instrument which are categorised as "promises to pay". Banknotes, bearer bonds, treasury bills and promissory notes are in this second category. A promissory note

> "is an unconditional promise in writing made by one person to another...engaging to pay on demand or at a fixed or determinable future time, a sum certain in money, to, or to the order of, a specified person or to bearer".[18]

The promissory note became famous in Ireland in 2010 when the government issued notes amounting to over €30bn to three financial institutions, and again in 2013, when the government restructured our banking debt in a way that would result in the taxpayer benefitting from lower interest rates on the notes as opposed to the rates on the bonds.[19]

In *Williamson v Rider*[20] the court considered a document which said:

> "In consideration of the loan of £100...from Mr. S.J. Garrod...I John Rider...agree to repay to Mr. S.J. Garrod the sum of £100... on or before Dec. 31, 1956".

The court decided that this document was not a promissory note according to the above definition because the words "on or before Dec. 31, 1956" gave the payer an option to repay on any day of his choosing before that date. This meant that it was not an unconditional promise to pay at a fixed future time. In *Claydon v Bradley*[21] the court considered a similar document. In that case, the promise was to pay money back "in full by 1st July 1983". The court again decided that the document contained an option to pay at an earlier date than the fixed date, and so some uncertainty was created and the promise was not one to pay at a fixed future time, therefore the note was not a promissory note.

---

[18] s 83, Bills of Exchange Act 1882.
[19] See *Hall v Minister for Finance* [2013] IEHC 39 (Kearns P).
[20] [1962] 2 All ER 268.
[21] [1987] 1 All ER 522.

The opposite conclusion was reached by the Irish High Court in *Creative Press Ltd v Harman*[22] where each of the defendants promised to pay the plaintiffs "on or before the 1st day of November, 1970" the sum of £2,000 for value received. The court stated:

> "In my opinion the fact that the defendants in the present case had an option to pay the sum of £2,000 before the 1st November, 1970, and that the plaintiffs would have had to accept such payment, does not mean that the defendants did not engage to pay the money at a fixed future time. They could not be made to pay on any date prior to the 1st November, 1970, and this in my opinion is the all-important factor. Therefore, I hold that the document is a promissory note and that the first point made by the defendants fails".[23]

This view expressed by the High Court in *Creative Press Ltd v Harman* would appear to be the correct statement of current Irish law.

Contrasting Promissory Notes with Bills of Exchange

A promissory note exists between two parties, the one who makes the promise (the promisor) and the one to whom the promise is made (the promisee); it is a promise to pay as opposed to an order to pay, and it is complete when delivered to the promisee. A bill of exchange, in contrast, involves three parties (drawer, drawee and payee), is an *order* to pay, and is complete once it has been drawn up and signed.

Conclusions

- A bill of exchange allows for trade credit by allowing payments to be made on agreed future dates.
- The law in relation to them was codified in the UK and Ireland in the Bills of Exchange Act 1882, so it is important to be familiar with the definitions provided there.

---

[22] [1973] IR 313, Pringle J, approving the decision of the five judges of the Supreme Court of Canada in *John Burrows Ltd v Subsurface Surveys Ltd* [1968] SCR 607 (Can).

[23] *Per* Pringle J, [1973] IR 313 at p 317. See also A H Hudson, "Time and Promissory Notes" (1962) 25 MLR 593, where it is suggested, referring to *Clayton v Gosling* (1826) 5 B & C 360, 108 ER 134, that a time of payment, in relation to a promissory note, is only contingent if it is a "time which may or may not arrive".

- A cheque is a payment direction.
- A cheque crossing is an instruction made to the bank by the drawer to make payment only to a banker.
- The relationship between bank and customer is governed by the law of contract (but note that a bank may be sued by a customer in tort—for negligence, for example, or in defamation).
- A promissory note is a "promise to pay" a specific sum of money at a fixed future time to, or to the order of, a specified person.

INSURANCE

Introduction

We have come across insurance contracts in Chapter 10. There we were learning about the rule that insurance contracts are contracts of the utmost good faith (*"uberrimae fidei"*), about the obligation to make full disclosure and the right of insurance companies to rescind a contract for non-disclosure. Insurance is a massive business. According to the most recent figures, insurance companies pay out more than €5.4bn in claims each year to Irish customers and contribute €1.6bn in tax to the Revenue. The insurance industry employs more than 27,000 people and holds €200bn in assets in Ireland.[1] But these are not the matters we are concerned with in this chapter. This chapter is about defining what a contract of insurance is and introducing various concepts that are important in this area of the law.

Definition of Insurance

One of the leading texts on insurance law says that a satisfactory definition of insurance is "elusive" but that a good attempt was made over a hundred years ago in *Prudential Insurance v Inland Revenue Commissioners*.[2] There, the judge offered this definition: a contract of insurance is one

> "whereby one party (the insurer) promises in return for a money consideration (the premium) to pay to the other party (the assured[3]) a sum of money, or to provide him with a corresponding benefit upon the occurrence of one or more specified events".[4]

Indemnity

One of the core principles of insurance is indemnity. By entering into a contract for insurance, a person will be indemnified for loss suffered. The insured will recover under a policy when he shows loss suffered. The courts have held that a person should be "fully indemnified but shall

---

[1] Insurance Ireland, Annual Report 2013.
[2] [1904] 2 KB 658 (Channell J).
[3] Note that "the assured" and "the insured person" are the same thing.
[4] Birds, *MacGillivray on Insurance Law*, 12th ed., Sweet & Maxwell 2012, at para 1-001.

never be more than fully indemnified".[5] The idea here is that—say in a case where property is insured—a person should not be paid more than the property is worth. Litigation can arise when the property had deteriorated in value since the insurance policy was entered into. In such cases, the contract might provide for the cost of re-instatement (i.e. rebuilding the building as good as new) or the contract might provide that the insurer will pay out in accordance with the market value of the building.

Insurable Interest

What is the interest of the insured in the subject matter of the insurance? The insured must have some legal relationship to the person or thing he is insuring. You might insure the life of your spouse, the health of your children, your house against flooding, your car against damage. In each case, the law recognises a relationship between you and the subject matter of the insurance. Our laws do not allow people to take out insurance policies on people they do not know or things they do not own. It might be that you do not own the property outright, but have a beneficial interest in it; that is still an insurable interest. For example, in *PJ Carrigan Ltd v Norwich Union Fire Society Ltd*[6], there were two plaintiffs. The first was a company, PJ Carrigan Ltd. The second was PJ Carrigan himself. The case concerned a house which burnt down; the house was owned by the company but insured by PJ Carrigan. The judge said that through the company, the second plaintiff "had a substantial if not the entire beneficial interest" in the house in question.[7] Therefore, the second plaintiff, Mr Carrigan, had an insurable interest in the house. The leading Irish text on insurance says that the Irish courts "have taken a liberal approach to finding an insurable interest, and a right to claim under fire insurance policies".[8]

---

[5] *Castellain v Preston* [1883] 11 QBD 380 (Brett LJ).
[6] Unreported, High Court, Lynch J, 11 December 1987.
[7] The plaintiffs' case was dismissed because the judge found "as a matter of high probability that the fire was started deliberately by the second Plaintiff".
[8] Buckley, *Insurance Law*, 3rd ed., Thomson Reuters, 2012, at para 4-35, citing *Brady v Irish Land Commission* [1921] 1 IR 56.

Subrogation

Subrogation is the right of an insurer to pursue a third party which caused loss to the insured party. In legal phraseology, we speak of the insured being subrogated into the insured's right of action. If the insurer pays out under the policy, but believes that other persons are also liable, the insurer is entitled "by subrogation to recover from the others a contribution of the proportions of what he has paid commensurate with the liability of such others" to the same person who had been insured.[9] Subrogation means that "the insurer [is] placed in the position of the assured".[10] In such situations, the case is still taken in the name of the insured person, even when it is the insurance company which is pursuing the action; the insured person might have agreed to assign his rights to the insured ("assignment"), in which case the insurer may bring proceedings in its own name. Often, an insurance contract will contain a clause which obliges the insured to take a case, for example, in material damages claims (e.g. one car crashes into another). If the insured person allowed the time limit to expire—meaning the claim would be out of time—the insurance company could recover damages against the insured because the insured's inaction meant it lost its opportunity to recover against the would-be defendant.

Contribution

A person may have taken out two policies with two different insurance companies on the one subject matter. If an event took place which entitled him to compensation under his policies, he would not be allowed to claim on both, on the basis that a person may not be compensated twice for the same loss (the principle of "unjust enrichment"). He would be entitled to be paid in full by one of the insurance companies, and that company could then seek a "contribution" from the other one. If Insurer No. 1 pays out, the liability of Insurer No. 2 is discharged. The right of Insurer No. 1 to insist on a contribution from Insurer No. 2 comes into being when Insurer No. 1 pays out under the policy.

---

[9] *Zurich Insurance Co v Shield Insurance Co Ltd* [1988] IR 174 at 177.
[10] *Per* Brett LJ, *Castellain v Preston* [1883] 11 QBD 380 at 388.

Proposal Forms and Cover Notes

A proposal form is the contract of insurance; it is offered to the person seeking insurance, who fills it out and returns it. When it is filled out, it becomes his application for insurance. It will have canvassed all relevant issues, and sought full disclosure on all matters. It will usually contain full details of the standard cover offered. A cover note is the provision by an insurer of temporary cover—for example, in fire, burglary and motor insurance contracts—for the period during which the insurer is considering the proposal form. Insurers may issue their agents with cover notes, impliedly or expressly conferring authority on them to issue this kind of temporary insurance cover.

Types of Insurance

Life Insurance

A number of acts govern the provision of life insurance: the Life Assurance (Ireland) Act 1886, the Assurance Companies Act 1909 and the Insurance Act 1936. Irish law says that you may insure the lives of almost all your close relatives (English law is stricter, and says that a parent must have some pecuniary interest in the life of a child to insure the child's life). The key concept is "insurable interest", discussed above. If a child under the age of sixteen is working, a parent will have an insurable interest on the child's life, but the insurable interest cannot exceed the value of the child's term of service, i.e. if the child is working on a weekly or monthly basis, that is the extent of the insurable interest—this is a piece of law that, to the modern ear, has a very Victorian ring to it.[11] A life insurance policy is payable upon proof of death (production of the death certificate) and the title of the claimant to the policy.[12]

Fire Insurance

For a person to recover under a fire policy there must be "ignition of insured property which was not intended to be ignited".[13] Damage

---

[11] *MacGillivray on Insurance Law*, at para 1-098.
[12] Life Insurance and Life Assurance are two different types of insurance from a financial viewpoint, however the principles of *upmost good faith* apply to both.
[13] *Harris v Poland* [1941] 1 KB 462 at 473.

caused by excessive heat, where there is no ignition, will not trigger the policy. If the ignition occurred on an adjoining property and spreads to the insured property, it does not matter that the ignition did not begin on the insured property. Damage caused by lightening is not damage by fire, unless the lightening causes ignition. The key question will be whether the fire was the proximate cause of the loss. If the fire gets worse as a result of bona fide attempts to extinguish it, that damage too will be included in the loss which is compensatable.[14] Deliberate acts causing fire are not compensatable. Negligence, however, is not necessarily fatal. The onus of proof is on the insurer to prove that the fire was started wilfully, once the insured has proven that loss by fire occurred.

Motor Insurance[15]

Motor insurance covers a number of factors: loss or damage to the vehicle, loss arising out of personal injuries or death, third party risks and litigation costs associated with third party risks, loss or damage to items contained in the car, the cost of a temporary replacement vehicle. Motor vehicle insurance is dealt with in Ireland in the Road Traffic Acts 1961–2006. Motorists are obliged to take out insurance (something that has been compulsory here since 1933).[16] It is a criminal offence not to be insured against causing injury to third parties while driving.

Conclusions

- A contract of insurance is one "whereby one party (the insurer) promises in return for a money consideration (the premium) to pay to the other party (the assured) a sum of money, or to provide him with a corresponding benefit upon the occurrence of one or more specified events".
- The courts have held that a person should be "fully indemnified but shall never be more than fully indemnified".

---

[14] *Stanley v Western Insurance Co* (1868) LR 3 Ex 71.
[15] For a comprehensive treatment, see Buckley, *Insurance Law*, Chapter 8.
[16] Road Traffic Act 1961, s 56(1); see also SI No 14 of 1962 and the SIs which implement EU directives.

- The insured must have some legal relationship to the person or thing he is insuring (a beneficial interest will do). This idea is known as the insurable interest.
- Subrogation means that the insurer is placed in the position of the assured.
- Contribution occurs where two insurers are insuring the same subject matter. When one of them pays out, it will seek a contribution from the other insurer. The insured is not entitled to compensation from both insurers, because this would amount to unjust enrichment.
- A cover note is temporary cover, issued for the period when the insurer is considering the proposal form which has been filled out by the insurance-seeker.

CORPORATE INSOLVENCY

Introduction

This chapter covers the three main areas of corporate insolvency: receivership, examinership and liquidation.

PART I

Receivership

When companies borrow from lending institutions there will usually be a term in the loan agreement which says that in the event of default the lender will be entitled to appoint a receiver. The most common event of default is a failure to make repayments. It usually signifies insolvency. In such cases, the lender will appoint a receiver, whose role is to take control of the charged asset and realise its value. The receiver may be appointed over one asset only, or over all the assets of the company, or over the business itself: it will depend on what the terms of the agreement say. The decision to appoint a receiver is a purely commercial one; there is no duty on the part of the lending institution to think of the consequences for the borrower.

A receiver has the power to do "all things necessary or convenient" which need to be done to attain the objectives for which he was appointed.[1] A list of the receiver's powers is set out in the CA 2014 at section 437. The following powers are a representative sample, indicative of the wide powers a receiver enjoys over a charged asset:

- To enter into possession and take control of property of the company in accordance with the terms of the debenture.
- To lease, let on hire or dispose of property of the company.
- To borrow money on the security of property of the company.
- To carry on any business of the company.
- To appoint a solicitor, accountant or other professionally qualified person to assist him.

The Companies Act 2014 states that a receiver is personally liable on any contract entered into by him in the performance of his functions,[2]

---

[1] CA 2014, s 437.
[2] CA 2014, s 438(3).

but in practice the receiver's contract with the debenture holder usually states that the receiver will not be personally liable for his dealings (as long as he is not negligent) and that he will receive an indemnity out of the assets of the company. The receiver is paid out of the assets of the company.

Notification of Receiver's Appointment

Where a receiver is appointed, every document on which the name of the company appears must contain a statement that a receiver has been appointed (for example: invoices, orders for goods, business letters).[3] Once a receiver is appointed, all emails sent by the company must state that the company is in receivership, and any website of the company must say it too. That information must be given a prominent position on the website. The idea behind this is that all third parties dealing with the company are fully aware of the state of play.

Agency of the Receiver

The receiver is the agent of the company, but a receiver's agency is different from all other kinds of agency.[4] He does not owe the company directors any duties. He does not have to consider alternative plans they suggest, keep them au fait with the company's affairs, or provide them with information (they are only entitled to the same information as every other prospective purchaser).

Duty of the Receiver

The key duty of a receiver is to exercise all reasonable care in selling the property of the company, in order to obtain the best price reasonably obtainable for the property as at the time of sale.[5] This duty was considered at great length in an Irish case called *Ruby Property Co. Ltd v Kilty*.[6] Among the points noted by the judge were the following:

---

[3] CA 2014, s 429. Default in this regard is a category 4 offence, i.e. liability for a fine of up to €5,000.
[4] *Irish Oil and Cake Mills Ltd v Donnelly*, Unreported, High Court, 27 March 1983, where at 6 Costello J said the receiver had an "exceptional status".
[5] CA 2014, s 439.
[6] Unreported, High Court, McKechnie J, 1 January 2003.

(1) Whether "the best price" reasonably obtainable was in fact obtained is a matter of historical fact to be established through admissible evidence. (2) The receiver is not required to postpone, defer or cancel a sale in the hope of the market improving. (3) The duty a receiver owes to guarantors does not extend to unsecured creditors. There is no duty owed to unsecured creditors. (4) A receiver is not bound in any preset way to adopt a specified approach in how he particularises the property or asset in sale, and there are no predetermined, fixed or rigid rules by which such disposal of property must take place.[7] In *Re Bula Ltd*[8] the sale by the receiver of the company's property was challenged, but the challenge failed because the bid accepted by the receiver was the only realistic one which had been made. In *Lambert Jones Estates Limited v Donnelly*[9] the allegations of negligence against a receiver failed because the alternative plan which was put forward by the directors and rejected by the receiver was dependent on a number of contingencies, and to opt for that plan could have resulted in more costs to the already insolvent company; furthermore, there was no guarantee the alternative plan would succeed. Similarly, in *Re Edenfell Holdings Limited*[10] the Supreme Court held that, where a receiver is faced with two offers, he is free to opt for the lower bid if the higher bid comes with conditions which render it uncertain.

PART II

Examinership

"Examinership" is neither a catchy title nor self-explanatory. This area of Irish law could be called corporate rescue. The idea is to save a company which is heading towards insolvency, or which is already insolvent, by affording it court protection for a short period of time during which the company's creditors cannot pursue their remedies against it and a qualified insolvency practitioner will be appointed to put forward a plan to save the company, which may involve restructuring and debt write-downs.

---

[7] Those points are part quotation, part paraphrase, and are not exhaustive. See pages 14–19 of the judgment.

[8] Unreported, High Court, Murphy J, 20 June 2002.

[9] Unreported, High Court, O'Hanlon J, 5 November 1982.

[10] [1999] 1 IR 443.

Criteria for Admission to Examinership

A company may apply for examinership if it can show the court that it is, or is likely to be, unable to pay its debts (the usual thing to do is to show inability to pay debts "as they fall due"). It must also show that no order for the winding up of the company has been made, and that there is no existing resolution to wind up the company.[11] The court will only admit a company into examinership where it is satisfied that "there is a reasonable prospect of survival of the company (or any part of its undertaking) as a going concern".[12] Even if a company can get past the test for admission to examinership, it is not entitled to admission as of right. The court has a wide discretion in this regard.[13] Examinership, which was introduced in Ireland in 1990, was only ever available in the High Court, but in an effort to reduce costs for small and medium companies, the government made the process available in the Circuit Court in 2014.[14]

Bringing an Examinership Petition

The person who asks the court to put the company into examinership is called "the petitioner". The company may petition on its own behalf, as may the directors, creditors, or a shareholder or shareholders, as long as he/she/they hold not less than 10% of the paid-up share capital of the company on the date of the presentation of the petition. The petitioner should come to court with an independent expert's report.[15] What should be included in this report is set out under s 511 of CA 2014, but the key thing is the independent expert's opinion that a "scheme of arrangement" would offer the company a reasonable prospect of survival as a going concern. While this is an opinion, it must be backed up with realistic projections, analysis and evidence, and not be "mere assertions" or couched in mere "management-speak".[16] It is important that the company will survive as a going concern; a company which would only survive to carry on low-level activity, such as receiving rental income on properties it

---

[11] CA 2014, s 509(1).
[12] CA 2014, s 509(2).
[13] *Per* Fennelly J in *Re Gallium Ltd* [2009] 2 ILRM 11.
[14] CA 2014, s 509(10).
[15] CA 2014, s 511.
[16] *Re Vantive Holdings* [2010] 2 IR 118.

owned while struggling to pay off outstanding interest on loans, would be considered "essentially passive", and would not be admitted to examinership.[17]

The petitioner and the expert have a duty to act in the utmost good faith,[18] but the aim of saving jobs is so important that sometimes the courts have had to overlook a lack of candour.[19] If a company fails to enter into examinership, it may be forced into liquidation; the courts are aware that, in a liquidation, the creditors may do even worse than if they have to take a write-down on the debt owed to them in examinership.[20]

Effect of Examinership on Creditors

Creditors must be heard before a petition is dismissed or an order appointing an examiner is made.[21] If a receiver stands appointed to the company, he can be displaced if the company seeks examinership within three days of his appointment (put another way, a receiver cannot be displaced if *in situ* for three working days or more).[22] In an examinership, all remedies of creditors against the company are frozen. Creditors can issue no proceedings to wind up the company, no receiver may be appointed, no action may be taken to realise any security, no steps taken to repossess goods in the company's possession.[23] The courts recognise that the entry of a company into examinership can have "serious consequences for the creditors, given the fact that their nominal remedies remain in abeyance",[24] but this recognition is small comfort to the creditors.

Powers of an Examiner

The examiner does not displace the board of directors, but he can apply to do so.[25] He has power to convene general meetings of the company, to

---

[17] *Re Tivway* [2010] 3 IR 49 at 72.
[18] CA 2014, s 518.
[19] *Re Seluwke Ltd*, High Court, Costello J, 20 December 1991.
[20] *Re Pelko Holdings Ltd* [2014] IEHC 226 (Hogan J).
[21] CA 2014, s 515.
[22] CA 2014, s 522.
[23] CA 2014, s 520.
[24] *Per* Keane J in *Re Butler's Engineering Ltd* (Unreported, High Court, 1 March 1996) at 10.
[25] CA 2014, s 528.

preside at board meetings and to propose resolutions at either. He is entitled to notice of meetings and entitled to take "whatever steps necessary" to halt, prevent or rectify the effects of any thing done which in his opinion is likely to be to the detriment of the company.[26] The examiner can repudiate contracts made before the protection period, and repudiate negative pledge clauses.[27] If the examiner thinks that selling off an asset which is the subject of a floating charge would facilitate the survival of the company, he may do so.[28] Officers of the company have a duty to produce documents and evidence to the examiner.[29] Any liabilities incurred by the company during the examinership—which the examiner certifies as having been necessary for the survival of the company—will be treated as expenses properly incurred.[30]

Scheme of Arrangement

As soon as the examiner is appointed, he must formulate proposals for a scheme of arrangement, or a compromise.[31] These must be put to the company's creditors and members. The examiner must report back to the court. Protection lasts for 70 days but, on the application of the examiner, the court may extend it to 100. Before the court confirms the examiner's proposals it must be satisfied that they are fair and equitable to any class of creditors which has not accepted them.[32] If the examiner is unable to secure agreement from the creditors to his proposals, the court might order than the company be wound up.[33] A successful examinership ends when the compromise or the scheme of arrangement comes into effect.

---

[26] CA 2014, s 524.

[27] CA 2014, s 525. (A negative pledge clause is a promise made by the company to the first lender not to pledge any more of its assets as security to an alternative lender, if such pledge would result in a decrease in the value of the first lender's security).

[28] CA 2014, s 530.

[29] CA 2014, s 526.

[30] CA 2014, s 529.

[31] CA 2014, s 539.

[32] CA 2014, s 541(4).

[33] CA 2014, s 535.

PART III

Liquidation: General Introduction

When a liquidator is appointed to a company, he takes the seal, the books and records, and all the company's property into his possession.[34] It is the liquidator's job to gather in all the assets and to distribute them to the creditors in accordance with the priority rules, and to make distributions in accordance with the *pari passu* principle when it comes to unsecured creditors.[35] In a liquidation the holder of a fixed charge stands outside the winding up, unaffected by it.[36] The liquidator's fees are paid first. Next to be paid are the preferential creditors (the employees, up to just over €3,000, and the Revenue). Next comes any floating charge holder, followed by the unsecured creditors. If any company asset was disposed of in any way, and the effect of this was to perpetrate a fraud on the company, its creditors or members, the court can order that the asset be delivered back to the liquidator.[37] If the liquidator is of the opinion that a related company should contribute to the debts of the company being wound up, the liquidator can ask the court to approve this, and the court will do so if it is "just and equitable".[38] If two or more related companies are being wound up, the liquidator can ask the court's permission to wind them up as if they were one company, i.e. to pool their assets.[39] Again, the court will allow this if it is just and equitable.

There are three different winding up processes: (1) court-ordered winding up, (2) members' voluntary winding up and (3) creditors' voluntary winding up. One of the innovations of the Companies Act 2014 is that once a court orders the winding up of a company, the winding up takes place like a members' voluntary winding up (previously there was more court supervision). The new regime makes creditors more involved, and the court less involved, in the winding up process. This is a very detailed and technical area, one which, in a leading company law textbook,

---

[34] CA 2014, s 596.

[35] The *pari passu* principle is that all unsecured creditors are paid an equal percentage of the debt owed to them.

[36] Unless the fixed charge is over book debts, in which case the Revenue can serve notice that debts owed to it must be paid out of the book debts.

[37] CA 2014, s 608.

[38] CA 2014, s 599.

[39] CA 2014, s 560.

receives an eighty-page treatment.[40] That, however, is a text for practitioners, which goes through the statute section by section and discusses all relevant case law. That level of detail is not possible or desirable in this context, where our aim is to provide an introduction to the area for business students, so what follows is an outline of the three ways companies can be wound up.

Court-Ordered Winding Up

A company may be wound up by the court in a number of circumstances.[41] The most common way is when a petition is presented by a creditor of the company stating that the company is unable to pay its debts. Other circumstances include: if the company has passed a special resolution resolving that the company be wound up by the court; if the court believes it is "just and equitable" to wind it up; if the Director of Corporate Enforcement petitions on the basis that the winding up is in the public interest. The minimum indebtedness threshold is €10,000. If a creditor to whom the company is indebted by €10,000 or more serves a letter of demand on the company, and within 21 days of that letter the sum remains unpaid, this will be proof of inability to pay debts.[42] The process should not be used for any ulterior motive, for example, a desire to stymie an action the company intended to take against the petitioner.[43] The debt should be bona fide and not disputed.[44] It is an abuse of process to petition where the debt is disputed. The company can sue in tort for "malicious presentation of a winding up petition".

An application to wind up a company is done by way of petition. The petition may be presented by the company, any creditor(s) or any contributory or contributories. It can be presented by any of them acting alone or all of them acting together.[45] If the court believes a winding up is the correct course of action, it may appoint a liquidator. A court-ordered

---

[40] Thomas B Courtney, *Law of Companies*, 3rd ed., Bloomsbury 2012.
[41] CA 2014, s 569.
[42] CA 2014, s 570. The alternatives are set out in s 570(b), (c) and (d).
[43] *Re Goode Concrete* [2012] IEHC 439; see also *Re Genport Ltd* (Unreported, High Court, McCracken J, 21 November 1996).
[44] *Re Pageboy Couriers Ltd* [1983] ILRM 510; *Re Forrest Lennon BSS* [2011] IEHC 523.
[45] CA 2014, s 571.

winding up commences at the time of the presentation of the petition.[46] The court can order that the winding up be conducted as if it were a members' voluntary winding up.[47]

Members' Voluntary Winding Up

A members' voluntary winding up ("MVW") is commenced by the Summary Approval Procedure.[48] This means that a resolution to wind up is passed by the company. Within fourteen days of the passing of the resolution, it must be advertised in Iris Oifigiúil.[49] The advantage of this kind of winding up is that the company gets to appoint the liquidator.[50] A company is only allowed to use this process where it will be able to pay its debts in full within a period of not more than twelve months after the commencement of the winding up.[51] The directors have to swear that this is true (the "declaration of solvency"). A voluntary winding up is deemed to commence at the time of the passing of the resolution for voluntary winding up.[52] Voluntary liquidations have always cost less than court-ordered liquidations, meaning creditors and shareholders have always stood a better chance of being paid a higher percentage of what they were owed.

Creditors' Voluntary Winding Up

If a creditor feels that the directors made the declaration of solvency without a sufficiently firm basis, the creditor may apply to court to have the members' voluntary winding up turned into a creditors' voluntary winding up ("CVW").[53] This application would have to be made within 30 days of the appearance in Iris Oifigiúil of the MVW notice. If that happens, and if a liquidator was in place, the liquidator must deliver a copy of the court order which converted the MVW into a CVW to the Companies Registration Office. In theory, it should not need to happen,

[46] CA 2014, s 589.
[47] CA 2014, s 572(4); see s 589(2) for the commencement of that kind of winding up.
[48] CA 2014, s 579(2) (unless the company was one of fixed duration—but this is not an issue that is usually investigated in a course which introduces aspects of business law).
[49] CA 2014, s 581—failure to do so is a category 3 offence.
[50] CA 2014, s 583.
[51] CA 2014, s 580.
[52] CA 2014, s 590.
[53] CA 2014, s 582.

because if the liquidator in a MVW forms the view that, in fact, the company will not be able to pay its debts in full within the period stated in the directors' declaration of solvency, he has a series of tasks to perform involving calling meetings, providing information to creditors, and ultimately, ensuring that the winding up becomes a CVW.[54]

A winding up can begin life as a CVW.[55] The company may pass a resolution resolving that it cannot continue business due to its liabilities, and should be wound up by CVW. The company might summon the creditors to that meeting, or schedule one for the following day.[56] The company has to give each creditor ten days' notice in writing of such a meeting. The directors prepare a full statement of the company's affairs for the creditors' meeting. It is the creditors who nominate the liquidator. If the company wants to appoint a different liquidator, it is usually the will of the creditors which prevails.[57]

Conclusions

- A receiver will be appointed upon the happening of an event of default. The most common event of default is a failure to make repayments. It usually signifies insolvency.
- A receiver has a broad range of powers which are set out in the CA 2014, s 437.
- The receiver's agency is exceptional. He does not owe the company directors any duties. His key duty is to exercise all reasonable care in selling the property of the company, in order to obtain the best price reasonably obtainable for the property as at the time of sale.
- A company can apply for examinership when it is, or is likely to be, unable to pay its debts. The key thing to show is that, if admitted to examinership, "there is a reasonable prospect of survival of the company (or any part of its undertaking) as a going concern". Court protection usually lasts for 70 days.

---

[54] CA 2014, s 584.
[55] CA 2014, s 586.
[56] CA 2014, s 587.
[57] CA 2014, s 588(2); see also ss 588(4) and (5).

- The remedies of creditors are frozen once a company is admitted into examinership.
- A successful examinership ends when the compromise or the scheme of arrangement comes into effect.
- It is the liquidator's job to gather in all the assets and distribute them to the creditors in accordance with the Companies Act 2014.
- The most common reason for the court to wind up a company is inability to pay its debts.
- The court can order that the winding up be conducted as if it were a members' voluntary winding up.
- A company should be solvent in order to begin a members' voluntary winding up.
- If creditors feel that a company which has begun a members' voluntary winding up is not solvent, it can apply to have the MVW converted into a creditors' voluntary winding up.

CHAPTER TWENTY ONE

Introduction to European Law

Development of the European Union

The EU is an economic and political partnership between 28 European countries (Member States) created out of the aftermath of World War II and a desire to create unity and avoid conflict in Europe. What began as a purely economic union has evolved into an organisation spanning different policy areas, from development aid to the environment. Reflecting this, the name of this partnership has changed from the European *Economic* Community to the European *Community* to the European Union.

Ireland joined the then European Economic Community (EEC) in 1973 after a constitutional amendment in 1972; this allowed European legislative supremacy over our domestic laws. Further treaties followed the original establishing treaties, which strengthened, enlarged and expanded the scope of the EU.[1] Since 2004 the EU had been struggling in its attempts to adopt a constitutional treaty; the treaty's rejection resulted in the compromise of the Treaty of Lisbon, which provided for some reforms, but in a more modest manner than originally envisaged.

The original European Union project, based on cooperation, freedom for working people and long-term goals of unity and strength, now faces an uncertain future, given the economic crisis and an increasingly German-led monetary policy.

---

[1] The following are the most notable EU treaties: The Treaty of Rome (1957); The Merger Treaty (1965): this treaty was signed between the founding states of the European Coal and Steel Community (ECSC) and the European Economic Community (EEC) on 8 April 1965 and resulted in the creation of the first joint institutions; The Schengen Agreement (1985): this treaty resulted in abolition of the border checks between the members of the then EEC; The Single European Act (1986): this treaty was signed between twelve members of the EEC—it revised the Treaty of Rome and provided the basis for the foundation of a single market. It also formalised European Political Cooperation, the precursor of the EU's Common Foreign and Security Policy; The Maastricht Treaty (1992) formally created the EU but also laid the foundation for the formation of the eurozone; The Amsterdam Treaty (1997) defined EU citizenship and individuals' rights in terms of justice, freedom and security. It also dealt with the Common Foreign and Security Policy and the reform of the EU institutions in future enlargements; The Treaty of Lisbon (2007) aimed to complete the reform process started by the Amsterdam Treaty. It entered into force on 1 December 2009.

Institutions of the EU[2]

The institutional framework is composed of seven different institutions, outlined below. It is worth taking an over-arching approach to looking at the EU institutions, considering them in constitutional terms. The European Parliament and the Council together make up the EU's legislature—they are like the two chambers or houses of a bi-cameral parliament; the Commission is the EU's executive—making policy, policing compliance with law and carrying out executive and other regulatory functions; and the Court of Justice is the EU's judiciary.

Figure 1: *The legislature and executive of the EU*

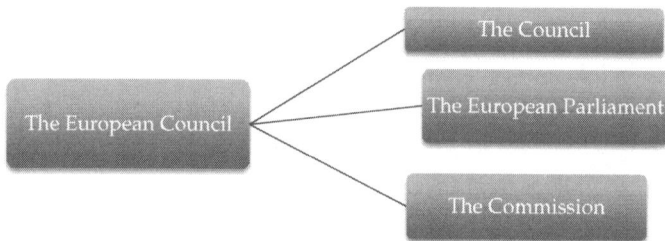

Figure 2: *Other institutions of the EU*

The European Commission

This is the executive of the EU, often seen as equivalent to the civil service. The Commission represents and upholds the interests of the EU as a

---

[2] What is outlined here is the bare bones of each institution: see http://europa.eu/ for further explanation.

whole; it is often called the "guardian of the treaties". It oversees and implements EU policies by:

(i) Proposing new laws to the Parliament and the Council;
(ii) Managing the EU's budget and allocating funding;
(iii) Enforcing EU law (together with the Court of Justice);
(iv) Representing the EU internationally, for example, by negotiating agreements between the EU and other countries.

The 28 Commissioners, one from each EU country, provide the Commission's political leadership during their five-year term. Each Commissioner is assigned responsibility for specific policy areas by the President. The President is nominated by the European Council. The appointment of all Commissioners, including the President, is subject to the approval of the European Parliament.

The Council of the European Union ("The Council")

This is where national ministers from each EU country meet to adopt laws and coordinate policies. This EU institution is often confused with the *European Council* which is another EU institution, where EU leaders meet in summit to discuss the EU's political priorities.[3]

The Council has the following functions:

(i) To pass EU laws;
(ii) To coordinate the broad economic policies of EU member countries;
(iii) To sign agreements between the EU and other countries;
(iv) To approve the annual EU budget;
(v) To develop the EU's foreign and defence policies;
(vi) To coordinate cooperation between courts and police forces of member countries.

The Council's main role is in the adoption of legislation, which (in most policy areas) it does jointly with the European Parliament. Much of the Council's legislative work is done in closed meetings of "working

---

[3] Although it also has the formal title "Council of the European Union", this is rarely used, and potentially causes confusion with the European Council. My preference is to call it simply "the Council", as it is called in the Treaty of the European Community (TEC).

groups", usually consisting of officials acting on behalf of their ministers, in which detailed negotiations take place before the Council reaches a "common position"; the role of political discussions cannot be underestimated here. Decisions in the Council of the EU are taken by qualified majority as a general rule, while votes on sensitive areas such as foreign policy and taxation are by unanimous vote.

The European Council

The European Council was originally not an institution of the EU; it was a summit-style meeting of EU Member State leaders that sought to define and influence the general political direction and priorities of the European Union. Since the Treaty of Lisbon it has become an institution of the EU. It meets twice a year, convened by its President. The European Council consists of the heads of state or government of the Member States, together with its President and the President of the Commission.

The European Parliament (EP)

The Members of the European Parliament (MEPs) represent the people of Europe and are directly elected for a period of five years. The Parliament is one of the EU's main law-making institutions, along with the Council of the European Union ("the Council"). The number of MEPs for each country is roughly in proportion to its population.[4] However, those living in smaller countries are currently better represented than the more populous countries; for example, Luxembourg has a population of 400,000 citizens and has one MEP for every 65,500 citizens, while Germany has a population of 82 million and has one MEP for every 828,000 citizens.

The European Parliament has three main roles:

  (i)   Debating and passing European laws, with the Council;
  (ii) Scrutinising other EU institutions, particularly the Commission, to make sure they are working democratically;
  (iii) Debating and adopting the EU's budget, with the Council.

---

[4] The current numbers in the Parliament were set, however, before the coming into force of the Lisbon Treaty. The numbers will be adjusted for the next mandate of the European Parliament. For example, the number of MEPs for Germany will thus be reduced from 99 to 96, whilst for Malta this number will increase from 5 to 6.

The Parliament exercises influence over other European institutions in several ways: it has powers of appointment, dismissal, litigation and inquiry. The Parliament has significant powers over the EU budget, along with the Council. If the members of the European Parliament disapprove of a nominee for the Commission, they can reject all the proposed nominees.[5] Parliament keeps a check on the Commission by examining its reports and by sometimes questioning Commissioners *via* various committees. MEPs can also look at petitions from citizens and set up committees of inquiry.

The EP's legislative powers vary according to the area of policy. "Co-decision" is the ordinary legislative procedure, which consists of the joint adoption by the European Parliament and the Council of a regulation, directive or decision on a proposal from the Commission. The Lisbon Treaty expanded the powers of the Parliament—by bringing over 40 new fields within the "co-decision" procedure, under which Parliament has equal rights with the Council.

The Court of Justice of the European Union (CJEU)

This judicial branch of the institutions is made up of three different courts—the Court of Justice, the General Court and the European Union Civil Service Tribunal. The General Court deals with cases brought forward by private individuals, companies and some organisations, and cases relating to competition law. The EU Civil Service Tribunal hears disputes between the European Union and its own staff.

The Court of Justice ensures that EU law is observed in all the Member States and that it is interpreted and applied uniformly. National courts can ask the Court of Justice to interpret a point of EU law that is before them in a domestic case—called "a preliminary ruling"—the Court of Justice gives an answer and then the national court decides the case before them based on this answer. The Court also hears actions brought against Member States for failing to apply EU law, actions against EU institutions for failing to make a decision, and actions brought by individuals against EU decisions or actions. From the beginning, the

---

[5] Its threats to use this power in 2004 forced the withdrawal of the proposed Italian Commissioner Rocco Buttiglione.

Court has interpreted EU law in ways Member States did not envisage, or actively fought against, in particular in relation to the four fundamental freedoms outlined below. It has given judgments affecting the day-to-day lives of schoolteachers,[6] the unemployed,[7] soccer players[8] and students[9] across the Member States.

The European Court of Auditors

The European Court of Auditors audits EU finances. It has no legal powers of its own and is entirely separate from the judicial branch of the EU. Its role is to improve EU financial management. It has the right to audit any person or organisation handling EU funds. It gives opinions on how to handle EU funds and has a role in fighting financial fraud.

The European Central Bank (ECB)

The European Central Bank's role is to manage the euro, the EU's single currency (currently adopted by eighteen EU countries), but also to safeguard financial stability in the EU as a whole. Much like a normal domestic central bank system, some of the ECB's tasks are to set interest rates within the Eurozone, manage foreign currency reserves, monitor price trends and, controversially, in the last number of years to ensure that national authorities adequately supervise financial markets and institutions.

The European Citizen's Initiative

Although not an EU institution, this initiative should be mentioned here. The initiative was conceived through the idea that every citizen should have the right to participate in the democratic life of the Union. In the past this was only achieved through voting in European Parliament elections. The Lisbon Treaty (Article 11.4 of the Treaty on European Union (TEU)) brought in this new mechanism, whereby, for the first time, citizens (with the proviso of not less than one million) can propose changes in European Union law.

---

[6] See Case 379/87 *Groener v Minister for Education* [1989] ECR 3967.
[7] See Case C-138/02 *Collins v Secretary of State for Work and Pensions* [2004] ECR I-2703.
[8] See Case C-415/93 *Union Royale Belge des Sociétés de Football Association v Bosman* [1995] ECR I-4921.
[9] See Case 66/85 *Lawrie Blum v Land Baden-Wurttemberg* [1986] ECR 2121.

The European Parliament adopted guidelines, including minimum numbers, age requirements and procedures relating to these matters in its resolution of 15 December 2010.[10] So far there have been a number of initiatives, involving economic policy, teaching and national budgets, and an initiative to legalise cannabis, although they are still at initial stages.

Sources of EU Law

The treaties themselves represent the fundamental or primary legislation of the EU. The EU would not exist outside of these treaties and many questions on the operation and powers of the EU can be answered by considering the text of the treaties themselves. Primary legislation of the EU takes precedence over national laws and this means that a national law can be invalidated if it conflicts with an EU law provision.

(i) *The Treaty of Rome - Treaty establishing the European Economic Community (TEEC)*
This Treaty founded the European Economic Community. It set out to harmonise the individual economic policies of the Member States and to encourage development of economic activities by creating a common market that facilitated the free movement of - goods, services, people and capital – the four fundamental freedoms at the heart of the idea of the European Union. It also set out to raise the standard of living for everybody living in the Member States, and established the EEC institutions. At Lisbon, the Treaty of Rome was renamed to the Treaty on the Functioning of the European Union (TFEU).

(ii) *The Single European Act 1987 (SEA)*
The aim of this Treaty was to advance European economic and political integration. The Treaty created policies, such as the removal of trade barriers between Member States to reduce competition, in order to achieve the objectives of the EC, and it also increased the voting power given to the European Parliament.

(iii) *The Maastricht Treaty 1993 Treaty on European Union—(TEU)*
This Treaty replaced "Community" with "Union" (EC became EU). The Treaty, like previous treaties, created policies to enhance economic and political integration; for example, the creation of the

---

[10] European Parliament Legislative Resolution passed 15 December 2010, EP-PE_TC1-COD(2010)0074.

idea of "European citizenship" and the implementation of a "single European currency".

(iv) *The Amsterdam Treaty 1997*

This Treaty involved policies on social integration, including immigration, public health, equality and employment.

(v) *The Nice Treaty 2001*

This Treaty did not introduce new policies but amended existing policies in previous treaties to cater for the enlargement of the EU from 15 to 27 Member States. The Treaty included, for example, changes regarding how power was to be divided between the EU institutions after enlargement.

(vi) *The Lisbon Treaty 2009*

This Treaty sought to make the European Union more democratic by raising its standards on accountability, transparency and participation. It made the EU Charter for Fundamental Rights, which lists the human rights recognised by the Union, a legally binding document.

There are five types of secondary legislation in the EU: regulations, directives, decisions, recommendations and opinions, and international agreements.

Regulations are binding on all EU Member States from the date they enter into force. They have direct applicability and automatically form part of the domestic law of each Member State. This means that the Member State usually does not need to transpose it by way of national legislation into their legal system. The regulation itself is the law and the source of rights and obligations.

Directives are binding as to the result they seek to achieve. However, it is open to each Member State as to how to achieve this goal; thus the Member State will adopt domestic legislation to reflect the directive's goals. This means that a directive only comes into force on the date stipulated by which Member States must transpose it into national law.

Decisions are binding on those to whom they are addressed, usually a specific Member State, although sometimes they can be addressed to private parties, usually in the field of competition law.

Recommendations and Opinions are not legally binding on those to whom they are addressed. They are usually drafted by an EU institution, recommending that a particular Member State take a particular course of action, without actually legally obliging them to do so and so are rather toothless.

International agreements have legal effects only for the part of the agreement which falls under the scope of EU competence.

CHAPTER TWENTY TWO

SIGNIFICANT CASE LAW OF THE EUROPEAN UNION

A Word on Some EU Cases

Many students seem to find EU law a dry topic, or somewhat confusing. The previous chapter introduced the EU institutions and the sources of law in the EU. For many business law students, that chapter will end the lesson on EU law. However, it is through its case law that that EU law comes alive and affects everyone in the twenty-eight Member States. There are many "grey areas" of EU law, and the court[1] (formerly the ECJ and now the CJEU) itself has been a driving force for change within the EU. The cases below are only a sample of how EU law has been driven by interpretations of the Court.

EU Law Reigns Supreme: *Costa v ENEL*[2]

In this famous decision involving the nationalisation of electricity in Italy, the Court established the *supremacy* of European Economic Community (EEC as it was at the time, now EU) law over the national law of Member States. How?

In 1962 the Italian government nationalised a private electricity company—ENEL. Mr Costa had owned several shares in the former corporation, yet lost all his rights due to the nationalisation. In protest he then refused to pay his electricity bill, which amounted to 1,925 lire (approximately €0.99 in 1964), and was sued by the newly created state company, ENEL. The money at stake in this case was unimportant; what was really at stake was the significance of the EEC. Costa argued *inter alia* that the nationalisation was against EEC law. The Italian government argued that the Italian law nationalising the electricity company was later in time than the Act which incorporated EEC law into Italian law. They said that, therefore, the Italian court was obliged to apply the later domestic law in preference to EEC law. The Italian court referred this question of priorities to the ECJ. Therefore, the ECJ was not deciding the dispute between Mr Costa and ENEL, but rather whether Mr Costa could invoke EEC law at national level to strike down a national law.

---

[1] The Court was formerly known as the European Court of Justice (ECJ); it is now called the Court of Justice of the European Union (CJEU).

[2] Case 6/64 *Flaminio Costa v ENEL* [1964] ECR 585.

If Italy's argument was correct, then every Member State could simply enact new legislation in order to sideline the European treaties. If any national legislation passed subsequent to the Member State's entering the EEC could take preference, then the Treaty of Rome and EEC law had no meaning. In answering Italy's objection, the ECJ more or less invented the doctrine of "supremacy".

> "By contrast with ordinary international treaties, the EEC Treaty has created its own legal system which, on the entry into force of the Treaty, became an integral part of the legal systems of the Member States and which their courts are bound to apply".

Thus, after the ratification of the Treaty of Rome, the Member States no longer had the power to create laws which contravened the legal order established by the European treaties.

Equal Pay for Equal Work in the EU: *Defrenne v Sabena (No.2)*[3]

The idea of equal pay for equal work is a no-brainer. But in the early 1970s many countries and companies in Europe did not subscribe to that principle. Gabrielle Defrenne worked as a flight attendant for the airline Sabena. The airline paid her less than her male colleagues who performed identical duties. Ms Defrenne complained that this violated her right to equal treatment on grounds of gender under Article 119 of the Treaty of the Rome[4], and claimed compensation.

The question for the court was essentially this: did Article 119 of the Treaty of Rome introduce directly into the national law of each Member State of the European Community the principle that men and women should receive equal pay for equal work, and could this sort of action be brought against a private company to enforce EEC (now EU) law?

---

[3] Case 43/75 *Defrenne v Sabena* (No. 2) [1976] ECR 455.
[4] Now Article 157 of the Treaty on the Functioning of the European Union (TFEU), which prior to the Lisbon Treaty was Article 141 of the Treaty of the European Community (TEC).

The Court found that Article 119 was mandatory in nature and therefore applied to both Member States *and* private companies. Article 119 was established as having "direct effect"; therefore, it required no implementing law at national level. Ms Defrenne was entitled to equal pay for equal work under EEC law.

State Liability for Breach of EU Law: *Francovich, Bonifaci and Others v Italy*[5]

Here Italy had failed to implement EC Directive 80/987 on the protection of workers in the event of insolvency. (The directive required the guarantee of payments of outstanding claims for remuneration and the creation of guarantee institutions to meet those claims.) Francovich and Bonifaci had outstanding claims against a company declared bankrupt in 1985. Unable to recover against the company, they brought actions in the Italian courts against Italy, requesting that Italy should pay them compensation in the light of the obligation in the directive. Both national courts referred questions to the ECJ to determine the extent of a Member State's liability. The ECJ held that Member States are obliged to compensate individuals for breaches of EC law for which they are responsible if three conditions are satisfied:

(i)   The objective of the directive must include the conferring of rights for the benefit of individuals;
(ii) The content of the rights must be identifiable from the directive;
(iii) There must be a causal link between the breach and the damage.

The Football Players Transfer System Violates EU Law: *Royale Belge des Sociétés de Football Association v Bosman*[6]

For anyone who follows soccer, this case changed the European transfer system forever. In 1990 Bosman's contract with RFC Liege (Belgium) came to an end and FC Dunkerque in France wanted to sign him, but the fee RFC sought was out of their price range. Thus, Bosman was stuck playing

---

[5] Cases C-6 & 9/90 *Francovich, Bonifaci and others v Italy [1991]* ECR I-5357.
[6] Case C-415/93 *Union Royale Belge des Sociétés de Football Association v Bosman* [1995] ECR I-4921.

for Liege. However, after this potential transfer deal fell through, Liege decided to lower his wage by 60%. He sued the Belgian Football Association (FA) and the club, and won. The FA and RFC appealed; Bosman won the appeal. The FA and RFC appealed again, this time being granted a reference to the ECJ.

The ECJ finally gave their ruling on 15 December 1995, more than five years after Bosman had initially tried to leave RFC Liege. The ECJ ruled that the football transfer system breached Article 45 of the TFEU, which provided for free movement of workers within the EU Member States, as it required the payment of a sum by a prospective acquiring team to a footballer's former club when his contract had ended. It was held that the rule was capable of impeding free movement of workers irrespective of the fact that there was no discrimination on the grounds of nationality and that there was no public interest justification. This ruling extended to all footballers making their living at football teams in the EU; once they reached the end of their contracts, they could leave. If their club wanted to keep them, they would have to negotiate a new deal.

Sadly, by 1995 Bosman had long since stopped playing football. The case seemed to consume his life, with hearing after hearing. His marriage broke down, and by the time he finally won his case, he was famously sleeping in his parents' garage. By that time, his career was over, but he had completely changed football forever, causing the inflation of footballers' salaries throughout the EU.

Hyperlinking on the Internet: Copyright and You: *Svensson v Retriever Sverige AB*[7]

When you read an article you like on the internet, do you re-post it to your Facebook or Twitter account, or to other social media? A few clicks is all it takes to make sure your friends and family are updated with what you are thinking about. What this case states—that linking to freely

---

[7] Case C-466/12, *Svensson v Retriever Sverige AB,* Judgment of 13 February 2014.

available content on the internet is permissible—is so obvious that at first one might think: how could this ever have been a problem?[8]

This case deals with the question whether a copyright holder may forbid people to link to public information. Retriever Sverige is a Swedish company which operates a website through which users receive hyperlinks to articles on other websites. Svensson and the other plaintiffs were all journalists who wrote articles published in the *Göteborgs-Posten* newspaper and on the newspaper's website, where they were freely accessible. Retriever Sverige provided hyperlinks to these articles on the *Göteborgs-Posten* website without the permission of the journalists. If the ECJ had followed what some copyright holders deemed sensible— that permission from the copyright holder is needed for redirecting internet users via hyperlinks to freely available information—it would have created huge difficulty for everyone using the internet. The court held that provision of hyperlinks could be considered a communication and that the website was aimed at enough people to constitute a public. This holding that hyperlinks were a communication could have been enough to breach Article 3(1) of Directive 2001/29/EC on the harmonisation of certain aspects of copyright and related rights in the information society.

However, the court also referred to case law and noted that

> "a communication … concerning the same works as those covered by the initial communication and made … by the same technical means, must also be directed at a *new public*, that is to say, at *a public not taken into account* by the copyright holders when they authorised the initial communication to the public" (emphasis added).

Here the initial communication targeted all potential internet users, as access to the *Göteborgs-Posten* website was not subject to any restriction (e.g. paywalls etc.). The hyperlinks, then, did not make the articles available to a *new public* and therefore there was no requirement for Retriever Sverige to obtain the journalists' consent.

---

[8] Hyperlinking made the internet what it is today—Tim Berners-Lee designed the world wide web based on the hypertext transfer protocol (http), and the ease of disclosure and communication of information, as well as the actual web, originated thanks to hyperlinks.

The court went on to explain that if the link allowed users to bypass restrictions designed to limit access to a protected work to, for example, a website's subscribers, those users *would be a new public not taken into account* by the copyright holders when they authorised the initial communication. The key element of the decision is that the links were provided to works which were already publicly available to all internet users.[9]

Data Retention and the Internet: the Digital Rights Ireland Case[10]

This case involved a challenge to the Data Retention Directive (Directive 2006/24 EC). The Data Retention Directive (DRD) required the collection and storage of telecommunications traffic data (for example, details on the maker and recipient of telephone calls) for the purposes of the prevention, detection and investigation of "serious crime". The preliminary reference to the Court in this case stemmed from actions taken by Digital Rights Ireland—an NGO—and just under 12,000 Austrian residents. The Court of Justice held that the EU legislature had exceeded the limits of the principle of proportionality in relation to certain provisions of the EU Charter for Fundamental Rights. The Court indicated that the retention of a broad range of data allowed by the directive provided an opportunity to construct a picture of a person's private life. As a result, the Court found the directive incompatible with the fundamental right to privacy. The Court considered whether there was any justification for the interference with these rights. While the directive aimed to tackle an important issue—the fight against serious crime—the Court considered that European lawmakers had gone beyond what was proportionate. However, critics have noted that the Court considered the "material objective"—crime prevention—rather than the stated objective of the directive—market harmonisation.

---

[9] Where the content linked to is not freely available elsewhere, such as on a site requiring a subscription, the linking website would be likely to be found to be communicating the work to a new public and therefore liable for copyright infringement.

[10] Joined Cases C-293/12 and C-594/12.

Conclusions

The above cases are just a sampling of some of the interesting ways EU law has affected the daily lives of people in the 28 member countries. The case law of the EU has also been used to guarantee the rights to work and to claim social welfare benefits, privacy rights, and many other rights of EU citizens over the years. The Court has contributed in ways that Member States certainly didn't envisage when signing up to the EU in the first place providing real meaning for the four fundamental freedoms and expanding in other directions including the concept of EU citizenship. Indeed, of all the EU institutions, the Court could be considered to have been the fiercest torchbearer for the rights of EU citizens.

INTRODUCTION TO EMPLOYMENT LAW

Introduction

Over the last thirty years there has been huge growth in the development of employment law. European legislation on equality and employment has been implemented via statute, and new forums for employment law disputes have been set up to try to reduce costs and speed up the process for all sides. The employee–employer relationship is essentially a contractual one, but the relationship has a special status in that many other provisions also apply to the relationship: health and safety legislation, common law duties, employment legislation, equality legislation and constitutional rights. This book cannot deal satisfactorily with all matters relevant to employment law, and so, instead, what follows in the next three chapters is an overview of some of the essential issues.

Employment Status

- Is the worker an employee or an independent contractor?
- Why is the distinction made?
- What are the determining factors?

This is the starting point for the examination of any employment law issue, as a worker who is deemed to be an independent contractor (*contract for service*) is not entitled to many of the statutory protections an employee (*contract of service*) is afforded.[1] Therefore, while the work being carried out may be similar or even identical in some cases, the legal basis on which it is being done is significantly different.

Usually the legislation refers to an employee as someone who works under a "contract of employment", meaning a contract of service (or a contract of service via an employment agency).[2] There is no statutory definition of "contract of service", but through case law we glean the essential steps in determining whether someone is an employee or an independent contractor.

---

[1] This differentiation between employee and independent contractor can also affect tax, social welfare status and employer liability in negligence for acts of employees.

[2] However, you should be aware that the definitions can vary across the statutes, with wider definitions given in the Payment of Wages Act 1991, the National Minimum Wage Act 2000 and the Employment Equality Acts.

The traditional viewpoint was to examine the level of control exercised in relation to the service being provided. However, this test of control has long been done away with and it is now only one factor of many that fall to be considered by the courts in deciding whether or not someone is an employee.[3] The integration test seeks to establish to what extent the individual is integrated into the organisation and the enterprise/economic test seeks to establish the extent to which the individual can be described as a person in business on their own account. It is this last test which is now the more commonly used test; however, these cases in practice are quite dependent on the individual facts and sometimes all three tests are combined in determining whether someone is an employee or not.

The leading Irish case is still the decision of the Supreme Court in *Henry Denny & Sons (Ireland) Ltd trading as Kerry Foods v The Minister for Social Welfare*[4]. Ms Sandra Mahon was hired by Henry Denny in 1988 as shop demonstrator, offering shoppers free samples of products. Ms Mahon's contract referred to her as an independent contractor and stated expressly that she was not an employee of Henry Denny & Sons. She was not eligible under her contract to become a member of the company pension scheme or a trade union. Ms Mahon was not supervised carrying out her work, but she was provided by the company with necessary clothing and equipment to carry out her function. She invoiced the company after carrying out the demonstrations and these invoices had to be signed off by the supermarket store manager. Ms Mahon was required to comply with any reasonable direction given by the store manager. Ms Mahon was not allowed to work for any competitors and could not routinely

---

[3] In the recent EAT case of *Doherty v Morris Oil Company Ltd* MN1815/2011, UD1768/2011, the level of control exercised over the worker was considered by the tribunal. Here the claimant, John Doherty, worked in a petrol garage owned by Morris Oil. However, he ran a car sales and car wash business from the same premises. He submitted his own VAT invoices, paid his own tax and PRSI, and did not receive annual leave. The EAT found that, although Morris Oil did exercise some element of control over Mr Doherty, it was more akin to a landlord rather than an employer. Mr Doherty was the one who decided what days to work and the amount of time to spend on the company's business versus his own. The company controlled the appearance of the garage, but again this was more akin to a landlord controlling the look of his premises rather than an employer. The element of control seems to have been a deciding factor in this case with the EAT holding Mr Doherty to be an independent contractor.

[4] *Henry Denny & Sons (Ireland) Ltd trading as Kerry Foods v The Minister for Social Welfare* [1998] 1 IR 34.

hire other people to carry out her work. She was found to be an employee of Henry Denny & Sons despite the written terms of the contract. The court held that the correct approach was to look beyond the written terms of the contract and to all the circumstances of Ms Mahon's employment.

Another key question is whether the worker was in business on his own account or working for another. The courts will consider the sort of obligations on each side and the parties' own descriptions of the relationship—a written contract which describes the worker as an independent contractor will not decide the issue (indeed in many employment disputes there may not be a written contract or the contract may not be signed). It will also be considered whether there is exclusive or personal service – whether the worker can delegate their work to someone else.[5]

For example in *ESB v Minister for Social Community & Family Affairs*[6] the ESB appealed a decision of the Social Welfare Appeals Officer to classify meter readers as employees for the purpose of social welfare contributions. The Officer had been particularly influenced by the fact that the meter readers had to have ESB approval, carried ESB ID cards and that any substitute had to be approved by the company. The High Court approved of this finding that the meter readers were employees despite the written terms of the contract stating that they were independent contractors.

All of the factors above fell to be considered in the decision of the Employment Appeals Tribunal (EAT) in *Hayes v Business & Shopping Guide Ltd.*[7] Hayes was taking a case for unfair dismissal, claiming he had been subjected to bullying and abusive behaviour. However, the EAT first had to determine whether the Unfair Dismissal Acts could apply to him, as the company maintained that Hayes was an independent contractor. Hayes had registered himself as a sole trader in 1962; he was what he himself termed "a career salesman". He started with the Business

---

[5] See two English decisions on this issue of delegation and personal service—*Ready Mixed Concrete Ltd (South East) v Minister of Pensions* [1968] 2 QB 497, [1968] 1 All ER 433 and *Kane v McCann* [1995] ELR 175.

[6] *ESB v Minister for Social Community & Family Affairs* [2006] IEHC 59.

[7] *Hayes v Business & Shopping Guide Ltd* UD177/2010.

and Shopping Guide as a sales agent in 1986 and informed the company of his work elsewhere. Eventually he was promoted by the company to manager, but he never signed a contract of employment, and was responsible for his own tax and social welfare affairs. He only attended the office once a year, and although the company maintained control over the price of his services, Hayes himself had complete discretion as to when and where to work. He owned his own sales, submitted VAT invoices in his name and claimed a self-employed old age pension at 66 years of age. Despite this, Hayes told the EAT that he considered himself to be an employee of this company. The company said it was their standard practice to engage sales agents on a non-employment basis, that sales agents received remuneration through sales and commission and were essentially left to their own devices.

The EAT here looked at the relationship between the company and Hayes. They held that it was a loose relationship, and that, given the lack of supervision along with the fact that he owned his own sales and paid his own VAT, PRSI and tax, Hayes was self-employed and not an employee of the company, and therefore that the EAT could not hear his unfair dismissal claim as they did not have jurisdiction.

Looking at the total overall picture rather then applying one single test was again upheld to be the correct approach by the High Court in *Minister of Agriculture v Barry*.[8] This was a somewhat complicated case factually, but the essential finding was that it is simply not possible to arrive at the correct result by testing the facts of the case in a rigid, formulaic way. This incorrect approach by the EAT was not a correct reading of the *Henry Denny* case in particular. *Henry Denny* never set out

---

[8] *Minister of Agriculture v Barry* [2009] 1 IR 215. Here the workers were temporary veterinary inspectors for the Minister of Agriculture at the Galtee Meats plant in Co. Cork. The meat plant closed in 2004 and they claimed redundancy payments and payments for minimum notice. When the claim came to be heard before the EAT, the Minister for Agriculture argued that the inspectors were not employees and therefore were not entitled to the payments under the Acts. The EAT found that they were employees; the Minister then appealed this to the High Court. It was a complex working situation and the High Court found that the EAT were wrong in the test they applied. Here the EAT applied a single composite test for determining whether a person is engaged on a contract of service or a contract for services. The tribunal found that the test "involves looking at the contract as a whole and asking, 'Is the person in business on his or her own account?' If the answer is yes, then the contract is one for services. If the answer is no, then the contract is one of service".

a single test for determining whether or not a worker was an employee or an independent contractor.

Contract with a Third Party?

Temporary agency workers are employed by the agency and usually then assigned to another entity to which they provide their services. Agency workers are entitled to equal treatment with any employees of the eventual hirer pursuant to the Protection of Employees (Temporary Agency Work) Act 2012.

Issues can arise in terms of the nature of the relationship between the worker and the hirer as there is no contract of employment between them; the contract of employment exists between the worker and the agency. Some legislation does make express provision for this sort of event and, for example, under s 13 of the Unfair Dismissals (Amendment) Act 1993, a claim can be brought by the worker against the hirer.

Generally, in claims involving an agency worker and their hirer, the courts have emphasised their approach as being based on the integration test rather than on locating an implied contract.[9]

Conclusions

- Determining whether someone is an employee or independent contractor is essential in every employment situation. For both employee and employer it is commercially prudent to have clarity as to the basis of the relationship, as this will impact on tax, social welfare and the legal obligations of both parties.
- The courts have moved away from the traditional test that looked to the level of control exerted over the worker and now use a combination of control, integration and enterprise tests to determine whether someone is an employee or independent contractor.
- Agency workers are entitled to equal treatment with employees, and the test will be one based on the integration model.

---

[9] See for example *Diageo Global Supply v Rooney* [2004] ELR 133; *Dacas v Brook Street Bureau (UK) Ltd* [2004] IRLR 358 and *James v Greenwich London Borough Council* [2008] ICR 545.

THE CONTRACT OF EMPLOYMENT

Introduction

As with all contractual matters, the foundation of the employment relationship is the contract of employment. Although various statutory developments have diminished somewhat the importance of the written contract of employment, it still remains the basic document the courts will examine in considering disputes.

Are Any Formal Requirements Necessary?

Generally there are no formal or special requirements necessary for the formation of a valid employment contract as opposed to any other sort of contract. As long as the formula for a contract has been met—offer + acceptance + consideration, intention to create legal relations and the absence of an illegal purpose—then a valid contract of employment is created.[1]

Terms of Employment (Information) Act 1994

As with all contracts, it is not necessary that there be a written document for a valid contract of employment to exist, but the law provides that *on the request* of an employee certain contractual information must be provided in writing. Section 3(1) of the Terms of Employment (Information) Act 1994 provides that within two months of starting employment, the employee should be given in writing all the particulars set out in s 3(1) (a) to (m), which include such information as address of the employer and employee, full names of the parties, job title, rate of pay, terms related to hours of work, etc. [2] Although this written statement

---

[1] See chapters on contract law for a discussion of these concepts.
[2] s 3(1): (a) the full names of the employer and the employee, (b) the address of the employer in the State or, where appropriate, the address of the principal place of the relevant business of the employer in the State or the registered office (within the meaning of the Companies Act, 1963), (c) the place of work or, where there is no fixed or main place of work, a statement specifying that the employee is required or permitted to work at various places, (d) the title of the job or nature of the work for which the employee is employed, (e) the date of commencement of the employee's contract of employment, (f) in the case of a temporary contract of employment, the expected duration thereof or, if the contract of employment is for a fixed term, the date on which the contract expires, (g) the rate or method of calculation of the employee's remuneration, (h) the length of the intervals between the times at which remuneration is paid, whether a week, a month or any other interval, (i) any terms or conditions relating to hours of work (including overtime), (j) any terms or conditions relating to paid leave (other than paid sick leave), (k) any terms or conditions relating to:

of terms may or may not be considered a contract of employment under the law, it would provide a court with strong evidence of the content of any such contract.[3]

Section 5 of the Act requires an employer to furnish an employee with written details of any changes in the terms or conditions of their employment to which the Act applies.

Unfair Dismissals Act 1977

Section 14(1) of the Unfair Dismissals Act of 1977 provided that an employer was obliged to furnish an employee with a notice in writing setting out the procedure that would be adopted prior to any dismissal of that employee. That obligation was largely ignored in practice, and the 1993 Amendment Act provided at s 5 that in adjudicating upon a claim for unfair dismissal, account shall be taken of the compliance or non-compliance of the employer with that procedure. A Code of Practice on Disciplinary Procedures exists by way of Statutory Instrument (SI 146/2000) and this provides a general framework for disciplinary procedures, including dismissal, with an emphasis on the need for compliance with the principles of natural justice.

Pensions (Amendment) Act 2002

Under the Pensions (Amendment) Act 2002 employers who do not provide an occupational pension scheme for their employees are obliged to provide access to at least one standard Personal Savings Account (PRSA) contract and to make deductions from the payroll at the employee's request of the employee's contribution to the PRSA. The employer is not obliged to contribute to the PRSA.

(i) incapacity for work due to sickness or injury and paid sick leave, and (ii) pensions and pension schemes, (l) the period of notice which the employee is required to give and entitled to receive (whether by or under statute or under the terms of the employee's contract of employment) to determine the employee's contract of employment or, where this cannot be indicated when the information is given, the method for determining such periods of notice, (m) a reference to any collective agreements which directly affect the terms and conditions of the employee's employment including, where the employer is not a party to such agreements, particulars of the bodies or institutions by whom they were made.

[3] *System Floors (UK) Ltd v Daniel* [1982] ICR 54, [1981] IRLR 475; *Robertson v British Gas Corporation* [1983] ICR 351, [1983] IRLR 302.

Express and Implied Terms of the Contract

Express Terms

Express terms are directly written into the contract, although some can be incorporated through staff handbooks, collective agreements, and custom and practice in the trade. The express terms of a contract are specific to that particular contract but there are some that can be considered standard terms, such as: date of commencement and parties to the contract, job specification, hours and place of work, probation periods, pay[4], sick pay, annual leave[5], retirement age[6], pension, notice[7], discipline and grievance procedures[8], and e-mail and internet usage.

Legislative Provisions

There are various provisions that should be included in an employment contract to ensure compliance with the many pieces of protective employment legislation. For example, employees must be paid a minimum level of pay pursuant to the Minimum Wage Act of 2000, and various rights to unpaid leave automatically arise upon the birth or adoption of children or for the care of relatives. In addition, if there is no express term in the contract, for example, dealing with equality legislation, such a term will be implied into the contract.

Restrictive Covenants/Non-Compete Clauses

Commercial or industrial secrets can fall into the hands of competing businesses through disclosure by former employees. Developments in technology or science, or a new design, can be worth millions in revenue, especially if launched first in a competitive environment. As a result many employment contracts contain an express restrictive covenant/non-compete clause to protect commercial secrets and interests. A restrictive covenant is a term or condition in a contract of employment which places restrictions on the right of an employee to compete with their employer *after* they leave employment. As they apply after the employment

---

[4] Subject to the Payment of Wages Act 1991 and the National Minimum Wage Act 2000.
[5] The Organisation of Working Time Act 1997.
[6] Must comply with the Employment Equality Acts 1998–2008.
[7] Minimum Notice (Terms of Employment) Act 1973–2001.
[8] s (14)(1) Unfair Dismissals Act 1977; the Industrial Relations Act 1990 sets out general guidelines on grievance and disciplinary procedures.

relationship is over, these clauses are controversial and involve a balancing by the courts between an employer's right to protect their legitimate business interests and an employee's right to move freely or set up in competition.

Courts usually treat these clauses as void unless they can be justified by the person seeking to enforce the clause, usually the employer.[9] The key factors in assessing whether or not such a clause is valid are whether it seeks to protect a legitimate proprietary interest of the employer, whether it is reasonable both between the parties[10] and in relation to the public interest, and also whether it is reasonable in its scope, i.e. its duration and geographical limitation.[11] Examples of legitimate proprietary interests that the courts have deemed valid for protection are: trade secrets and confidential information, trade connections and existing employees. Careful drafting is still required by an employer if they wish such a clause to be upheld in the courts.

In *Net Affinity Ltd v Conaghan and Revmac Limited t/a Avvio*[12] the court looked at a restrictive covenant in a contract which sought to restrain the first defendant, Ms Conaghan, from working for *any* competing business for twelve months after ceasing employment with Net Affinity Ltd. Net Affinity was a small company providing digital services such as online booking systems to the hotel sector in Ireland. The company had become the leading expert in the area of new social media such as Facebook and Twitter, and had designed a unique social media module which was added to the online booking engine that they sold to hotels. This had yet to be replicated by other companies in this area of business. Ms Conaghan had received specialist training in this new social media module and in how to drive this aspect of the business. In February 2011 Ms Conaghan informed her employer that she was leaving Net Affinity to work for their main competitor, Avvio. Net Affinity then tried to prevent Ms Conaghan taking up employment with Avvio before the twelve-month period in the covenant was up. The court here held that the non-compete clause in the employment contract was void as there

---

[9] *John Orr Ltd and Vestcom BV v John Orr* [1987] ILRM 702.
[10] *Stenhouse Ltd v Phillips* [1974] AC 391.
[11] *Murgitroyd & Company Ltd v Purdy* [2005] 3 IR 12.
[12] [2011] IEHC 160.

was absolutely no geographical limitation in the clause and therefore it was too wide to protect the legitimate interests of Net Affinity. Ms Conaghan was prevented from taking up employment anywhere, either inside or outside Ireland, whether dealing with Irish companies or otherwise. The extent of the territory covered by the clause must at all times be reasonable.[13]

Sometimes, even though the clause may be restricted to a particular geographical area, it will still fall on the wrong side of the balancing line. In *Murgitroyd & Company Ltd v Purdy*[14] the company was a large law firm dealing solely with intellectual property and trademark law. Barry Purdy was employed under a three-year service agreement as a European Patent Agent with the firm and there was a clause which provided that he would not work within the Republic of Ireland for a period of twelve months after his employment, either on his own account or for a competing company. Purdy resigned from Murgitroyd and immediately set up practice as "Purdy and Associates" on Adelaide Road, Dublin. At the time this case was decided, there were only about ten patent attorneys operating in Ireland, and they all operated from Dublin. The court in this case therefore took the approach that a geographical restriction based upon the extent of jurisdiction of the Irish State was not unreasonable. In regard to the duration of the restriction, the court considered that due to the specialised nature of the business a period of twelve months was also not unreasonable. However, the company still lost their application to enforce the clause. Why? Clarke J held that:

---

[13] However, while the non-compete clause was invalid, the Court did go on to grant injunctions regarding the protection of confidential information. See also two cases on this issue of geographical scope: (1) In *Office Angels Ltd v Rainer-Thomas & O'Connor* [1991] IRLR 214, a restraint of 1,000 metres was considered excessive when applied to the city of London. The restraint ruled out the possibility of the employee seeking similar employment anywhere in the city of London. Such a clause was deemed not to be necessary to protect the employer's clients, as most of the work was conducted with them over the telephone and as such the location of the office was not important to them; (2) *Isitt & Anor v Ganson* (1899) 43 Sol Jo 744: where a business is carried on by a small number of people and with customers widely distributed, a very large area will be allowed, and a wider restraint may be considered reasonable in a business carried on by agents or by correspondence than in one necessitating constant attendance in person. All of England was regarded as an acceptable area of restriction for an accountant in this case.

[14] *Murgitroyd & Company Ltd v Purdy* [2005] 3 IR 12.

"Covenants against competition by former employees are never reasonable as such. They may be upheld only where the employee might obtain such personal knowledge of, and influence over, the customers of his employer as would enable him, if competition were allowed, to take advantage of his employer's trade connection: see Kores Manufacturing Co. Ltd v Kolok Manufacturing Co. Ltd [1959] Ch. 108".[15]

Here, the prohibition on all competition was too wide; a prohibition on dealing with customers of the plaintiff would have been reasonable, and sufficient to meet any legitimate requirements of the plaintiff.

The dim view taken by the courts of these types of clauses in employment contracts can be seen in the recent decision in *Hernandez v Vodafone Ireland Ltd*[16], where even a three-month restriction was enough for the court to assess at the interlocutory stage that there was a fair issue to be tried.[17]

Implied Terms

Sometimes the express terms in the contract of employment will not cover the particular situation in which the employee or employer find themselves. In certain circumstances the courts will imply a term into a contract of employment to fit the situation. This is similar to the general situation of implied terms in contract law, although in employment cases, certain statutes and the Constitution imply terms not expressly provided for in the contract.

---

[15] *Murgitroyd & Company Ltd v Purdy* [2005] 3 IR 12, at para [21].

[16] *Hernandez v Vodafone Ireland Ltd* [2013] IEHC 70.

[17] In *Hernandez v Vodafone Ireland Ltd* [2013] IEHC 70, the plaintiff had worked for Vodafone for seven years and had been offered employment by its competitor O2 in December 2012. There was a non-compete clause in his contract which prevented the plaintiff taking up employment with a competitor for six months. Vodafone and O2 engaged in communications which provided that Mr Hernandez could take up employment with O2 in May 2013. This meant that he would be without pay or social welfare benefits (as the case concerned a resignation) for three months. He was a married man with two young children and financially supported his ill parents in Mexico. As this was an interlocutory application the court could not determine whether or not the clause was enforceable but it did consider that there was a fair issue to be tried and that damages would not be an adequate remedy in this situation as it was crucial to the plaintiff and his family that he have a continuous source of income.

Terms Implied by (Case) Law

As the courts have been dealing with employment contracts over the years they have developed certain "default rules" in relation to these types of contracts. However, a term will only be implied when it is necessary to make the contract workable and effective. The courts have implied a term that the employer must act reasonably in his dealings with an employee and a separate duty to act fairly. There is also an implied term in employment contracts of mutual trust and confidence owed by the employer to the employee and by the employee to the employer.[18] Duties such as an implied duty on the employer to provide an employee with a safe and healthy work environment[19]; a duty to obey lawful and reasonable orders[20] and a duty to adhere to natural justice and fair procedures[21] have also been "read" into employment contracts by the courts.

Terms Implied by Statute

Various terms have been implied into employment contracts via employment legislation over the last 30 or so years. These terms are implied regardless of the intentions of the parties to the contract. For example The Minimum Notice and Terms of Employment Acts 1973–2001 imply a graduated scale of notice periods according to length of service into all contracts of employment[22] and the Unfair Dismissals Acts 1977–2008 imply the right not to be unfairly dismissed into every employment relationship.

Terms Implied by Custom and Practice

For a term to be implied by custom and practice it must be "so notorious, well known and acquiesced in that in the absence of agreement in writing

---

[18] *Malik v BCCI* [1998] AC 20, [1997] ICR 606, [1997] IRLR 462.
[19] *Kielthy v Ascon Ltd* [1970] IR 122.
[20] *Pepper v Webb* [1969] 1 WLR 514, [1969] 2 All ER 216.
[21] *Glover v BLN Ltd* [1973] IR 388.
[22] For example, one week's notice is the statutory requirement for someone with between thirteen weeks and two years' service; for between two and five years' service, two weeks' notice is required; five to ten years requires four weeks' notice; ten to fifteen years requires six weeks' notice and anything over fifteen years requires eight weeks' notice under the legislation.

it is to be taken as one of the terms of the contract between the parties".[23]
Terms usually implied into a contract of employment by custom and
practice include rights to sick pay, the right of an employer to suspend an
employee, and the rights of employees in relation to *ex gratia* termination
payments, particularly in situations of redundancy. For a term to become
part of the contract it must reflect a clear, recurring, uninterrupted
practice that has been the norm for a number of years in that particular
industry or business.

Varying the Terms of the Contract of Employment

Every alteration to the terms of the contract as originally signed amounts
to a variation of terms. There must be an informed consent to the
variation and there should be evidence of this consent. The reality of
working life must be reflected, and employees cannot expect work
practices to always remain the same as a business strives to become more
efficient. This means that employers can make unilateral changes to *work
practices* that have built up over time but have not gained contractual
status.[24]

Terminating a Contract of Employment

Under the common law, a contract of employment can be terminated in
the following ways:

(i) *Agreement by Notice*
This is the most usual way a contract of employment comes to an end.
The correct notice required by the terms of the contract must be given
by either party, or reasonable notice where no specific notice is set out
in the contract. Alternatively, an employer can pay wages in lieu of the
notice period, subject to the provisions of the Unfair Dismissals Acts
1977–2008.

(ii) *Death of Employer or Employee*
Death of either the employer or the employee will automatically end
the contract unless there is a specific term in the contract that provides

---

[23] *O'Reilly v Irish Press* (1937) ILTR 194.
[24] *Creswell v Board of Inland Revenue* [1984] 2 All ER 713; *Kenny v An Post* [1988] IR 285; *Rafferty v Bus Eireann* [1996] IEHC 33, [1997] 2 IR 424.

otherwise. This does not apply if the employer is a company as companies continue to exist in law after the death of a member or director.

(iii) Frustration

If either party is incapable of performing their part of the contract due to circumstances beyond their control, the contract will be terminated due to frustration. Illness, injury and imprisonment can all result in frustration of a contract, depending on the particular circumstances.

(iv) Insolvency

Insolvency or bankruptcy of either employer or employee will only end the contract where it is provided for in specific terms in the contract. However, the reality of an insolvency situation means that it will be unlikely that an employer will be able to pay an employee.

(v) Breach of Contract

A contract of employment can be ended by breach if an employee resigns without giving reasonable notice and without sufficient reason, goes on strike, or fails to perform the contract and observe the terms. Breach by the employer can occur when he dismisses the employee without notice with no justifiable reason, or changes some essential term of the contract.

Conclusions

- Generally there are no formal or special requirements necessary for the formation of a valid employment contract beyond those that apply to any other sort of contract.
- The Terms of Employment (Information) Act 1994 provides that employees may request certain information in writing from their employer.
- Express terms are those written in the contract of employment and implied terms are those that may not be in writing but are "read" into the contract by virtue of legislation, the Constitution or case law.
- The courts take a dim view of restrictive covenants because they try to regulate the behavior of an employee <u>after</u> the employment relationship has already ended.

- An employer can vary the terms of the contract of employment if an employee gives informed consent.
- An employment contract can be terminated in a number of ways: by agreement, frustration, death, insolvency or breach.

CHAPTER TWENTY FIVE

EMPLOYMENT LAW: EMPLOYMENT LAW DISPUTES

Introduction

Currently there are over 40 individual pieces of employment legislation governing all aspects of the employment relationship. Employment disputes can arise in various circumstances, including prior to the employment relationship—at interview stage, and can include matters such as payment of wages, redundancy payments and redundancy selection, payment of various statutory entitlements, equality of treatment or pay at work, unfair dismissal, and various claims regarding treatment in the workplace.

Prior to 2015 the system for bringing different claims was quite unwieldy and complex, involving varying time limits for taking claims, varying remedies, different avenues for appeals and different methods of hearing disputes.[1] The new Workplace Relations Act 2015 has remedied this complex system somewhat in that there is now only one first-instance forum, the same time limit for bringing all complaints and a simplified appeals process.[2]

What follows here is a examination of some of the types of disputes that can arise and the ones that are frequently asked about by people learning employment law.

Equality Claims

The Employment Equality Acts seek to prevent discriminatory treatment on any of the nine prohibited grounds in quite a broad-reaching manner. The Acts cover not only existing employment relationships but also the termination of those relationships, and even the treatment of former employees. The Employment Equality Acts regulate the employment relationship itself and also the circumstances in which an employer may

---

[1] See T Mallon, "Employment Law Reform" (2012) IELJ 3 7680 and F Sheehan, "Transforming the Employment Rights Dispute Resolution System—Part I" (2013) ILT 31 74–77.

[2] However, the new system is not without criticism and it remains to be seen if it will withstand any legal challenges. See Employment Bar Association, "Submission to the Minister for Jobs, Enterprise and Innovation, Mr. Richard Bruton TD, on Reform of the State's Employment Rights and Industrial Relations Structures and Procedures" (2011) at p 1, Mark Hilliard, "Workplace Relations Bill set to radically overhaul employment disputes" *The Irish Times*, 15 December 2014.

seek to recruit an employee.[3] Section 8(1) of the Employment Equality Act prohibits discrimination in relation to access to employment, conditions of employment, pay, training or experience for or in relation to employment, promotion or regrading, or classification of posts. Discriminatory dismissal (which includes constructive dismissal on any of the protected grounds) is also prohibited by the Acts.

Discrimination is defined in section 6 of the Act as occurring where one person is treated less favourably than another is, has been, or would be treated on any one of the nine specified grounds. The discriminatory grounds are set out in s 6(2) and comprise what are now commonly referred to as the nine discriminatory grounds: gender, civil status, family status, sexual orientation, religion, age, disability, race/nationality/ ethnicity and membership of the Traveller community. The Act provides for certain exemptions to the discriminatory grounds, for example many employers offer higher pay to employees with superior qualifications and this is permissible under the Act.

The simplest and best definition of unlawful discrimination was provided by the European Court of Justice (CJEU) in *Gillespie v Health and Social Services Board and Others*[4] where it was said that:

> "It is well settled that discrimination involves the application of different rules to comparable situations, or the application of the same rules to different situations".

While the less favourable treatment must be based on one of the nine specified grounds, it is not necessary for the claimant herself to fall within these grounds. In particular, the Act covers discrimination both by imputation and by association. Discrimination by imputation arises when a person is treated less favourably on the basis of one of the discriminatory grounds because the employer believes that they fall within one of these grounds, even though they do not. For example, if a Muslim is treated less favourably by an employer because the employer believes she is Jewish, this will constitute discrimination on the religion ground within the

---

[3] See *Conlon v University of Limerick* [1999] 2 ILRM 131 which involved a claim of indirect sex discrimination in relation to a requirement for an academic post that the candidate would have several years' experience at senior level.

[4] *Gillespie v Health and Social Services Board and Others* C-342/93 [1996] EUECJ, [1996] ECR 475.

meaning of the Act. Discrimination by association arises where a person is treated less favourably than another due to her association with persons falling within the discriminatory grounds.

The Need for a Comparator

In general, a complainant must prove less favourable treatment as compared with another person in a similar position to the complainant. Therefore, without a comparator, the claim may fail and the choice of comparator is of significant importance to the success of any claim. However, this does not apply to allegations of pregnancy-related discriminatory treatment, where the law in general accepts a hypothetical non-pregnant comparator.[5] Examples of discrimination between the victim and an actual comparator include:

Scanlon v Bests Ltd[6]—where the claimant had been rostered for fewer days than her male co-employees.

Phelan v Michael Stein[7]—where the claimant had been asked questions about her children and child-minding arrangements, and where no equivalent questions had been asked of the male competitors for the position.

Field v Irish Carton Printers[8]—where a free taxi service was provided for female employees, but none was provided for the male employee.

A hypothetical comparator may sometimes be used where there is no actual comparator. In *Barry v Board of Management, Virgin Mary Schools*,[9] a female candidate was questioned at an interview about her ability to reconcile childcare and working obligations, but there were no male candidates who could provide an actual comparator for the purpose of establishing whether the questioning was discriminatory. The Equality Officer found discrimination on the basis that a hypothetical male comparator would not have been similarly questioned.

---

[5] Section 6(2) provides that less favourable treatment on pregnancy or maternity leave issues is deemed to constitute discrimination on the gender ground.

[6] [1997] ELR 14.

[7] [1999] ELR 58.

[8] [1994] ELR 128.

[9] *Barry v Board of Management, Virgin Mary Schools* DEC-E2001-031.

Types of Claim

The types of claim which can be brought under the Employment Equality Acts can be categorised as follows:

(1) Direct discrimination;
(2) Equal pay;
(3) Indirect discrimination;
(4) Harassment;
(5) Victimisation.

Direct Discrimination

Direct discrimination is concerned with less favourable treatment experienced by a complainant on one of the protected grounds set out in the Employment Equality Acts. In making the connection between the alleged less favourable treatment and the protected ground, the Equality Tribunal and Labour Court have been clear in expressing the view that there is no need to establish an intention, subjective or otherwise, on the part of the alleged perpetrator to discriminate.[10]

Equal Pay Claim

First, it must be proved by the claimant that the comparator does like work. Section 7 of the Act requires that the work be identical or interchangeable in nature, or the work performed must be similar in nature or of equal value. "Pay" is a concept which is defined widely both at EU level and in Irish legislation and jurisprudence, and "remuneration" is defined in the Act as including any consideration whether direct or indirect (cash or in kind) which the employee receives from the employer in respect of employment.[11]

---

[10] *St. James's Hospital v Eng* EDA023.

[11] The following matters have been held to be pay: sick pay (C-171/88 *Rinner Kühn v FWW Special Gebäudereinigung Gmbh & Co KG*); grading systems (C-243/95 *Hill and Stapleton v The Revenue Commissioners*); inconvenient hours supplement *(C-236/98 Jämställdhetsombudsmannen v Örebro läns landsting)*; termination/redundancy payments, *(Osterreichische Gewerkschaftsbund v Wirtschafts Kammer Osterreich)*; bonus payments (C-333/97 *Lewen v Lothar Denda);* statutory and non-statutory redundancy pay *(R (Seymour-Smith) v Secretary of State for Employment* [2000] UKHL 12 *and (1999)* C-167/97).

Indirect Discrimination

Section 22(1) of the Act provides that:

(a) Indirect discrimination occurs where an apparently neutral provision puts persons of a particular gender (being As or Bs) at a particular disadvantage in respect of any matter other than remuneration compared with other employees of their employer.

(b) Where paragraph (a) applies the employer shall be treated for the purposes of this Act as discriminating against each of the persons referred to (including A or B), unless the provision is objectively justified by a legitimate aim and the means of achieving that aim are appropriate and necessary.

Section 31 of the Act has an identical provision in relation to all the other protected grounds.

So how does indirect discrimination work in practice? In *70 Named Female Employees v Superquinn*[12] the employer, Superquinn, assumed responsibility for cleaning uniforms of staff in fresh food departments but not in other departments. Clearly the requirement that an employee work in the fresh food department is a neutral requirement, unrelated to any of the discriminatory grounds. However, the claimants showed that in reality, the requirement meant that male employees were more likely to have their uniforms cleaned, as 70% of the employees in the fresh food department were male, while the other departments were 65% female. The practice was therefore discriminatory and so it was up to the employer to establish that it was objectively justifiable by a legitimate aim and that the means of achieving that aim were appropriate and necessary. Here the employer was able to provide objective justification, since it was required to ensure that fresh food uniforms were cleaned daily under regulations implementing a European Community food hygiene directive.

In *Ice Group Business Services Limited v Czerski*[13] the complainant was a Polish applicant to an employment agency who claimed discrimination

---

[12] *70 Named Female Employees v Superquinn* DEC-E2001-028.
[13] *Ice Group Business Services Limited v Czerski* [2010] 21 ELR 8.

on grounds of her race arising from the agency's requirement that she furnish two employment references. The Equality Tribunal upheld her claim that she was indirectly discriminated against on the grounds of her race in that the requirement for two employment-related references operated to the disadvantage of a non-Irish national as compared with an Irish national, and could be complied with by a substantially smaller number of non-Irish employees. However, on appeal to the Labour Court it was held that, as the agency had informed the complainant that a character reference would be acceptable as one of the references, the court could not see how a non-Irish person would be placed at a greater disadvantage than an Irish person.

The question of what constitutes a legitimate aim will depend on the facts of each case, and, even if an aim is legitimate, the measure itself must also be necessary and proportionate.

Harassment

Harassment (apart from sexual harassment) is defined as any unwanted conduct related to any of the protected grounds and "being conduct which in either case has the purpose or effect of violating a person's dignity and creating an intimidating, hostile, degrading, humiliating or offensive environment for the person".[14]

In a recent case involving harassment on the ground of gender and family status before the Equality Tribunal a financial controller who was demoted to a debt collector role after taking maternity leave was awarded €80,000. Ms. Mullen had been subjected to a range of discriminatory treatment from the time she told her employer she was pregnant and his reaction was "Jesus Lisa, you don't hang around".[15] This, along with other comments made regarding her job, pregnancy and family status constituted harassment in the view of the Tribunal.

In the case of *Attila Marton Ajtai v McDonnell Brothers Agricultural Suppliers Ltd*[16] focused on racial harassment. The claimant was a Roma-

---

[14] s 14(7)(b).

[15] "Employee awarded €80,000 over 'range of unlawful treatment'" The Irish Times, 17 March 2014

[16] *Attila Marton Ajtai v McDonnell Brothers Agricultural Suppliers Ltd* DEC-E2013-167.

Hungarian man, who had been subjected to Nazi salutes and other racially based slurs from Polish co-workers, as well as suffering physical assaults and (possibly) having soap slipped into his sandwich. Some enquiries had been made by management, but no records or notes of these were kept and there was no policy in place to deal with such behaviour. It was found he had suffered harassment due to his race, and was awarded €20,000.

Victimisation

Victimisation protects employees from fear of retaliatory conduct on the part of their employer should they rely on discrimination law or raise complaints of discrimination with their employer. The key elements of victimisation provided for in s 74(2) of the Acts are as follows:

(i) The employee had taken action of a type referred to at section 74(2) of the Acts (a protected action—such as a complaint of discrimination, legal proceedings related to discrimination, or support for another employee who has alleged discrimination);

(ii) The employee was subjected to adverse treatment by the respondent; and

(iii) The adverse treatment was in reaction to the protected action having been taken by the employee.[17]

Unfair Dismissal

Before the enactment of the Unfair Dismissals Acts 1977–2013, employees had limited protection from arbitrary dismissal. The common law remedy of wrongful dismissal was unwieldy and did not deal with a fundamental element of constitutional justice—the *fairness* of procedures and the manner in which the employee was treated.

Who is Covered by the Legislation?

In assessing an unfair dismissal claim, the first thing to be dealt with is whether or not the legislation applies to that employee. Section 2(1) of the Act sets out a long and comprehensive list of those excluded from its

---

[17] *Department of Defence v Barrett* EDA1019.

remit; for example, members of the defence forces and the Gardaí, and people employed by a family member, are all excluded.[18] Section 2(2) provides that an employee engaged under a fixed-term or specified-purpose contract will not fall under the remit of the Act where the employment ends because the contract expires. The criteria that applies to all employees is that, in order to fall under the Act, the employee must, at the date of the dismissal, have at least fifty-two continuous weeks service with the employer.[19]

Types of Dismissal

The Unfair Dismissal (UD) Acts provide for three different types of dismissal:

---

[18] s 2(1) This Act shall not apply in relation to any of the following persons:
  (a) an employee (other than a person referred to in section 4 of this Act) who is dismissed, who, at the date of his dismissal, had less than one year's continuous service with the employer who dismissed him and whose dismissal does not result wholly or mainly from the matters referred to in section 6 (2) (f) of this Act,
  (b) an employee who is dismissed and who, on or before the date of his dismissal, had reached the normal retiring age for employees of the same employer in similar employment or who on that date was a person to whom by reason of his age the Redundancy Payments Acts, 1967 to 1973, did not apply,
  (c) a person who is employed by his spouse, father, mother, grandfather, grandmother, step-father, step-mother, son, daughter, grandson, granddaughter, step-son, step-daughter, brother, sister, half-brother or half-sister, is a member of his employer's household and whose place of employment is a private dwellinghouse or a farm in or on which both the employee and the employer reside,
  (d) a person in employment as a member of the Defence Forces, the Judge Advocate-General, the chairman of the Army Pensions Board or the ordinary member thereof who is not an officer of the Medical Corps of the Defence Forces,
  (e) a member of the Garda Síochána,
  (f) a person (other than a person employed under a contract of employment) who is receiving a training allowance from or undergoing instruction by An Chomhairle Oiliúna or is receiving a training allowance from and undergoing instruction by that body,
  (g) a person who is employed by An Chomhairle Oiliúna under a contract of apprenticeship,
  (h) a person employed by or under the State other than persons standing designated for the time being under section 17 of the Industrial Relations Act, 1969,
  (i) officers of a local authority for the purposes of the Local Government Act, 1941,
  (j) officers of a health board, a vocational education committee established by the Vocational Education Act, 1930, or a committee of agriculture established by the Agriculture Act, 1931.
[19] This restriction does not apply to employees dismissed because of trade union membership or activity, pregnancy, or exercise of rights under the Maternity Protection Acts 1994–2003 and the National Minimum Wage Act 2000.

(i)   Fair dismissal;
(ii) Unfair dismissal;
(iii) Constructive dismissal.

(i) Fair Dismissal

Section 6(1) of the UD Acts sets out the grounds on which it may be fair to dismiss an employee. Section 6(4) provides specific grounds on which, if an employer can prove that the dismissal resulted mainly from such ground, a dismissal will be deemed a fair dismissal:

a.   *The Capability, Competence or Qualification of the Employee*
     The *incapability* of carrying out the work he is employed to do must be inherent in the employee and cannot arise through the fault of the employee such as medical illness.[20]
     Competence relates to the employee's ability to do the work satisfactorily; continued under-performance with no sign of improvement can be grounds for a justifiable dismissal. The method of evaluating performance then will be crucial to whether the dismissal is, in fact, fair.
     If the dismissal is based on *qualification*, the employee must be lacking the *necessary* qualification to do the work he was employed to do. If the nature of the work changes making it necessary for the employee to undergo further training, then he must be given a reasonable amount of time to obtain the further qualification.

b.   *The Employee's Conduct*
     Conduct will usually refer to something which has affected the relationship of trust and confidence between employee and employer.[21] The court or tribunal will look particularly at the conduct, whether fair procedures were used during the investigation, and whether the employer's actions were in all the circumstances reasonable.

---

[20] See *Reardon v St Vincent's Hospital* UD74/1979.
[21] For a discussion of various types of conduct that may justify a dismissal, see Cox, Corbett and Ryan, *Employment Law in Ireland*, Clarus Press 2009, pp 742–750.

c. *Redundancy of the Employee*

If it is a *real redundancy* as opposed to a "sham" redundancy, then under the Act the dismissal will be fair. If the redundancy is real but the *selection procedures* were unfair, then it cannot be a fair dismissal.

d. *The Employee's Continued Employment Would be in Contravention of Statute*

A dismissal may be justified where continued employment might contravene a statute; for example, where a driver loses his driving licence or an employee's work permit expires or is revoked.[22]

In assessing a dismissal which an employer claims was made under one of these grounds, the court will look both at whether the ground on which the decision was based was fair—substantive fairness, *and* whether the manner in which the decision was made was fair—procedural fairness. Even if the substantive ground is considered fair, if the employee was denied procedural fairness the dismissal will be considered unfair.[23]

This two-pronged approach to any claim of unfair dismissal can be seen in *Miskella v Keahal Limited T/A Tír nÓg Crèche and Montessori School*.[24] Here the Employment Appeals Tribunal (EAT) examined whether a childcare assistant in a crèche had committed an act of gross misconduct, and then whether her subsequent dismissal was procedurally fair.

---

[22] The issue of work permits has been decided in recent cases, with the application for or renewal of the employee's work permit deemed at least an implied term of the contract—see *Dubyna v Hourican Hygiene Services t/a Master Clean Services* UD 781/2004, and a similar decision was reached in the case of *Golovan v Porturlin Shellfish Ltd* UD 428/2006.

[23] In addition to substantive and procedural fairness in an unfair dismissal, an employer owes his employees duties under the Health and Safety legislation, and failure to fulfill these and comply with the legislation can also result in a finding of unfair dismissal. In *Stobart (Ireland) Driver Services Limited v Keith Carroll* [2013] IEHC 581 (High Court, Kearns P, 20 December 2013) the employment of the driver of a truck was terminated by the haulage company after he had made a complaint of being tired and unable to fulfil his driving duties under the Health and Safety Acts 2005. The company argued that Mr Carroll's withdrawal of labour was a refusal of a reasonable request (a common law duty of an employee to his employer) and that this amounted to gross misconduct. Mr Carroll argued that his dismissal was a penalisation for making the complaint and that under the Health and Safety Acts 2005 this was an unfair dismissal. The High Court agreed and found that any penalisation by an employer for a complaint by an employee under the Health and Safety Acts 2005 could amount to an unfair dismissal.

[24] *Miskella v Keahal Limited T/A Tír nÓg Creche and Montessori School* UD1072/2012.

The owner of the crèche stated that she observed Ms Miskella being rough with one of the children in her care, and two days later, following only one conversation, Ms Miskella was dismissed. There was no written contract, nor were there any written procedures for discipline or grievances. Ms Miskella denied any inappropriate behaviour had occurred and she claimed that she had approached her employer to talk about it and was repeatedly refused. The EAT held that because there were no written procedures, there had been no investigation of the incident, the employee had not been given an opportunity to be heard and was not notified of the fact that there was going be a decision on her dismissal, and there was no right of appeal, there was procedural unfairness in this case. In addition to this the EAT found on the evidence put forward that the conduct complained of in this case was not gross misconduct and therefore the response of summary dismissal was disproportionate.

In *Kelleher v An Post*[25] both the reasons for the dismissal and the procedures involved were examined by the court. However, in this case the procedures were in fact "scrupulously fair". Mr Kelleher had been the postmaster in Newcastle West, Co. Limerick for about nineteen years. There was a kidnapping incident in the post office while Mr Kelleher was on holiday, where his son was threatened. However, the subsequent investigation found that the staff had not been trained by Mr Kelleher as to what to do in this scenario. It also transpired that some monies lost during this kidnap should have been deposited on an earlier day, and that Mr Kelleher had taken an advance of his salary with him on holidays from the company funds. Mr Kelleher was accused by An Post of misuse of funds and failing to follow security procedures in the course of the kidnap, which resulted in the loss of €105,000 to the company. An Post terminated his contract and sought to make him liable for half of the loss (€52,000). Mr Kelleher claimed that his dismissal was unfair as there was procedural unfairness; however, the High Court held that.

> [H]e was informed of the issues of concern in a very comprehensive manner. He was invited at every stage to give any responses or observations he wished, and he did so

---

[25] *Kelleher v An Post* [2013] IEHC 328 (High Court, Peart J, 16 May 2013).

at length before his volte face on the 12th October 2011. He was afforded the opportunity of an oral first instance hearing which he at first indicated a wish for, but later declined. He was afforded an oral appeal hearing and a full opportunity to make both oral and written submissions. Taken in the round, this process was scrupulously fair.

(ii) Automatically Unfair Dismissal

Section 6(2) of the 1977 Act provides for nine grounds upon which if a dismissal is based, either wholly or mainly, then it will be deemed to be unfair:

(i)   Trade union membership or activities;
(ii)   Civil or criminal proceedings against the employer;
(iii)   Religious or political beliefs of the employee;
(iv)   Race, colour or sexual orientation of the employee;
(v)   Employee's pregnancy and pregnancy-related issues;
(vi)   Exercise of other statutory rights;
(vii) Age of the employee;
(viii) Membership of the Travelling community; or
(ix)   Unfair selection for redundancy.

(iii) Constructive Dismissal

This type of dismissal applies where an employer might wish to "get rid" of an employee but also wishes to evade liability for an unfair dismissal. An employee is not actually dismissed but her working life and position is made unbearable to the extent that she is forced to resign. Under the Act, if this occurs an employee can bring an action for constructive dismissal, essentially arguing that because of the behaviour of her employer she had no other option but to resign. A constructive dismissal is a type of unfair dismissal based on the unreasonable actions of the employer. In these types of cases the employee must prove that, but for the employer's behaviour, she would not have resigned and that in fact she was dismissed. This is slightly different to an unfair dismissal claim where the burden falls on the employer to prove the dismissal was fair. It is a somewhat more difficult case to take for an employee because of this evidential burden.

Workplace Bullying

"It is important to record at the outset that bullying is one of the more obnoxious traits in human behaviour. That is so because it involves a deliberate and repeated course of action designed to humiliate and belittle the victim..... Any rational person who has seen the effects of bullying will agree that it is an activity which carries a grave risk for the victim's health and for his or her ability to function in a normal way".[26]

Bullying, harassment and stress at work continue to take up a significant amount of time for human resource departments, and are also a significant legal issue. There is no legislation dealing with the specific issue of bullying or stress at work and claims are usually made within other causes of action, commonly in the arena of personal injuries (as part of tort law), which was never designed to deal with this area of interpersonal relationships. Depending on the facts of the case and the particular injuries caused, actions can be grounded on: the Health and Safety at Work Act 2005, a personal injuries claim if there is a recognisable psychiatric illness, bullying as a legal wrong, or breach of the duty of mutual trust and confidence. In *Glynn v Minister for Justice Equality and Law Reform and Others* Kearns P pointed out the difference between bullying, occupational stress and workplace stress; he said these "are all things which, conceptually at least, are quite different from each other, though on occasion they can overlap and coincide".

Employers should note that although there is no specific legislation in this area, a number of codes of practice have been introduced in the general area of bullying and harassment, for instance, the code of practice under the Industrial Relations Act 1990.[27] Whilst codes of practice are not legally binding, being more like indications of best practice, they can be admitted in legal proceedings, and an employer's failure to have regard to them can assist an employee in making a case. Further, where an employer has their own code of practice in place and

---

[26] *Per* Kearns P in *Glynn v Minister for Justice Equality and Law Reform and Others* (High Court, 21 March 2014).

[27] SI 17 of 2002; also, the Health & Safety Authority's Code of Practice on Bullying in the Workplace is frequently cited in court and contains the same definition of bullying as the Industrial Relations Act Code of Practice.

it is disregarded or not used correctly, this can have legal implications in these sorts of claims.

A plaintiff must establish that the treatment which they claim has caused their injury constitutes an actionable wrong. A plaintiff may be able to establish a statutory breach of duty, such as one based on the Health and Safety at Work Acts. In establishing a breach of the common law duty of care, the conduct complained of must come within the code of practice's definition of bullying as endorsed by the Supreme Court in *Quigley v Complex Tooling and Moulding*[28]:

> "Workplace bullying is repeated inappropriate behaviour, direct or indirect, whether verbal, physical or otherwise, conducted by one or more persons against another or others, at the place of work and/or in the course of employment, which could be reasonably be regarded as undermining the individual's right to dignity at work.
>
> An isolated incident of the behaviour described in this definition may be an affront to dignity at work but as a once off incident is not considered to be bullying".

Stress and bullying claims commonly take the form of claims for personal injuries, including psychiatric injury. The test to establish liability for psychiatric injury in the workplace in Irish law was set out by Clarke J in *Maher v Jabil Services Limited*[29] (endorsed more recently by the High Court in *Browne v Minister for Justice Equality and Law Reform*[30]) as follows:

(a) Has the Plaintiff suffered an injury to his or her health as opposed to what might be described as ordinary occupational stress;
(b) If so, is that injury attributable to the workplace; and
(c) If so, was the harm suffered to the particular employee concerned reasonably foreseeable in all the circumstances.

---

[28] *Quigley v Complex Tooling and Moulding* [2005] ELR 305.
[29] *Maher v Jabil Services Limited* [2005] 16 ELR 233.
[30] *Browne v Minister for Justice Equality and Law Reform* [2012] IEHC 526.

Foreseeability in this context depends on the particular characteristics of the employee, the particular demands the employer placed on her, and the extent and frequency with which the employee complained to the employer. (In *Maher* the plaintiff had complained to his employer, but it was held by the High Court that these complaints were not frequent or numerous enough to make his employer aware of the danger of psychological injury.) The court examines whether the employer then acted reasonably in the situation.

In one of the first cases in Ireland dealing with psychiatric injury due to bullying at work—*McGrath v Trintech Technologies Limited*[31]—foreseeability was the key to the success of the case. The defendants were involved in the information technology sector and operated on a worldwide basis. The plaintiff's contract of employment contained an express provision that his employment could be terminated on one month's notice. During his employment with the defendant, the plaintiff suffered bouts of ill health of a physical nature. While on sick leave, he was asked by the defendant to go on an assignment to Uruguay. The plaintiff claimed that when he took up the assignment in Uruguay, the terms of his contract of employment were varied, in that he was guaranteed that the defendant would retain him in employment for a period of one year following his return. During the period of his assignment the plaintiff alleged that he was subjected to grave work-related stress and pressure which resulted in injury to his psychological health and well-being. On his return from Uruguay in June 2003, the plaintiff was absent from work on certified sick leave. In August 2003 he was informed by the first defendant that he was being made redundant. The plaintiff was of the view that the method of his selection for redundancy was wrongful and/or unfair. Laffoy J in the High Court was prepared to hold that, despite inconsistencies in the opinions and diagnosis of the medical experts, the plaintiff had established that he had suffered a "recognisable psychiatric illness". More recent case law suggests that there has been a move away from the strict requirement for a "recognisable psychiatric illness" and that damages will be awarded for conditions such as stress and adjustment disorders.[32]

---

[31] *McGrath v Trintech Technologies Limited* [2005] 4 IR 383.
[32] See *Browne v Minister for Justice Equality and Law Reform and Others* [2012] IEHC 526 and *Kelly v Bon Secours* [2012] IEHC 21.

However, despite this finding of a "recognisable psychiatric illness", the plaintiff in *McGrath* failed to win because the court found that there was no evidence to suggest the defendant employer knew or ought to have known that the plaintiff's bouts of ill health were the result of stress at work. The High Court took note of an English case, *Hatton v Sutherland*[33] where four employers appealed against findings of liability for four employees who had psychiatric illnesses caused by stress at work. The Court of Appeal allowed the employers' appeals in three of the cases, *Hatton*, *Barber* and *Bishop*, in a composite judgment. Essentially, the court laid down sixteen practical propositions to provide guidance as to the principles applied in occupational stress claims.[34] These propositions emphasise the subjective element of foreseeability; there must be signs from the employee herself. These propositions, endorsed by the Irish High Court, are seen as quite favourable towards the employer—there is no obligation to act until a "real risk" exists.

An example of where a number of complaints went unheeded and did result in a finding of negligence against an employer can be seen in *Keenan v Power and Ors*[35] where the plaintiff was awarded damages to compensate him for injuries sustained by him as a result of the State's negligence in allowing the plaintiff to come into regular contact with a colleague who had been previously found to have bullied him.

In the recent case of *Ruffley v Board of Management St Anne's School*[36] liability was imposed based on a breach of mutual trust and confidence, in this case the wrongful manner in which a disciplinary process was conducted. The plaintiff claimed damages for bullying and harassment which allegedly occurred over a one-year period in the course of her work as a special needs assistant ("SNA"). There were no disciplinary or grievance issues during the plaintiff's eleven-year employment with the defendant until September 2009 when the defendant's principal informed the plaintiff that she was treating the plaintiff's locking of the door to the school's sensory room whilst inside with a pupil as a

---

[33] *Hatton v Sutherland* [2002] All ER 1.
[34] Mr Barber appealed. The House of Lords (Lords Bingham, Steyn, Scott, Rodger and Walker) endorsed the principles laid down by the Court of Appeal in *Hatton*, describing them as "a valuable contribution to the development of the law" (Lord Walker).
[35] Decision of 5 October 2011.
[36] *Ruffley v Board of Management St Anne's School* [2014] IEHC 235.

disciplinary matter. There was an initial meeting after which the plaintiff felt her explanation had been accepted by the principal and that no further action was to be taken. The court found the principal's subsequent dealings with the plaintiff, in the context of a review of the child's programme, to be irrational, and her inclusion of "trumped up" charges relating to performance and conduct to be reprehensible. The court was satisfied that the principal informed the plaintiff that the matter was to be brought to the next meeting of the defendant in November 2009. However, the plaintiff was not provided with any detail of what was being brought to the board; was not afforded an opportunity to represent herself in any way; nor was she informed that there might be an adverse disciplinary outcome for her. At the said meeting, under the heading "any other business", an issue relating to the plaintiff's performance was recorded, together with the defendant board's support for the principal's recommendation that a disciplinary sanction issue in the circumstances. The court did not think that the defendant board members could have come to the conclusions it did without the principal's account of the situation being grossly misleading and unfair to the plaintiff, and the locking of the sensory room being presented as an instance of individual misconduct on the part of the plaintiff. The court considered the principal's conduct in the lead up to the defendant's board meeting, and what happened during the meeting, to be a departure from all of the norms of natural justice. The court was further satisfied that the principal's treatment of the plaintiff throughout the disciplinary process was entirely inappropriate within the meaning of workplace bullying. The court found that the persistent, inappropriate behaviour of the defendant wholly undermined the plaintiff's dignity at work. The court awarded the plaintiff the total sum of €255,276 in general damages for the psychiatric injury suffered and special damages for loss of earnings, the largest award for bullying in the State to date. This case is a good demonstration of the importance of natural justice and fair procedures during any disciplinary process. It is currently being appealed by the defendants and one of the many grounds of appeal is that as some of what occurred was not in the presence of the plaintiff (at the Board meetings) this could not undermine her dignity at work. It will be interesting to see the determination of the Court on this point.

Conclusions

In this chapter a number of different workplace disputes have been introduced—equality claims, unfair dismissal and bullying at work. Some of the cases should serve as a warning for employers that codes of practice should be in place and used correctly, but also that their procedures must involve fundamental fairness.

- Various claims can be taken under the Equality Acts:
  - Direct discrimination
  - Equal pay
  - Indirect discrimination
  - Harassment
  - Victimisation
- The Unfair Dismissal Acts provide for three different types of dismissal: (i) fair dismissal, (ii) unfair dismissal, (iii) constructive dismissal.
- Dismissals must be both substantively fair and also procedurally fair.
- Constructive dismissals are a form of unfair dismissal but involve an onus of proof on the employee not present in a "normal" unfair dismissal claim.
- Bullying and stress claims taken as personal injuries cases are on the rise. However these types of claim must meet a three-point test of a recognisable psychiatric injury, causation (through workplace bullying as defined by the courts) and forseeability.

Index

and fixed charges 192–3
negligence 203
negligent misstatement 34–6, 97
and negotiable instruments 199–201
paying and collecting functions 202–3
registration of charges 191
use of undue influence doctrine against 122–3, 125–6
Bankruptcy *see* insolvency; insolvent liquidation
Bargaining power, and exclusion clauses 87, 139
Barristers
dual duty of 36
professional negligence 36–7
vs. solicitors 11–12
"Basis of contract" clause 102–3
Battle of the forms 57–8
Bills of exchange 199–200
certainty 200
vs. cheques 200–1
definition 199–200
parties 200, 205
vs. promissory notes 205
Bills of Exchange Act (1882) 199
definition of cheque 200
Book debts, fixed charges on 192–3
Books and records
failure to maintain 171, 176
liquidation 223
Bosman ruling 245–6
Breach of contract 133–9
affirmation 134
and agency 185
anticipatory breach 134
of conditions 89, 111, 135, 139
consideration 63

damages 111, 143–6
discharge by 133–7
by employee 269
by employer 269
exclusion clauses 139
injunctions 148–9
limitation period for claims 32–3
and negligence 28–9
quantum meruit 149–50
remedies 143–50
repudiatory breach 137–9
rescission 146–7
right of election 134–5
specific performance 147–8
substantially the whole benefit test 137
Breach of duties
by directors 168
by fiduciary 179
statutory 286
Breach of mutual trust and confidence 285, 288–9
Breach of warranty 83, 84–5, 135, 136
Bullying at workplace *see* workplace bullying
Burden of proof, civil *vs.* criminal law 10

C

Campus oil test 149
CCPC *see* Competition and Consumer Protection Commission
Central Bank of Ireland *see also* bank(s)
role in enforcement of Consumer Protection Act (2007) 78–9

damage assessment 144–5
fundamental breach and
    exclusion clause 139
negligent misstatement 97
packaging and design 43
promissory estoppel 68

I

Illegal acts, and consideration 65
Immunity from suit, barristers'
    36–7
Implied conditions 74–5, 83
    description of goods 74
    quality of goods 74
Implied terms *see* Implied
    warranties
Implied terms in employment
    contracts 266
    by case law 267
    by custom and practice 267–8
    by statute 267
Implied warranties 74, 83, 84,
    86–7
    breach of 84–5
    definition 86–7
Improvident transactions 127
Indemnity 209–10
Independent contractors, *vs.*
    employees 253–7
Indirect discrimination, in
    employment 277–8
Industrial Relations Act (1990) 285
Informed consent, to alterations
    in employment contracts 268
Injunctions
    against government 23
    breach of contract 148–9
    Campus oil test 149

definition 148
interim 149
interlocutory 149
mandatory 148
passing off case 24
perpetual 149
tort law 22–4
work context 23–4
Innocent misrepresentation 85,
    98–9
Innominate terms *see* intermediate
    terms
Insolvency *see also* examinership/
    examiners; liquidation;
    Insolvent liquidation;
    receivership/receivers
    EU Directive 269
    and termination of employment
        contracts 269
Insolvency Protection Directive
    (80/987) 245
Insolvent liquidation 223–6
    see also liquidation;
        liquidators
    advertisement in *Iris
        Oifigiúil* 225
    application to wind up 224–5
    court's role 223, 224–5
    creditors' voluntary liquidation
        225–6
    malicious presentation of
        winding up petition 224
    member's voluntary
        liquidation 225
    pari passu 223
    proof of inability to pay
        debts 224
    and restriction of directors
        170–1